Chiricahua and Janos

BORDERLANDS AND TRANSCULTURAL STUDIES

Series Editors:

Pekka Hämäläinen
Paul Spickard

| Lance R. Blyth

Chiricahua and Janos

Communities of Violence in the
Southwestern Borderlands,
1680–1880

University of Nebraska Press | Lincoln & London

Library of Congress Cataloging-
in-Publication Data
Blyth, Lance R., 1966–
Chiricahua and Janos: communities of violence
in the southwestern borderlands, 1680–1880 /
Lance R. Blyth.
p. cm.—(Borderlands and transcultural studies)
Includes bibliographical references and index.
ISBN 978-0-8032-3766-7 (cloth: alk. paper)
1. Chiricahua Indians—Mexico—Janos—
History. 2. Chiricahua Indians—Mexico—
Janos—Government relations. 3. Chiricahua
Indians—Violence against—Mexico—Janos.
4. Violence—Social aspects—Mexico—Janos.
5. Janos (Mexico)—History. 6. Janos
(Mexico)—Race relations. 7. Janos (Mexico)—
Politics and government. I. Title.
E99.C68B59 2012
305.897'25607216—dc23   2011051695

Set in Sabon by Bob Reitz.

For my mother
Carolyn Louise Blyth
1935–2009

Contents

Maps

| Preface

For over two hundred years the descendants of Spanish settlers and Apache Indians did violence to each other in the region known as the Southwestern Borderlands; historical, cultural, and geographical shorthand for the area on either side of the current U.S.-Mexican border. From the 1680s to the 1880s members of both communities regularly committed acts of violence, even as they often negotiated or traded. It may be illustrative to many to map this two-century scale of time onto the history of the United States. Consider a New England in 1875 that had just concluded King Phillip's War with the Wampanoag begun two hundred years prior. Think of a South in which the Creek towns of Alabama remained at war with American settlements in Tennessee until 1975. Or consider the Front Range of the Rocky Mountains, where I write these words today, still being the scene of Cheyenne raids and Anglo revenge until at least the late 2060s, with flare-ups into the next decade. It is mind-boggling to think of a conflict running for that length of time.

As I confronted this reality I turned to David Nirenberg's *Communities of Violence: Persecution of Minorities in the Middle Ages*, which provides the central insight of this work. Nirenberg looked at conflicts and violent episodes in the relations among Christians, Jews, Muslims, and lepers in northeastern Spain and southern France in the fourteenth and fifteenth centuries. He studied "cataclysmic" violence that featured attacks on Jews, lepers, and Muslims, motivated by rebellion against the monarchy and social conflict, and "systemic" violence, which arose from "everyday transgressions of religious boundaries" via conversion, interfaith sexuality, commensality, dress, and topography. As Nirenberg studied religious communities who were members of a single society and subjects of a medieval state, his categories and methods of analysis did not readily transplant to the Southwestern Borderlands. But his central thesis, that violence was not a sign of intolerance but was, instead, "a central and systematic aspect of the coexistence of majority and minorities in medieval Spain" and that "a constructive relationship between conflict and coexistence" prevailed, did cause me to rethink my assumptions about violence.[1]

I took from Nirenberg the realization that violence is instrumental in establishing, maintaining, and changing relationships both within and between communities. Violence can be a useful tool for communities to employ, particularly in areas where no single political organization or cultural group has a monopoly on its use, such as borderlands. It is just such communities to which I apply Nirenberg's appellation of "communities of violence." While I focus on a borderland, called the Southwestern Borderlands in expectation that most readers will view the region from this geographical viewpoint, there are many other borderlands at other times and other places. Even a cursory study of those borderlands will likely reveal their own communities of violence.

The study of the Southwestern Borderlands—and borderlands in general—is no stranger to violence, yet I seek to take a different tack. I try to identify individual members from the two communities whenever possible in the text. I attempt to braid the strands of these individuals and their respective communities, both native and settler, into a single narrative thread, emphasizing their similarities and common humanity, even as they attempted to do violence to one another. I treat violence as a readily available tool in the human survival toolkit. And I believe this is the main contribution of my work. By taking a deep, unblinking view of violence, showing not only its negative aspects but also the potential positive outcomes for the individuals and communities involved, I hope to help us understand and account for violence better, both in the Southwestern Borderlands and in others—yesterday, today, tomorrow.

A disclaimer: in accordance with Title 5, Code of Federal Regulations, parts 2635.807(b) and 3601.108, while I am currently employed by the Department of Defense, the views presented in this work are my own and do not necessarily represent the views of the Department of Defense or its components.

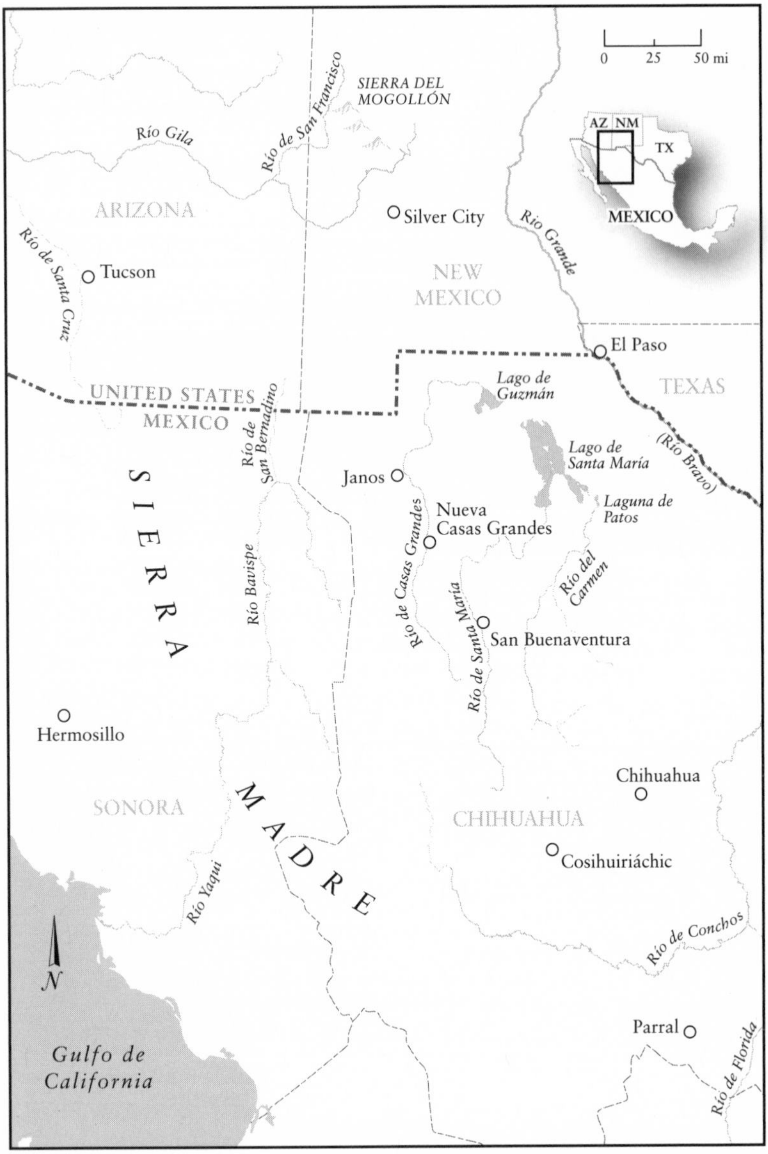

Map 1. Northwestern Mexico and southwestern United States

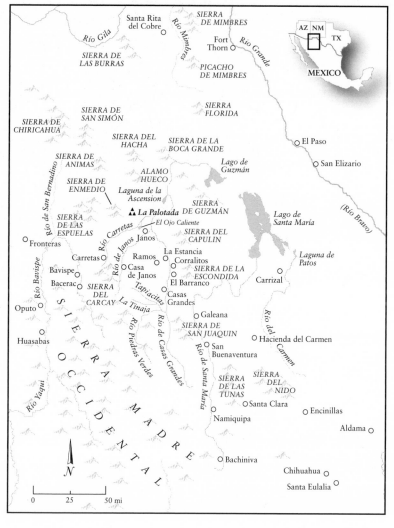

Map 2. Northwestern Nueva Vizcaya region, ca. 1800

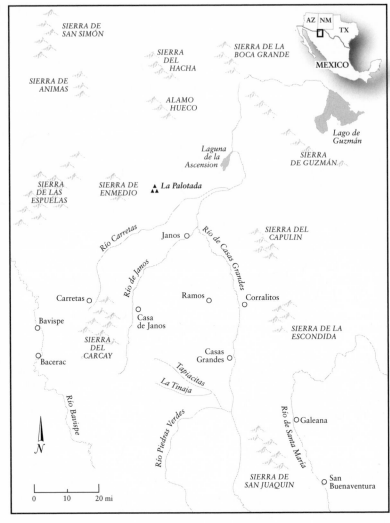

Map 3. Part of the Janos jurisdiction

Chiricahua and Janos

| Chapter 1

Communities of Violence
Apaches and Hispanics in the Southwestern Borderlands

With guns on their saddle-bows and lances at their stirrups the Sonorans rode over the mountains in the half-light of morning. The target of their wrath was the group of Chiricahua Apaches encamped outside the town Apaches called Kaskiyeh. As the Sonorans descended the pass they split into two parties: one to surprise a camp southeast of town, the other targeting Apaches to the west.

The Killings at Kaskiyeh

The first contingent found the campsite abandoned and so pressed on to Kaskiyeh, killing two Apaches and capturing several more along the way. The second group of Sonorans charged into the western Apache camp, brutally brushed aside an attempted parley, and killed four men and four women. While most Chiricahuas escaped into the hills, some fled to Kaskiyeh and found refuge in the houses of its Mexican inhabitants. As the sun rose the Sonorans converged on Kaskiyeh—Janos, as its Hispanic inhabitants called it—a long-time garrison community in northwestern Chihuahua. Since they outnumbered the garrison, the Sonoran mob ignored the protests of the commander of Janos and his lieutenant, Baltasar Padilla. They invaded Janos and forcibly took Apaches from houses, killing several.

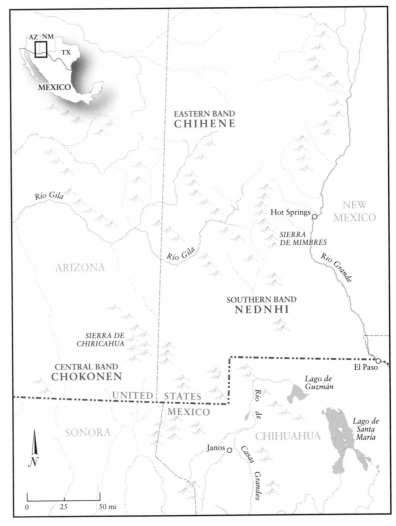

Map 4. Chiricahua, ca. 1850

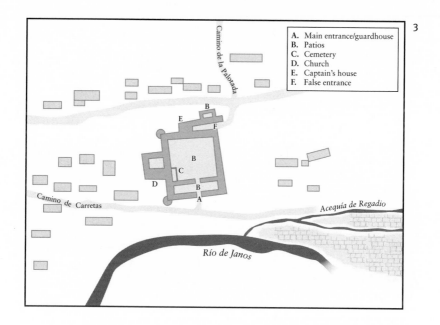

Map 5. Janos, after a drawing by José Urrutia, 1766

After nightfall the surviving Chiricahuas—including a man known as Goyahkla—rendezvoused in the woods along the river. These survivors discovered many of their men and women were dead and many more had been captured, including Goyahkla's wife, mother, and three children. Realizing they were outnumbered in the heart of enemy country the Chiricahuas retired northward to their homeland on the headwaters of the Gila River. Meanwhile, the Sonorans occupied Janos and uncovered the contraband trade between Chiricahuas and Janeros. After five days the Sonorans departed Janos with their Chiricahua prisoners—six men, four women, and fifty-two children—and more than three hundred head of livestock, including thirty-eight horses and mules with Sonoran brands taken from citizens of Janos, leaving Chihuahuan officials vainly protesting the Sonoran incursion to the central government.[1] But Goyahkla was not done.

Nearly a year later Goyahkla inspired Chiricahuas to avenge the killings of their kin at Kaskiyeh in a climactic battle against the Sonorans, during which he earned the sobriquet of Geronimo. This battle was the start, as Geronimo remembered it, of decades of conflict with the Mexicans and eventually the Americans that led to his ultimate exile and imprisonment by the United States. Since Geronimo recounted the events during his captivity nearly fifty years after the fact, either his memory was playing tricks on him, or he may have been playing tricks with his memory. The battle Geronimo presented as revenge almost twelve months after the Sonoran attack likely took place six weeks prior to the killings at Kaskiyeh. So what he recounted as retaliation was a provocation. Reversing the order of events in his recounting, Geronimo illustrated the primacy of violence in Chiricahuas' dealings with Hispanic communities in the Southwestern Borderlands, including Janos.[2]

Geronimo was not alone in "re-remembering" events in light of the killings at Kaskiyeh. Baltasar Padilla, stung by accusations and evidence of coexistence and active cooperation with Chiricahuas, went beyond his habitual one-sentence synopsis of his actions in that year's service record. With a different pen Padilla proceeded to list every expedition, campaign, skirmish, or pursuit against the Apaches he either led or participated in over the previous decade. Padilla filled up the page with his recollections before he ran out of space, breaking off in midsentence and midword: "Hay otra camp . . ." (There was another camp[aign]).[3] Faced with evidence of nonviolent interaction with the Apaches, Padilla wrote an addendum to his services rendered insisting on the dominance of violence in Janos's relations with Indian communities, especially Chiricahua.

Communities and Violence

The memories and remembrances of Geronimo and Padilla are emblematic of Chiricahua and Janos as "communities of violence" where violence drove relations—both conflictive and cooperative—not only between but also within the two communities.[4] The experiences of both men suggest that violence did not mean the end of interactions between Janos and Chiricahua, but was instead "an essential means by which that interaction occurred."[5] Violence often drove the two communities to peaceful dealings—negotiations, trade, treaties—which had the possibility of future violence looming over them, as these contacts between the two could lead to acts of violence, which in turn might carry the potential of future peace. As James F. Brooks noted, "borderland violence was not solely destructive but produced enduring networks of economic and social relations."[6] In this work I argue similarly for the centrality of violence in the relationships and exchanges between and within borderland communities.

The community of Janos was a European-derived, Hispanic *presidio* (garrison community) in present-day northwestern Mexico, with connections to other towns and settlements southward along the valley of San Diego, the valleys of Santa María and Santa Clara to the east, El Paso to the northeast, southeast to Chihuahua, and west over the sierras to Sonora.[7] Chiricahua was an Athapaskan-descended, Apache community that lived to the north-northwest of Janos along the upper drainages of the Río Gila and Río Mimbres and whose descendants live today in Oklahoma and southeastern

New Mexico. The Chiricahua tribe was historically divided into three bands. The Eastern Band, also called the Chihene (Red Paint People), lived in present-day southwestern New Mexico, the Central Band or Chokonen in present-day southeastern Arizona, and the Southern Band or Nednhi (Enemy People)" in northwestern Chihuahua and northeastern Sonora.[8]

Both Chiricahua and Janos were collections of several hundred families, whose total population never topped more than several thousand, living within socially determined boundaries. Chiricahua was a region where camping areas for families and groups of families changed with the seasons. Janos was a town with houses gathered around a plaza, itself centered on the presidio, with streets, fields, and pastures farther beyond. While they were different in form, Janos and Chiricahua were the same in function. Communities are not just a people in a place but are best understood as sets of relationships. The primary purpose of these relationships was to ensure cooperation in order for the members of the community to survive.

Chiricahuas and Janeros experienced their community as a set of increasingly extended kinship ties, a shared ethnic identity, familiar language, and common moral and material culture, all of which provided visual, audible, and olfactory clues as to who was a member of the community — one of "us" — and who was one of "them," cueing members how to act appropriately.[9] The more altruistic a community the more likely it would survive and allow its members to reproduce, even at the cost of individual deaths in conflict with outsiders, since in-group cooperation possessed a dark side: out-group aggression.[10] The willingness of humans to kill those they perceive as "beyond the pale" of their community is well attested to in the paleographic, archeological, ethnographic, and historical records.[11]

The communities of Chiricahua and Janos lived in the region referred to in this work as the Southwestern Borderlands. From the seventeenth to the nineteenth centuries the Southwestern Borderlands was a region betwixt and between Indian, European, and

Euro-American polities and cultures with overlapping, interacting, ever-shifting, and conflicting geographic, political, demographic, cultural, and economic boundaries.[12] The sheer flux of the region, combined with the negative aspect of communal identity, meant violence would dominate any relations as no one had a monopoly of violence over the entire borderlands.

Apaches were spatially and socially distributed across the Southwestern Borderlands to take maximum advantage of all available resources, and they relocated each season. Chiricahua economic, social, and religious institutions thus lacked the ability to create or maintain the physical power to dominate or control more territory or population than was needed at the immediate moment in their food quest.[13] Since the Southwestern Borderlands lay beyond the resource-producing mines, settled Indian villages, and haciendas of central Mexico, it simply did not pay for either the imperial Spanish or national Mexican state to secure the area fully. While Janos was a state-sponsored presidio from the seventeenth to the mid-nineteenth centuries, there were never enough presidios to dominate the region, and they rarely had the manpower needed to cover the complex terrain.

This lack of power in both polities meant neither had "an enduring monopoly in the use of violence."[14] Thus either community could use violence to pursue their own self-interest. Both therefore had ample reason to distrust the other, to stand ready to do violence at any time, or to strike before being struck. If they suffered violence, both communities knew they would have to take an implacable revenge to reestablish some level of deterrence and maintain a reputation of toughness in the hope of deflecting future violence.[15] Violence was thus the primary option and may have been the only means for both settler and native communities to establish, sustain, or change relations with each other.

An understandable tendency exists to think of violence as "anomalous, irrational, senseless, and disruptive." When viewed in a cross-cultural perspective, however, violence emerges as a human universal, a constituting element of societies, and a critical ingredient for their realities. Violence in this view, far from being meaningless, is full of meaning. Violence creates and constitutes relations, to the extent that violence is often intrinsic in relationships; determining, dominating, driving, dictating. As meaningful action, violence is a "form of interaction and communication." As an "experienced reality," violence is best understood via "its incorporation in the streams of human life" and history.[16]

Neither Janos nor Chiricahua is a historiographical stranger. Anthropologist William B. Griffen earlier studied the Apache experience at Janos presidio and its jurisdiction, seeking the basis of the conflict between Apaches and Hispanics. As Griffen was careful to paint Apaches as historical actors in their own right, he located heart of the matter in Indian social, cultural, and economic organizations. While he concluded that violence was central to Apache culture and economy, the scope of his work was the experience of Apache leaders, society, and culture with Spanish and Mexican policies and administration. Janos presidio was the site, not a subject of his work.[17] A quick perusal of the notes in the present work, however, reveal its debt to Griffen's efforts.

Recent scholarship on the Southwestern Borderlands has been sensitive to the role of violence. James F. Brooks's path-finding work cast the Southwestern Borderlands as a field of relationships among Indian peoples, Spaniards and then Mexicans, and finally Americans. Slavery, captivity, and redemption, interacting with and interpenetrated by cultural ideas of gender, kinship, honor, and subsistence, defined these relationships. Slavery bound societies together in the borderlands; it created bonds that violence did not break but enhanced. Violence, for Brooks, formed the basis of his relational field.[18]

Juliana Barr used gender as a lens to view relationships between Indians and Spaniards in eighteenth-century Texas. Natives dictated relationships via a gendered kinship system. Indians brought gendered understandings and practices to their relationships—contact, diplomacy, alliance, peace—with Spaniards. Barr covered violence as part of gendered "practices of peace."[19] Pekka

Hämäläinen explored a wide range of relationships—ecological and environmental, kinship and gender, captives and labor, trade and raid—between the Comanche and their neighbors in the borderlands. These relations allowed for political construction and cooperation among Comanches and alliances with other Indian peoples and Spanish colonial authorities. The Comanche were thus able to establish a regional indigenous hegemony, a "Comanche Empire." Hämäläinen showed violence as one of many calculated, rational, and orderly policies.[20]

Other scholars have focused on violence in the borderlands. Ned Blackhawk used violence as the "overarching theme," but saw pain, especially Indian pain, as the "object" of his study of Great Basin Indians. Utes initially raided New Mexico in retaliation for Spanish attacks but soon turned to raiding more distant Indians for slaves to trade in New Mexico. Utes thus "displaced" Spanish violence by attacking other natives. These waves of violence pulsing out from Spanish settlement shattered and reshaped Indian peoples, bringing them into the orbit of the Spanish and then American empires. Blackhawk emphasized the role of violence as one of Indian displacement and colonization.[21]

Brian DeLay centered violence in his history of the Southern Plains, Mexico, and the United States in the first half of the nineteenth century, seeking the origins of the U.S.-Mexican War of 1846 to 1848. Indian raiders laid waste to northern Mexico, killing and capturing thousands of Mexicans and taking innumerable livestock, creating a thousand man-made deserts of abandoned ranches, mines, and settlements. DeLay noted that native warriors sought not only plunder but also vengeance on Mexicans for past wrongs and status among their people. Yet the violence of the "War of a Thousand Deserts" ultimately allowed American expansionists to justify their programs and so weakened Mexico that it was unable to resist American aggression.[22] Karl Jacoby too employed violence to focus his study of Spanish, Mexican, American, Western Apache, and Tohono O'odham interactions. All these communities lived in harsh terrain where practices of agriculture, pastoralism, and raiding overlapped, deepening the conflict and hatreds among all the groups. This hatred exploded in the Camp Grant massacre of April 30, 1871, with which Jacoby begins his work. He anchored his work firmly and effectively in questions of genocide and massacre, history and memory.[23]

This work is intended to build upon the efforts of these scholars. It traces how violence dominated the relations between two borderland communities by which both increased in size via incorporation and captives; the relations of violence also reproduced each community by establishing a path to male adulthood and marriage; sustained both communities by providing for families; maintained interactions by revenge and retaliation; and ultimately placed both communities in a "security dilemma." By foregrounding violence, this work aims to extrapolate through illustration what violence was in a borderland setting in all its forms, types, and consequences by and for both natives and settlers.[24] Ultimately, for Chiricahua and Janos, violence created their social and economic meanings and constituted their cultural realities for over two hundred years in the borderlands.

The histories of this violence between Chiricahua and Janos are found in two "archives." The Janos archive is the traditional type well known to historians. It consists of more than forty thousand documents in archives and libraries and on rolls of microfilm. The archive includes official correspondence, troop reviews, ration issues, Indian affairs, criminal proceedings, daily diaries, campaign reports, financial accounts, instructions and orders, regulations, inventories, records of military service, censuses, and lists of equipment, supplies, horses, students, and so forth. The Janos archive speaks in the official voice of who, what, when, where, and occasionally why.[25] While much about Chiricahua can be found in the Janos archive, the Chiricahua archive is quite different. It consists of myths, tales, and stories, glossed as "oral history," along with ethnographic reports, all from the early part of the twentieth century. While this archive lacks much historical specificity, it is invaluable in transmitting the historical experience and memory of Chiricahuas. The Chiricahua archive may not tell much of the when or where of an event but is rich in how it would be remembered.[26] This work therefore combines information and insights from these two archives, allowing each community to speak with its own voice by alternating their shared experiences. And one set of experiences they shared were the histories of violent interactions both communities had long before they settled alongside each other.

The Last Conquistadors

With a simple wooden cross in the ground between them, two groups of mounted men faced each other across the plaza of San Juan Pueblo in the September sunlight of 1598 to perform a play. The *Moros* (Moors) led by the Sultán, in faux flowing robes and turbans, took their places on one side of the plaza. Sitting astride their horses on the other side, dressed in what finery survived the months on the trail northward from New Spain, were the *Cristianos* (Christians) under their lord Don Alfonso, watching as one Christian posted himself as a sentinel near the cross. The Sultán announced to the watching crowd that it was evening as he gave the orders to form his men for battle, but first he decided to send a spy to capture the cross. The Moorish spy approached the Christian sentinel, telling him he wished to convert. With the aid of the wineskin he carried, the spy put the sentinel to sleep and returned with the Holy Cross to the Sultán. Declaring it was a new morning as he rode forth into the plaza a few moments later, Don Alfonso learned of the loss of the cross from his lieutenant and ordered an immediate attack: "Onward, my brave soldiers, to vanquish the foe. By our valor, these infamous hordes shall be destroyed." Three times the Christians charged their foes that day, swirling around the Moors, swords clashing, to the "olés" of the watching crowd. All three times the Moors repulsed them.

Announcing it was the start of a second day, and certain of victory, the Sultán offered to ransom the Holy Cross, only to be rebuffed by Don Alfonso, who directed a new assault on the Moors. Both sides clashed three more times, the dust from their horses' hooves mingling with sweat, spittle, and blood from accidental wounds. After the third skirmish the Christians prevailed, capturing the Sultán and all his men, with Don Alfonso personally recovering the cross. Brought before Don Alfonso, the Sultán exclaimed: "Christian, your valor has me prostrate at your feet. I beg you, by your Cross, and by your almighty God, give me freedom, for I am convinced that only your God is true." Don Alfonso, with the Holy Cross in his hand, dismounted, helped the Sultán to his feet, and pardoned him and his subjects. Remounting, Don Alfonso led both groups united in religion and allegiance twice around the plaza, before riding out. It is unknown what the Pueblo Indians watching from the roof tops thought of the strange spectacle before them, but the Spanish audience knew exactly what they had just witnessed: the drama of *Moros y cristianos* (Moors and Christians), a theatrical enactment of conquest, assimilation, and reconciliation.[27]

Spaniards performed mock battles between Christians and Moors from the earliest days of the *Reconquista* (reconquest); the centuries-long recovery of the Iberian peninsula from its Muslim conquerors.[28] The conquerors of Mexico performed *Moros y cristianos* and Hispanics continued to perform the festival in the borderlands, including in the province of Nueva Vizcaya during the colonial period and in New Mexico well into present times.[29] The play's emphasis on total victory and the ultimate conversion of Hispanic foes was completely at odds with the borderlands reality of undefeated and often hostile Indian peoples. This did not matter, as the outcome of *Moros y cristianos* was less important than the relationship it envisioned with Indian peoples: confronted and defeated by Hispanic military prowess but not annihilated—rather, integrated and assimilated.[30] Yet the participants in the first *Moros y cristianos* in New Mexico at the foot of the Sangre de Cristo Mountains on September 8, 1598, were not just reenacting a conquest; they were enacting one: the conquest of New Mexico under Juan de Oñate.[31]

This fact was not lost on the Indians watching the festivities, among them men from the western pueblo of Acoma, who were less than impressed with what they saw. The war faction at Acoma failed to convince the rest of the pueblo to kill Oñate when the Spaniard visited their mesa-top village several months later and received an oath of submission from its elders. After this, the war faction finally convinced their people of the necessity to fight the invaders. When the next party of Spaniards climbed up the mesa to visit Acoma the Indians ambushed them, hunted them down, and killed them one by one. Only the three watching the horses at the base of the mesa escaped to tell the tale. Oñate promptly held a judicial proceeding on what to do about Acoma. One of his captains testified that if the Spaniards did not attack, they would have no security anywhere in New Mexico. The Franciscan fathers insisted that Acoma first had to be given the chance to surrender. If they refused, then any attack on them would be a just war. Hence, when a force consisting of more than half of the Spanish fighting men in New Mexico approached Acoma, they marched around the mesa three times, then called upon Acoma, again three times, to surrender and submit. Each time the people of Acoma refused, yelling insults, shooting arrows, hurling spears, and throwing rocks from atop their seemingly impregnable natural fortress.[32]

The next day, with the low winter sun slipping toward the western horizon behind them, the Spanish main body feinted at one side of the mesa, drawing all the Indians to defend against them, allowing twelve selected men to climb, unmolested and unspotted, up the other side. This number included Gaspar Perez de Villagrá, who would later write an epic poem of the conquest, the *Historia de la Nueva México*. Villagrá's forlorn hope secured a foothold on the mesa against desperate Acoma counterattacks. By dawn the next day more Spaniards joined the twelve and began a brutal, house-to-house fight. Villagrá's tortured rhymes described the scene:

No skillful reapers do more swiftly yield
Their curving sickles, flashing rapidly,
When they do quickly knot within their arms
One handful after another and do so
Set up their sheaves in a thousand places

As these brave, haughty combatants
Who, stumbling upon a lofty mound
Of bodies now dead, never ceased
To shed apace a might sum
Of fresh red blood, by which the wall
Was everywhere, upon all sides,
Bathed and ensanguined, and nothing
Remained that was not sprent with it.[33]

Hauling two small cannon, culverins, up onto the mesa tipped the battle in the favor of the Spaniards, and the cannons' burning wadding set the pueblo afire. As the sun set on the second day of fighting, the flickering flames revealed some 600 to 800 Acomas dead, with another 600 captured, mainly women and children.[34]

To this point the Acoma Revolt followed the paradigm of the *Moros y cristianos* these same men had celebrated only months prior—treachery, battle, and retribution—but repentance, forgiveness, and assimilation did not follow. Oñate placed the surviving Acomas on trial at Santo Domingo Pueblo, found them guilty, and ordered a series of brutal punishments. Men over the age of 25 had one foot cut off and were condemned to 20 years of personal servitude. Males aged 12 to 24 years received 20 years of servitude, as did women over 12 years of age. Children under the age of 12, not guilty due to their youth, fell to the Franciscan fathers for a Christian upbringing. The Franciscans soon dispatched sixty small girls to Mexico City, never to return home to their kin. Oñate instructed that two Hopi Indians captured during the fight at Acoma be sent back to their pueblos to carry the news of the punishment, minus their right hands. Oñate directed that the mutilations of the twenty-four men be carried out over a number of days at several nearby pueblos to have as wide an impact as possible. While Oñate may have intended this to cow the Pueblo Indians, the conquerors lost whatever sense of ease they might have had in New Mexico.[35]

The parallel performance of *Moros y cristianos* and the story captured in Villagrá's *Historia* illustrate the primacy of violence in relations with Indian peoples by Janos's ancestors. The last conquistadors, descendants of whom would come to found Janos some eighty years later, sought to dominate Indian peoples, but in order to assimilate them, and bring them into the dual embrace of the Spanish crown and Christian cross. Under cross and crown all would be reconciled, all would live in harmony, all would prosper, in this world and the next. Faced with treacherous resistance and dangerous defiance, carefully proven to be illegal, the Spanish seemingly turned reluctantly to violence — or wished it to seem that way — to establish and maintain the preferred relationship between themselves and the Indians. Yet Indian peoples, including Chiricahua ancestors, had their own historical understandings of the need to do violence.

Killer of Monsters

One spring a band of ancestral Apaches, Apacheans, called Querechos by the settled peoples along the great river to the west, camped on the Southern Great Plains, their buffalo-hide lodges spread along the banks of a narrow and shallow but flowing river. When they spotted a group of oddly dressed strangers approaching, some riding on animals like large dogs, they came out to see the newcomers. They had likely heard of these folk who came into the land of Tiguex during the previous year when the Apacheans went to trade buffalo hides, deer skins, and jerked meat for corn and blankets with the inhabitants of Cicuicue to the west. Among the strangers was a man the Apacheans recognized as one of the peoples to the northeast so they communicated with him via hand signs. They informed El Turco, as the strangers called him, that if the strangers followed the river eastward they would eventually reach a great river with many towns.

El Turco, in turn, likely told the Apacheans of the bloody war waged by these strangers on the people of Tiguex over the winter and of the demands for food and goods they placed on people they encountered. The Apacheans were therefore wary when the leader of the strangers caught up with his advance party and questioned them again about lands to the east. So the next morning they loaded their lodges and goods onto travois hauled by a pack of protesting dogs and moved away from the new people. The Apacheans probably reasoned that they already had one enemy on the plains, the Teyas, and they did not need any more. These ancestral Apaches, descended from killers of monsters as remembered in their tales, understood communities of violence.[36]

As Geronimo told the story, "In the beginning the world was covered with darkness. There was no sun, no day. The perpetual night had no moon or stars." In this land ancestral Chiricahuas tried to live, but the tribe of the beasts and the serpents kept killing them. The beasts and serpents met often in council with the feathered tribe of the birds, led by the eagle. The birds wanted daylight admitted to the world, but the beasts continually refused. Finally, the birds made war against the beasts. "The beasts were armed with clubs, but the eagle had taught his tribe to use bows and arrows. . . . They fought for many days, but at last the birds won a victory." The birds killed many beasts and monsters, but they proved unable to kill them all. The birds, however, now controlled the council and they admitted light to the world. Only with daylight and most of the monsters killed could Chiricahua forebears begin to live in the world.[37]

When and where the Apacheans entered the world of the Southwestern Borderlands is uncertain. They migrated from the Arctic southward across the Great Basin, on the plains across the Texas Panhandle and eastern New Mexico, or down the Front Range of the Rocky Mountains, and onto the Southern Great Plains sometime before their initial encounter with Spaniards from Francisco Vázquez de Coronado's expedition that May day in 1541.[38] Wherever and whenever they entered the plains, the Apacheans did so as an invasion that "*did* involve violence," as the land was already occupied by the Teyas.[39] Sometimes they traded with the Pueblo Indians along the Rio Grande and sometimes they raided. As the Pueblo villages were capable of producing an annual surplus of corn to trade, trading meat for corn was a "less costly means" for the Plains Indians to gain calories than year-round hunting. This made hunting grounds valuable and contributed to the violence between the Apacheans and the Teyas.[40] For ancestral Chiricahuas the Teyas with their tattooed faces and bodies could have been seen as yet another set of monsters that would not let them live in the world.

As Chiricahuas later told it, since the birds did not kill all the monsters, four remained, killing their ancestors. One monster, Giant, kept eating the children of White Painted Woman, the first woman. The Creator brought White Painted Woman a child via a rainstorm and when he was born she named him Child of the Water. White Painted Woman kept Child of the Water from Giant via various subterfuges until he turned four, when he took up a bow and arrows made of grama grass and set out to kill the monsters. While hunting in the forest he provoked Giant to a duel. Giant, secure in his four-layer flint coat, fired his four arrows made of pine trees at Child of the Water, but missed all four times. It was then Child of the Water's turn. "Child of the Water shot at him. The topmost layer of his flint coat slid off him. The next layer, as he shot at him again, this one slid off him also. He shot at him again for the third time. The third time, his coat again slid off him. Then his heart could clearly be seen beating. Child of the Water shot at him for the fourth time. He shot the arrow right into the center of his heart." Giant crashed to the ground, dead.[41]

To kill the second monster, the monster eagles, Child of the Water covered himself in deer entrails and was carried by the father monster eagle to his nest high in the mountains as food for his children. There Child of the Water killed the little monster eagles, sparing only the littlest. He then ambushed and killed the father and mother monster eagles, before having the littlest monster eagle carry him to the ground, where Child of the Water killed it too. The next monster was the buffalo bull, who lived in the middle of the plains and killed people with his eyes by just looking at them. Gopher helped Child of the Water by digging four tunnels, each one deeper than the previous one, under the buffalo. "Then Child of the Water went in. There was the buffalo lying right there. You could see the heart beating. Child of the Water shot that buffalo right through the heart. Then the buffalo was furious and began to dig into that tunnel."[42]

But the buffalo died before he reached Child of the Water in the fourth, deepest, tunnel. The last monster, the antelope, who also killed with his eyes, Child of the Water killed with the help of Lizard, who shot an arrow in all four directions. The antelope chased each arrow in turn, before dying from exhaustion. White Painted Woman sang and danced upon his returning home for Child of the Water killed all the monsters that would not let Chiricahuas live.[43]

Experiences on the Southern Plains and the memories recorded in the battle of the birds and the beasts for daylight and in Child of the Water's exploits illustrate the importance of violence for Chiricahua relations with other peoples. White Painted Woman simply wanted to live with her family but faced terrible and powerful monsters who preyed upon them. Child of the Water turned to violence to allow his family to live. The Chiricahua ancestors thus understood that they might have to use violence to ensure the proper relations with their neighbors, whether tattooed Teyas, town-dwelling Pueblos, or the new Spaniards, if these peoples would not let Chiricahuas live as they wished.

Chiricahua and Janos

The rest of this book considers what happened after both Apache and Hispanic populations settled in the northern Sierra Madre region in the later seventeenth century: the people of Janos as refugees from the Pueblo Revolt in New Mexico, the Chiricahuas as migrants. In the low-yield environment of the Southwestern Borderlands adequate resources required a large territory for subsistence, even with the small populations of both communities. Further, the low population of both communities meant they especially required a critical resource: people, particularly women and children. Chiricahuas and Janeros therefore made their communities throughout the first half of the eighteenth century by incorporating the original indigenous populations and their territories via parallel processes of "Apache-ization" and "Hispanic-ization."[44] Violence dominated these processes since both communities were incorporating the same populations in the same territory, including each other's.

In borderland communities that lived under the threat of violence, such as Chiricahua and Janos, families preferred that their daughters marry men who could not only provide for a wife but also protect her. For the young men of both communities—as it was they who were inclined to greater risk taking to acquire a wife and establish their place in life—violence provided the opportunity to do both, even at the risk of losing their lives.[45] During the later eighteenth century the Janos garrison continually filled its muster roll after the death of soldiers, ultimately trebling in size during a time of demographic collapse, as men sought the status and opportunities of military service—especially access to the supply system—before they sought out a marriage partner. Among Chiricahuas an increase in raiding opportunities allowed more young men to become adults and acquire the necessary material goods and status to marry. Violence also provided the means for experienced warriors to become leaders of their own groups of families. However, the responsibilities of families and leadership forced both Janeros and the Chiricahuas into closer relations.

These closer relations resulted from the creation of peace establishments at presidios, including Janos, across New Spain's northern frontier by the end of the eighteenth century. In order to maintain the families and the status raiding had brought them, many Chiricahuas settled near Janos, reduced their violence, and were gifted with what they had previously raided for. Janeros, also wanting to keep their rank and households, accepted the nearby presence of their erstwhile enemies. While the peace establishment at Janos reduced violence, it did not and could not end the violence altogether as rivalry for rank and status within both communities continued. Since harming the community's enemies was seen as

positive, violence continued to carry social esteem and was carefully accounted for by both communities. Violence continued to
dominate the means to gain and maintain status within each community, even in a time of relative peace.[46] Chiricahuas and Janeros were not, however, always each other's enemies. Chiricahuas
joined in Janos's campaigns against other Apaches, while the Janos
soldiery fought insurgents in north-central Mexico in the counter-
insurgency that led to Mexican Independence.

With independence national support for presidios and peace establishments steadily eroded. The failure to provide adequate gifts
and ensure ample exchanges saw the rise of a generation of Chiricahuas who once again sought to gain position and ensure survival via ever-increasing violence. The steadily weakening garrison at
Janos, joined by a growing number of armed civilians, retaliated
for this violence, with the hope of eliminating the Apaches or at
least establishing deterrence. From time to time Janos worked out
local peace arrangements with Chiricahuas, but these rarely lasted
as retaliation more often simply provoked revenge. Revenge caused
more retaliation, more revenge, and even more retaliation. In the
absence of any authority to enforce cooperation or separation, or
at least minimize the damage, retaliation served as the only rational option for either community.[47] This cycle produced a "grinding,
long sustained apprehension" which neither Chiricahuas nor Janeros escaped, feeding the instinctive desire to strike back; to redirect
their apprehension at the first available target.[48] Retaliation and revenge provided "spiritual fulfillment" for both communities, re-cre-
ating the moral and psychological balance by reassuring their members that although they had been attacked, they could strike back.[49]

The border dividing the borderlands into the United States and
Mexico did not initially change the potential for conflict between
Janos and Chiricahua. Centuries of violence gave rise to endemic
suspicion and insecurity, inviting not only retaliation but also pre-
emptive strikes, in turn magnifying the mutual suspicion and insecurity between the two communities. Each community regarded
the other as a potential enemy, the very existence of which posed a

threat since "they" might attack any day and destroy "us."[50] This "security dilemma" meant that both Janeros and Chiricahuas, while motivated by defensive concerns, often chose to attack to eliminate or severely weaken the other. However violence, while a promising choice and often a rational act for both communities, was not the optimal one, as actions both communities took to provide security for themselves ultimately threatened their survival.[51] If Chiricahuas stayed on the Mexican side of the border they faced treachery and attacks. But if they crossed to the American side seeking security for their families, they could not live the way they wanted. For Janos the dilemma was different, but no less threatening to the community's survival in the long term. The creation of the border and subsequent political turmoil in Mexico only continued the steady decrease and eventual dissolution of the Janos garrison. This made Janeros solely responsible for their own security, a development that would ultimately threaten the Mexican state.

The willingness of both the Mexican government and the United States to enforce the border by the later nineteenth century signaled the end to both Janos and Chiricahua as communities of violence. Neither the United States nor Mexico accepted the role of violence in driving relationships between the two communities. Indeed such communities of violence were the antithesis of the modern nation-state and its claim to a legitimate monopoly on the use of violence.[52] While the Chiricahuas' primary foe was now the United States, their preferred opponent remained Mexican communities across the border. This situation ultimately resulted in their final imprisonment and exile. Janos moved from confronting Chiricahua to facing the expanding power of the Mexican state; ultimately by violence during the Mexican Revolution, in which ex-presidial communities such as Janos played a leading role. The finale for both communities of violence, after two centuries of violent relations, was thus predictably—but understandably—violent.

Ultimately both Chiricahua and Janos gained resources, including population and territory, from each other by violence. Both communities increased by recruiting young men who would then become adult males via violence, gaining the status and material resources necessary to claim a wife. Violence was the means to maintain these families at Janos and Chiricahua by way of competition for rank and status. Both communities used violence to secure themselves in the face of attacks by the other by striking out in retaliation and for revenge. Finally, Chiricahua and Janos deployed violence to handle the dilemma that, regardless of what they did or did not do, they could be attacked by the other, so it was best to attack them first. Both communities stood ready to do violence to each other, a fact that allowed violence to dominate their relations in the Southwestern Borderlands through two hundred years of confrontation, conflict, and cooperation.

Chapter 2

Refugees and Migrants
Making Hispanic-Apache Communities, 1680–1750

Both Chiricahua and Janos made their communities via violent competition over the most basic resource: people. Refugees from the New Mexican Pueblo Revolt of 1680 created Janos presidio in 1686 in response to an Indian rebellion. Apaches continued to migrate from the Southern Plains to the Rio Grande Valley to the mountains above Janos during the seventeenth century, resulting in conflict with Hispanics. Both Chiricahua and Janos were thus made in the cauldron of war between the Spanish crown and re-sisting Indians. Initially both communities incorporated the original inhabitants of the region into their communities; Chiricahua as wives, Janos as part of a caste system that included the offspring of an increasing number of ethnic intermarriages. Both then turned to taking each other's population into their own via violence in raids and campaigns. While Janos and Chiricahua would occasionally take adult captives, especially women, both preferred to seize young children to add to their populations and increase their communities. This meant that the two communities were ultimately related, at least at the genetic level, a relation brought about by violence.

Refugees

Under the late summer sun a sad dispirited parade made its way into the *paraje* (campsite) of La Salineta, three leagues north of El

Paso. More than two thousand men, women, and children filled
the site that September day in 1680, all refugees from a revolt by
northern Pueblo Indians in the Kingdom of New Mexico. Although
they had been alerted to the coming uprising, its size and vehemence
surprised the Hispanic settlers as Indians killed several hundred on
isolated ranches and farmsteads. Those who could fled to Santa Fe,
where Governor Antonio de Otermín defended the capital against
a loose siege for a week. He then led a retreat southward through
scenes of devastation and desecration, catching up with those settlers from the Río Abajo (downriver area) who had survived the rebellion. United, the refugees continued their month-long disheart-
ened withdrawal southward before coming to rest at La Salineta.[1]

As descendants of the last conquistadors, 90 percent of whom
were born in the province, these refugees had been the dominant
class in New Mexico. By virtue of conquest the settlers enjoyed
aristocratic status, although this was at best a local honor, plus
access to Indian labor and *mercedes* (royal grants of land). They
maintained these privileges for over four generations by continual campaigns against enemy Indians, especially Apaches, who had
come to surround the province.[2] Now they were refugees, without
the status they had enjoyed in New Mexico and therefore likely to
remain landless and laborless. Thus many of these Hispanic New
Mexican refugees exploited kinship ties and continued beyond La
Salineta, into the province of Nueva Vizcaya.

Governor Otermín immediately realized many of his kingdom's
subjects were going on southward from La Salineta on their own.
He informed the governor of Parral, who ordered Captain Andrés
López de Grasia, *alcalde mayor* (magistrate) of Casas Grandes, or
in his absence Captain Alonso Pérez Granillo, *alcalde mayor* of
Carretas and Janos, to go to El Paso to prevent anyone from leaving. It is unknown if either López or Pérez went to El Paso, and it
might not have helped stem the tide if they had, as Casas Grandes
and Carretas, which was on the road to Sonora, were the very places to which New Mexican refugees were retreating. Upward of five
hundred Hispanic refugees from the Pueblo Revolt came to settle

in the river valley of Casas Grandes, named for the nearby ancient Indian ruin, along the northeastern flank of the Sierra Madre.[3]

The connections between Casas Grandes and New Mexico went back almost two decades to when the Suma Indians of the region had asked for a mission. Franciscan friars built one, San Antonio de Padua de Casas Grandes, downstream of the ancient Indian ruin, with corresponding lands for corn and wheat and pastures for sheep, goats, and cattle. At the same time Andrés López de Grasia of El Paso settled his family and several others at Casas Grandes south of the mission lands, separated by an irrigation ditch. López became the first *alcalde mayor*.[4] By 1681 Francisco Ramírez de Salazar, López's son-in-law, served as magistrate, but López was quite active in settling his kin among the New Mexican refugees in the district. And there they became quite comfortable for, when Governor Otermín ordered all citizens of New Mexico to report to El Paso a year after the retreat, only three from Casas Grandes appeared. Many, Otermín claimed, were "maliciously" remaining in the valley, some pretending to be sick. Despite Otermín's order to "send at once all the people belonging to New Mexico," it appears that Ramírez failed to do so.[5]

Having fled one Indian rebellion, the New Mexican refugees soon found themselves in the midst of another. The influx of so many new families into the district, all hungry for land, labor, and water, combined with the example of the Pueblo Revolt, upset the delicate ecological and political balance between Indians and settlers in the Casas Grandes valley. The stirrings of rebellion came in early 1684, but the first to rebel were the Jano Indians of the mission of Nuestra Señora de Soledad on May 6, supported by some Sumas. The rebels killed Fray Manuel Beltrán, Captain Antonio de Alviso, and a servant, and carried off six females and two or three boys. Francisco Ramírez did not learn of the incident for nearly five days. During the night of May 13 all the Sumas fled the mission at Casas Grandes after burning their houses. Rebel Indians once again surrounded the New Mexican refugees.

Other New Mexican refugees saved them from seemingly certain destruction: forty from Parral, thirty from El Paso, including allied Piro and Tewa Pueblo Indians who had also left in 1680, and thirty from Sonora, the latter led by militia Captain Juan Fernández de la Fuente, who would soon feature prominently. By early June this force located the rebel Indians, reportedly numbering two thousand, on the Sierra del Diablo, thirty leagues from Casas Grandes. Concerned that the community could be attacked at any time, Ramírez only took twelve Casas Grandes settlers to guide and accompany the nearly one hundred mounted gunmen and Indian auxiliaries to the Sierra del Diablo. After an attack on the rebel Indians, in which one Hispanic and several Pueblo Indian auxiliaries were wounded, Ramírez neither continued the assault nor laid siege but returned the forces to their homes to guard against further attack.[6]

Yet with the rebel Indians still at large and growing in strength, the settler community at Casas Grandes remained insecure. Ramírez therefore sought and received the assistance of Juan Fernández and his thirty men from Sonora after the summer rains began. Ramírez and Fernández then spent "days campaigning," trailing the rebel Indians north by northeast "from one mountain range to another." However the Suma and Jano rebels doubled back on the Hispanic forces, falling on Casas Grandes in mid-September while Ramírez and Fernández were still fifty leagues distant. The New Mexican refugees were in grave danger once again. The Indians bludgeoned some settlers to death with war clubs and set fire to the storage *jacales* (huts), a fire that eventually consumed the settlers' houses. Rebel Sumas and Janos also took horses out of the corrals and drove away the sheep and the goats to their stronghold in the sierra, five leagues away.[7]

Ramírez and Fernández hastily returned to Casas Grandes, along with Captain Roque Madrid of El Paso, with whom they had joined forces while on campaign. Further reinforced by men from the presidio of Sinaloa, Ramírez, Fernández, and Madrid reached the rebel stronghold at dawn on September 30 and attacked an hour later. All day the soldiers, settlers, and Pueblo Indians fought the

Suma and Jano rebels on foot among the rocks of the sierra. Without the tactical advantage of fighting mounted, Hispanic forces suffered nearly thirty badly wounded casualties, including Madrid, and were forced to withdraw. Two weeks later Ramírez tried again, with a few more Indian allies. He also convinced Madrid to stay and fight, in return for six hundred head of cattle for El Paso. The rebels moved their camp to another sierra in the meantime, but Ramírez, Fernández, and Madrid led their forces into another all-day fight, this time killing many of the rebels and scattering the rest. They rescued women and children taken captive, recovered cattle and horses taken from Casas Grandes, and reclaimed items from the Janos mission, including a chalice.[8]

Even with this success, Ramírez did not feel the community and Casas Grandes were secure. He wrote to the governor of Nueva Vizcaya "on the great peril we faced," asking for either more assistance or permission to abandon Casas Grandes altogether. Neither proved forthcoming, but the governor did authorize any New Mexican refugee who wished to do so to settle at the abandoned Janos mission. On December 1 Ramírez learned that a "great number" of Indians were gathering at Ojo Caliente. Able to spare only twelve men from guarding the community, Ramírez conscripted eight lance-armed *vaqueros* (cowboys) and more than a hundred Indian auxiliaries. He attacked ten days later, surprising the Indian rebels; Ramírez again estimated their number at over two thousand, and he forced them to sue for peace. The Christian Indians among them he ordered back to their villages in fifteen days and "the rabble to return to their own territory." Yet April 1685, after nearly a year of rebellion, found the community of Casas Grandes "awake every night guarding what few horses we have left as well as our lives and the church," into which they had moved after their houses burned the previous September. Many in the community lived in fear of Indian "cruelty," and Ramírez again asked for more help, believing "we risk our very lives to remain here past August."[9]

Ramírez was right to fear the Suma who had returned to Casas Grandes supposedly in peace, although he got the month wrong.

In September a Suma man threatened to cut a priest's throat, while others went around stating they were going to kill the Spaniards to avenge the deaths of relatives the Spaniards had killed. Some among them said the Suma were going to go war again to impress the other Indians with their valor and bravery. By October the refugees at Casas Grandes feared all the Indians in the area would revolt at the next full moon. For the next two months the Spaniards hunted down suspected Suma conspirators, killing some seventy-seven men. At Casas Grandes the refugees executed fifty-two of these, clubbing some to death in revenge, taking the Suma women and children as slaves.[10] While the presumed Suma conspiracy unfolded, events across the ocean would lead to the creation of a new community.

On June 16, 1685, in response to ongoing rebellions, King Carlos II of Spain ordered the establishment of two new presidios of twenty-five men each at Cuencamé and Gallo. Although these were far to the south of Casas Grandes, the precedent was set. By December the royal council learned that the king's orders had not been implemented and so castigated the viceroy, reiterating the command. The council added orders for the creation of a third presidio farther north, on the Río Conchos, to have fifty men armed with newer firearms. By early 1686 work was underway on all three, and the viceroy added a fourth at Casas Grandes. Consisting of fifty men under the command of Juan Fernández de la Fuente, whose Sonoran militiamen had succored Casas Grandes in its darkest times, the presidio moved within a few months to the old mission site of Janos, likely taking much of the Casas Grandes community with it, nearer to the Sonoran passes and the growing Apache threat.[11] For while the New Mexican refugees dealt with the rebellion in front of them, they kept an eye out for an old foe, Apaches. On his August to September campaign in 1684 Ramírez had watched for signs of Apache enemies the whole time. He voiced his concern that the Suma and Jano rebels would eventually join forces with the Apaches.[12] This fear would come to consume the new community at Janos, and they were right to be concerned, for

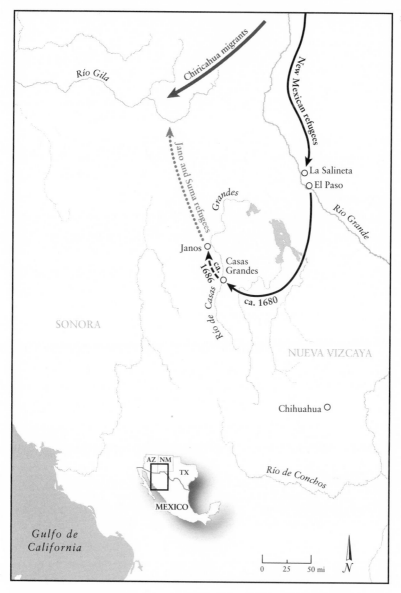

Map 6. Refugees and migrants, ca. 1690

Apaches did join the New Mexicans in the region—not as refugees but as migrants.

Migrants

In late summer, about two generations after the initial encounter with the Spaniards of Coronado's expedition, a band of Apaches encamped among the ridges three days' travel east of Pecos Pueblo. Four men set out to hunt and had traveled about a day away from their families when they spotted a large party of strangers leaving the mountain pass and heading out onto the plains. Through their trading connections at Pecos the Apaches had undoubtedly heard of the return of Spaniards to the Rio Grande valley. While it is unknown whether they knew of Spanish desires to conquer the region, they took precautions before meeting the party of sixty men. One Apache hid in the Spaniards' path while the other three fell back and concealed themselves where they could cover him with their bows and arrows if necessary. When the Spaniards were close enough to hear him, but not close enough to attack, the first Apache rose out of the grass and called to them. Determining they were not hostile, he then called to his three other companions. These four then escorted the Spaniards to their *ranchería* (settlement), where three more Apaches met them on the opposite side of the ridge from the camp. When the Spanish leader, Vicente de Zaldívar Mendoza, Oñate's *sargento mayor*, elected to go into the camp escorted by only one other Spaniard, the Apaches asked him for assistance against their ancestral enemies, the "Xumanos . . . Indians who are striped." Zaldívar demurred, leaving the Apaches the next day and, since the Spanish would not help them in their fight against their enemies, leaving the Apaches cautious in any future dealings with the newcomers to the region.[13]

The Spanish conquest of New Mexico did not end Apache migrations. They continued to move off the Southern Plains over the Sangre de Cristo Mountains to settle in the hinterlands between the northern Rio Grande Pueblos. Within a decade of their encounter with Zaldívar, Apaches lived near Pecos, Taos, and Picuris pueblos.

On the Southern Plains the Apaches incorporated the settled farmers into their subsistence patterns via the dual means of raiding and
trading. This made the Pueblo Indians quite wary of and somewhat hostile to the Apaches in their encounters, as Apache memories show. The Jicarilla Apaches, having lived the longest in contact with the Pueblos, remembered when their cultural hero visited
Picuris Pueblo. The Picuris "decided to use him in evil ways" and
lowered him over a cliff to steal some eagle chicks from their nest.
At Taos Pueblo the hero, dressed in rags, fled from the Taoseños,
who cried, "You get out, you old Apache." Further, they treated
him like a dog, forcing him to beg for scraps to eat. Despite this
initial mistreatment, in both cases the cultural hero did render assistance to the Pueblos, in much the same way as Apache trade
proved beneficial.[14]

The arrival of Spanish trade goods in the Rio Grande Valley
likely prompted the migration of some Apaches closer to those
Pueblos with which they had the longest relationships. Given the
relative poverty of the province and lack of any exploitable min-
eral deposits, however, the Spanish saw the Pueblo-Apache trade
as a potential source of profit and so attempted to bring it under
their control, upsetting the delicate balance of trade and raid between Pueblos and Apaches. Because of this Apaches saw Spaniards as "scoundrels," "people concerned only with their own in-
terests." To retaliate against these "monsters" who would not let
them live, they struck at livestock, the most vulnerable and most
valuable Spanish possession.[15]

As Chiricahuas later remembered it, there were initially no cattle on earth. The crows kept the cattle in the ground under a big
stump. Killer of Enemies, Child of the Water's older male kin, got
into the ground with the help of Coyote. There he regaled the keepers of the cattle with stories of prairies, grass, canyons, mountains,
and water on the surface. Why keep the cattle below, penned up
with no grass? Why not let turn them loose onto the world where
they could get fat? The old man who was the crow leader agreed,
and Killer of Enemies herded all the cattle together and turned them

out. At this point Coyote ceased helping and starting killing cattle—he was after all a coyote—but nearly all the cattle were now out of their subterranean corral. It was late in the evening and the crows, who made noises like cowboys herding cattle, were unable to do anything to stop the cattle from coming onto the earth.[16] Chiricahua ancestors saw themselves as liberating livestock from Spanish "scoundrels" in retaliation for their disruption of the profitable raid and trade relationship between Apaches and the Pueblos. But Apaches soon had another reason for taking revenge on Spaniards.

Slaves were one item of the Apache-Pueblo trade that the Spanish particularly wished to control. Earlier, Apaches had occasionally traded Caddoan-speaking captives from the east at the Pueblos, but after the arrival of the Spanish the slave trade quickened. Yet Apaches could not provide enough captives to meet Spanish demands, and they began to suffer slave raids. These raids reached the extent that the Spanish population of New Mexico soon came to include several hundred Apache slaves. One of the first known instances of a slave raid took place nearly twenty years after the conquest, when a Spanish governor sent out a strong party of Pueblo Indians to attack an Apache encampment. Despite the professed desire of the Apaches to become Christians, the slavers killed their chief and took many others as captives to be sold to the silver mines of Nueva Vizcaya.[17] The shock of such attacks reverberated in Apache memory.

Chiricahuas told of these encounters in "Foolish People" stories; stories intended to be instructive of proper behavior told about people who did not know how to act in a given situation. One story told of when many white men came to a big Foolish People camp and began to shoot at them. The Foolish People decided to do nothing, so as not to annoy their attackers. The white men then rode into their camp, attacking them with swords. The Foolish People were aghast at this, asking why they would do such a thing. It was only once they were being killed that the Foolish People realized they had to run away. Another story told of some Foolish People who were encamped on a plain when men on horseback rode down on them. They escaped only by running over the small hills scattered about the plain, tiring out the horses of their pursuers.[18] To avoid such attacks many Apaches continued to migrate away from the main Spanish settlement along the northern Rio Grande, but still remaining close to the Pueblos with whom they had grown increasingly interdependent.

The travels of one community of Apaches, including that which would be known as Chiricahua, took them south of the northern Pueblos and to the west side of the Rio Grande. Under their captain, Sanaba, they came to occupy lands several days' travel west and north of the Pueblo of Senecú, near present-day Socorro, New Mexico, identified as Gila Apaches by the Spanish. Sanaba apparently "ordinarily attended" happenings at the pueblo, including the preaching of Spanish friars. Possibly because he thought they could intercede with the secular authorities, Sanaba became enamored with the priests, giving one a *gamuza* (treated deerskin) painted with a green sun and a grey moon, each decorated with a cross. If Sanaba had hoped his gift would allow his people to maintain their trade and raid relationship with the Piro pueblos around Senecú without Spanish interference, he was ultimately disabused of this prospect. Within a few years most Apaches were at war with the Spanish and their Pueblo allies, and over the decades Apache attacks on the roads threatened communications between Santa Fe and El Paso.[19]

A new factor entered the relations between the Spaniards and Pueblos: horses. Apaches had previously raided for horses along with other livestock, primarily to eat. Around the time of Sanaba's encounter with the friars at Senecú, Apaches began to ride horses. Chiricahuas recollected that their Plains Apache cousins showed them how to ride. The Foolish People in the story were unfamiliar with a horse they took, unsure of what it ate or what to do with it. A Mescalero Apache who was with them demonstrated how to ride the horse, to the amazement of the Foolish People. Thus the Gila Apaches had a new means to raid and a new motive for raiding. Mounted warriors could strike and withdraw much more quickly on horseback than on foot and over much longer distances. Trade relations become less and less important, although they did not disappear, as mounted raiders could exploit larger areas. Apaches now used horses to get more horses, which they used to trade or to eat.[20]

The continuing poverty of New Mexico meant continuing Spanish and Pueblo slave raids, increasingly met with raids by increasingly mounted Apaches. Gila Apaches continued to live along the routes out of New Mexico, but under a new leader, El Chilmo. They now relied upon the mobility of their horses, abandoning their settled rancherias and increasing their mounted attacks. On one occasion a force of Gila Apaches under El Chilmo surprised a Spanish convoy carrying the new governor to Santa Fe, killing four Spaniards and running off all their mules. On another El Chilmo led a coordinated, mounted assault on Senecú, driving off all the livestock in the pueblo. Waiting Apaches ambushed a combined force of Spaniards and Piros that set off in pursuit, forcing them to retreat. Campaigns against the Gila Apaches yielded nothing, and for the decade before the revolt they carried out continuous raids against the Spaniards and their Pueblo Indian allies, contributing to the abandonment of six pueblos. Yet Gila Apaches took no part in the Pueblo Revolt, being far to the south, and limited themselves to harassing the Spanish refugees as they passed out of the province.[21]

The Gila Apaches now faced a conundrum. Their greatest enemy was gone, but they had grown reliant upon relations, both violent and in trade, with the Spaniards. From their settlement near the hot springs at present-day Truth or Consequences, New Mexico, the Gila Apaches split into the bands that would collectively come to be known as Chiricahua. One band stayed around the headwaters of the Gila River, one came to rest in the Sierra de Chiricahua, and one would ultimately come to reside on the northern slopes of the Sierra Madre.[22] Those Apaches moving south soon found themselves in range of the New Mexican refugees and using guides, both willing and unwilling, from among the local Suma and Jumano Indians. The winter after the Spaniards retreated through their territory south of Senecú, Apaches struck at El Paso, taking two hundred head of livestock, having "done as they always do." A few months later they attacked a ranch near the refugees at Casas Grandes, something never reported before.[23] The Chiricahuas had arrived and now joined Janos in the first steps of a deadly dance that would eventually lead to a violent embrace.

Communities Made by War

For the next ten years both communities would be made in a crucible of war. Janos kept one eye cocked for migrating Chiricahuas to their north as the new presidio continued to engage rebels: Suma, Jocome, and their namesake Jano Indians. In March 1688 Captain Fernández led a campaign against the rebellious Indians with forty soldiers from his new command, thirty settlers, and two hundred Indian allies from Casas Grandes. Four months later the Jano and Jocome Indians struck back, attacking the Casas Grandes region, killing one soldier and wounding Fernández. Despite his injuries Fernández led a force in August to defeat an alliance of Jano, Jocome, and Suma Indians, killing two hundred and capturing many women and children.[24] The Jano and Jocome fled northward to seek refuge along the Gila River. There they intermingled with Apaches. Chiricahua migrants took advantage of these natives' knowledge of the region, traveling to Janos presidio to sell deerskins and make off with horses when possible. One party took fifty horses in the spring of 1691.[25]

Chiricahuas considered such events to be par for the course. The Foolish People, as they remembered, went to the south to raid for horses and cattle. After a number of misadventures, including losing packs of food and trying to kill a dragonfly, they came upon a horse. As they prepared to take the horse, some Hispanics came after them and began killing them. Rather than running, the Foolish People just stood there, asking why they were being killed. After most were killed, a few realized that they had better run. That, Chiricahuas remembered, is "why they didn't last."[26]

Lasting, or survival, was at the heart of Apache raiding. It was, in the words of one observer, a "recognized and integral part of the economy" and was seen as a "stern economic necessity."[27] However, it would be erroneous simply to think of the raids by the Apaches along the Gila as purely subsistence. Raids were deeply embedded in a larger network of exchange stretching far beyond the Spanish settlements out onto the Great Plains, as evidenced by the testimony of a Jumano Indian enslaved by the Plains Apaches, traded to the Gila Apaches for horses, and taken by a Spanish expedition. This Jumano reported that Gila Apaches made horse raids since Plains Apaches were now dependent upon horses. They had previously acquired horses from New Mexico, but with the Pueblo Revolt and the retreat of the Spaniards, the Plains Apaches "come now to have it [trade for horses] with the Apaches of the Sierra of Gila."[28]

It was thus "common knowledge" at Janos that the Apaches were in league with all the rebellious Indians of the north, and the community sought the assistance of the exiled New Mexican government at El Paso to wage war "with fire and sword until they seek peace with us" since "a hard war ensures a secure peace." The new governor of New Mexico, Diego de Vargas, felt it was not his place to go to the aid of Janos. The viceroy, however, overruled him. So Vargas placed his plans for a reconquest of New Mexico on hold and reported to Fernández that he would be ready to campaign "where the enemies' opposition and resistance is greatest" against "the Gila Mountain Apaches." But Vargas carefully insulted the captain of Janos by addressing him as "vuestra merced" (your honor), a polite form, but lacking the connotation of nobility in "vuestra señoría" (your lordship).[29]

Vargas's annoyance lay not just in his spoiled plans of reconquest but also in his thwarted desire that the New Mexican refugees, gone from the exiled colony in El Paso for over ten years, would return. While the viceroy had issued an order that all were to return to the kingdom with Vargas, and Vargas ensured a copy went to Casas Grandes, he warned the viceroy that magistrates in Casas Grandes would contest it. Too many of the refugees were now working on *ranchos* (ranches) and *haciendas* (farms), whose owners would be loath to lose them. Many others were "living under the protection of the royal standard, having enlisted in the presidial companies," including that of Janos. Vargas realized that the order to recall refugees could not, and thus should not, be enforced in the presidios, haciendas, and ranchos of jurisdictions confronting the Indians.[30]

Those Indians, including Chiricahuas, were unaware that the united forces of Fernández and Vargas marched northward out of Janos and crossed the Continental Divide into the Gila River basin. Encamped along both sides of the river, several rancherias awoke one crisp dawn in late fall to discover Spaniards struggling through the rough terrain beyond their camp in an attempt to surround them. The Spanish surprise attack turned into a pursuit as the Apaches fled, many praying to the *Gahe* (Mountain Spirits). The Chiricahua told of the *Gahe* coming out of their mountain to the prayers of an old man and some women who were chased by soldiers. The *Gahe* opened up a cave in the mountain and with their swords, like those the soldiers carried, forced the Spaniards into the cave, which they then sealed up, trapping all the soldiers inside. Whether it was due to the loss of surprise or the *Gahe*, the Janos presidials managed to capture only twenty-three women and children and just two warriors. Yet the Apaches did not stay captured for long, rising up in force against the Spaniards who "brawled," killing sixteen. An early season storm with wet and swirling snow forced an end to the campaign and its withdrawal back to Janos. But the sally confirmed the fears of Fernández and the community of Janos, for the "Apaches made a formable union of all the people of their nation and that of the Janos, Jocomes, and Sumas."[31]

In late July 1692 Janos learned of a concentration of rebel Indians at Carretas, an old Suma settlement to the west near the crest of the Sierra Madre. Fernández planned a campaign for the next month using his soldiers, supported by Casas Grandes settlers and Concho Indian auxiliaries. However, patrols spotted an encampment only eight leagues away at the *aguaje* (water hole) of Palotada, and on July 26 a small party of soldiers "sallied forth" to attack.

They soon ran into a force of several hundred Indians on foot and on horseback. The Janos soldiers managed to fight their way clear and retreat, but at the cost of several wounded. Fernández quickly mustered the rest of the garrison and led a stronger force back to Palotada, where they discovered the large village of Indians three leagues beyond the *aguaje*. Spotting the soldiers, the Indians sent their women and children scrambling to the safety of a nearby hilltop and drew up in a number of tribal groups to await Janos's attack. The first clash wounded a soldier and several horses but killed many Indians. Faced with such losses, the Indians expressed a desire to talk.[32]

Peace talks went on for several days, with both sides exchanging goods. The village totaled some three hundred adult males, a combination of Janos, Jocomes, Mansos, and Sumas, with some Apaches and Pimas. Two Indians of each nation accompanied the soldiers back to Janos, where they received tobacco, clothing, and other gifts. All agreed to return to their own lands since, as Fernández noted, the village with its women and children totaled nearly a thousand people and was too big to support itself without resorting to raiding. For the next two weeks parties of Indians came into the presidio to affirm the peace plan, but the principal Jano chief and El Tabovo of the Jocomes wished Fernández would visit them in their villages. On August 11, Fernández did so, and all reaffirmed the peace agreement, with the Jano Indians agreeing to settle near the presidio, which was, after all, on their ancestral lands. However, within a few days the peace fell apart as the Indians, as Fernández had predicted, resorted to raiding and "returned to the sierras and places where they were living before."[33]

A year later the uncertain situation remained unaltered. When Fernández received an order sending him with many of his company to Sonora to deal with an uprising of the Pimas, he chose to await reinforcements before heading out, believing he did not have "enough forces to leave this place [Janos] secure from the Apaches and other nations." Ironically, this order came from an inspector, *Maestre de Campo* (Field Marshall) Don José Francisco Marín, sent to the northern frontier by the viceroy of New Spain to determine if the newly erected presidios, including Janos, should be suppressed and their forces combined into a single *compañía volante* (mobile company) to patrol the road, escort travelers, and respond to attacks.[34]

Most of the men queried by the *maestre de campo* believed the presidios had to be retained, especially Janos, since it faced "the frontiers of divers rebellious nations and the Apache Nation." Another noted that the presidios were "very necessary" as the captains led campaigns into enemy country, from which the soldiers and their horses could recuperate at their presidio. Marín agreed with the leading men of New Spain's northern frontier that the presidios needed to stay. War, he believed, had to be waged continuously against the Indians in their own lands, pursuing them to where they hid, so that the Indians could not make raids against the king's subjects. Each presidio would keep ten men as a guard and the remaining forty would search the hills for Indian settlements, primarily during the rainy season when water for horses and men would be available. Once the Indians surrendered they were to be placed into settlements, under the watchful eyes of a presidio.[35]

Both communities were now made by war. By viceregal fiat, Janos was secure in its place on the slopes below the Sierra Madre. No longer a community of refugees from New Mexico, the Janeros were now a garrison intended to wage war against Chiricahua Apaches, "a widespread nation." Chiricahuas, having "named the mountains, named the springs, the rivers, plants, trees, and berries" from the Gila River to the edge of the Chiricahua Mountains, were at home, no longer migrants. They had come south to maintain their ability to raid and trade with the Spaniards and with it their ability to survive. Settled by violence into their new homes, the people of both Janos and Chiricahua set about creating multiethnic borderland communities, often by violence.[36]

Making Borderland Communities

In the season of Many Leaves the Apache leader known as El Salinero listened to a tale of woe under the pines in the Gila country.

The teller of the tale, the Jocome elder called El Tabovo, led a mixed settlement of Jano, Manso, Suma, Chinarra, and his own Jocome Indians in the central Chiricahua Mountains, all in open rebellion against the Spanish for over ten harvests. Around the summer solstice these nations gathered together for security as most of the adult men and some women, nearly one hundred in all, set out to raid settlements on the western slopes of the Sierra Madre. Their timing was unfortunate, as a Spanish campaign discovered their trail and pursued them in a running battle that lasted all morning and killed almost half of the Indians. The Spaniards then followed the trail back to the Chiricahua Mountains, forcing El Tabovo's charges to flee among the arroyos and mesas. He himself led the captains of the Janos, Jocomes, Mansos, Sumas, and Chinarras to negotiate with the Spaniards. For seven days they asked that their captured kin be released and their seized horses be returned, while accepting gifts of tobacco, bread, blankets, meat, and pinole. The Spaniards, however, abruptly departed. But with so many men dead or captured—there were only nineteen men left among the Jocomes—an ailing El Tabovo led the Indians to the Gila River country to join the Apaches. Having listened to this tale, El Salinero welcomed the Jocomes to his band, promising his men would support them and protect them from the Spaniards, who he insisted "were not men." Within a few weeks, after El Tabovo's brother left the band, El Salinero became the recognized leader, *gobernador* (governor) in the Spanish rendering, of this unified band of Jocomes and Apaches.[37]

El Salinero's actions were not unique. All across the Southwestern Borderlands Apaches made their communities by replacing, incorporating, or acculturating many of the previous native inhabitants of the region in a process of "Apache-ization." At one point the Apaches offered to help the Spaniards fight the Mansos, apparently so as to make former Manso lands available to the Apaches. Apaches did incorporate people by force; after all, it was a Jumano Indian from the Plains, enslaved by Apaches, traded for horses, and rescued by the Spaniards, who had explained why the Apaches were raiding for horses. Apaches also acculturated other Indians by creating kinship relations. Yet the most direct means for the Apaches to create a borderland community was to take wives from among the original inhabitants of the region.[38]

Genetic evidence shows that "extensive female" migration accompanied Apache contact with other Indian groups in the Southwest. Most of the migration, by factor of at least 10:1, consisted of women moving from surrounding groups to the Apaches, rather than Apache women moving into other groups. One estimate suggests that approximately 2 percent of mothers in each Apache generation over the last five hundred years originated in surrounding groups. In the first decades of contact the number was likely much higher, with many wives and mothers coming from the surrounding Uto-Aztecan speaking Janos, Sumas, Mansos, Chinarras, and Jocomes. This suggests Chiricahuas required wives urgently enough to acquire them through trade, or warfare, or indirectly in the case of El Salinero's men.[39]

El Salinero's band may well have needed women from outside the Apache community as wives, for more men than women migrated into the borderlands. An old Jocome woman reported "many more" Apache men than Jocomes in El Salinero's mixed ranchería. These men would have needed women to create a viable community, especially given all the labor women provided. A man normally got access to a woman's labor via marriage. But marriage to a Chiricahua wife meant joining her family with all the primary avoidances that entailed.[40]

For Chiricahuas a son-in-law was "one who carries burdens for me," and every relative of the wife was entitled to address him as such. Adding to this was the requirement that a husband had to avoid totally his wife's mother, her father, her mother's mother, and her father's mother. These four, of whom three may have been at his new bride's home, were known as "the ones to whom I do not go." Yet these affinal relatives determined a husband's actions, using his wife as a messenger, to the extent that a husband was "the man ruled by them [the relatives]." A son-in-law had to support his wife's relatives, although he could take anything they had in turn. The requirement for a husband to support his wife's relatives, even while avoiding them, could continue even after the death of the wife.[41]

Chiricahuas told of when Coyote married. He had a camp of his own, but his mother-in-law's camp was nearby. "Of course, he didn't see her." One day Coyote went hunting and chased a rabbit into a hollow log. Coyote tried to reach the rabbit in the log but could barely touch it. He went back to his camp and told his wife to ask her mother to see if she could get the rabbit out; "maybe her arm was longer than his." When his mother-in-law left camp, Coyote circled back and watched as she crawled into the log. When she was about half in, Coyote ran over, had intercourse with her, and ran back to his camp. She did not know who did it, but she located the tracks. Coyote's mother-in-law took a stick and measured the footprint she found. She took the stick back to her camp and called her daughter over. She gave the stick to her daughter, who took it back to her wickiup. She found Coyote lying on his bed, singing. She began to measure his foot in every way. Coyote asked, "What are you doing?" His wife told him that while her mother had been trying to get the rabbit, someone "played a trick on her." Then Coyote told his wife, "Don't talk like a witch! That's witch talk. Go away and don't bother me. You folks have witch mouths!"[42]

Coyote's outburst stemmed from the fact that Chiricahuas considered anyone who committed incest to be a witch, along with anyone who dwelled on the subject, or anyone who was suspected of failing to obey the avoidance taboos. Public exposure and beatings were "the mildest punishments meted out to those discovered in incest."[43] Thus wives from outside the community, who often came without their families and who may not have necessitated any avoidance behavior patterns, may well have proven attractive to Chiricahua men. The Jumano women likely appealed to those men with El Salinero that summer day in the Gila Mountains. No matter how attractive they may have been, El Salinero himself did not live long to take advantage of their arrival.

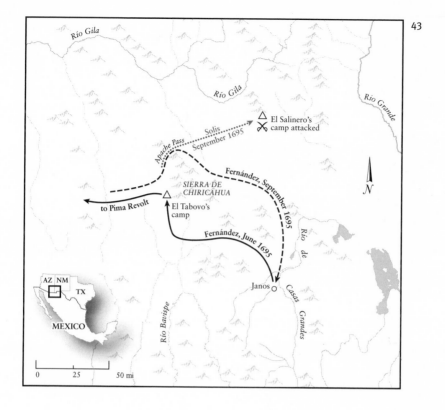

Map 7. Fernández, El Tabovo, and El Salinero, 1695

His demise came from the actions of Captain Fernández of Janos presidio. In mid-June Fernández led thirty-six of his own soldiers, forty under Don Domingo Terán de los Rios, commander of Gallo presidio, and sixty allied Indians, including thirty Conchos under their war captain Juan Corma, out of Janos on a campaign against the Janos, Jocomes, Mansos, Sumas, Chinarras, and Apaches. This force, after scouring the mountains and valleys to the north and northwest of Janos for a week, located, pursued, and devastated the raiding party from El Tabovo's ranchería. While negotiating with El Tabovo in the Chiricahua Mountains, Fernández and Terán learned of the revolt of the Pima Indians and left to put down their rebellion. However, after two months, Fernández returned to the Chiricahua Mountains in mid-September, alarmed that rebel Indians were increasingly joining the Apaches. A patrol took several captives, and from these Fernández learned that the Jocomes, Janos, Sumas, and Chinarras had gone to the Gila River country. Further searches discovered El Tabovo's brother, who informed Fernández that El Tabovo was ill but that the Jocomes, Janos, and Sumas wanted peace. The next day troops seized a Jocome man and woman who told them of the Jocomes' joining with El Salinero's band of Apaches. The woman also informed Fernández that the Apaches did not want peace, but "vengeance for those killed and captured" by the Spanish.[44]

It was now the twentieth of September and Fernández's force was encamped at the northern end of the Chiricahua Mountains near the western end of present-day Apache Pass. Many men were ill with chills and fevers, likely due to a viral infection from drinking contaminated water in the heat, humidity, and violent rains of the summer monsoon season. Terán was too sick to ride a horse and nearly a hundred Pima allies had abandoned the campaign. Fernández determined to send another strong patrol to find the Jocomes to see if they really wanted peace. Lieutenant Antonio de Solis led out sixty-four men with three horses each and a hundred friendly Opatas, Conchos, and Pimas, all with four days of rations. For three anxious days Fernández waited, but Don Pablo

Quique of the Opatas and Juan Corma of the Conchos returned to camp to announce a victory. While scouting for Solis's force, Silvestre Pacheco of Janos presidio spotted the Jocomes' settlement at midmorning. The rest of the soldiers closed rapidly and pursued the Indians, who fled their camp. Soldiers and allied Indians killed twelve, including both El Tabovo and El Salinero, and captured forty-four women and children and two old men. Solis released one old man to tell the Indians that if they wanted their people back, they had to come and negotiate. He then returned to Fernández's camp, with the women and children captives in between two columns of soldiers, flanked by the Indian auxiliaries "carrying the scalps of those they had killed as a sign of victory."[45]

Fernández then questioned the old man, asking if the Jocomes wanted at peace, why were they taking horses? The old man replied that it was the young men who were raiding "and the governors and captains could not stop them." Besides, the old man went on, the Apaches did not want peace. Fernández set off through the pass the next day, ordering three Jocome captives and two old women shot so as not to impede his progress. Terán had to be carried in a litter, and many of the men were still sick with fever and chills and could not travel far. The campaign emerged from Apache Pass onto the eastern side of the mountains on September 26 and reached the San Simón springs the next day. There Fernández decided to rest until the sick soldiers could travel, and he sent out patrols to the north and south. These patrols returned on September 28 having found nothing. Fernández determined that all the Indians had fled to the Gila River, "the Apache country." With Terán unable to speak, Fernández convened a Council of War with Don Domingo Jironza Petriz de Cruzate of Sonora, *Alférez* (Ensign) Pedro de Villegas of Terán's company, Captain Nicolás de la Higuera, commander of Sinaloa presidio, Lieutenant Solis, *Alférez* Francisco de Acuña, Sergeants Diego Lopéz Zambrano and Cristóbal de Vargas of Janos presidio, and "many other officials experienced in this kind of war." Since many soldiers were sick and most of the Indian allies had already left, all agreed to recommend abandoning the campaign until enough forces could be assembled to invade the Gila country. Terán died just after midnight the next day, but Fernández determined not to bury him in Indian territory and sent his body on to Janos with an escort of seven soldiers to bury him there. As the campaign force prepared to depart the springs, they distributed the captured Jocome women and children among themselves. "Everyone was pleased," Fernández reported. With his soldiers and captives in tow, Fernández returned to Janos on October 3, after three and a half months in the saddle.[46]

Perhaps wishing to be reunited with their captured kin and perhaps desiring to escape from Apache men taking their women as wives, three years later in October 1698 the remaining Janos and Jocomes, along with some Sumas, about 120 families in all, came to Janos to make peace. A Jocome presented Fernández with a deer skin painted with symbols representing all those nations and families who wished to make peace. Fernández accepted it and settled the Jano Indians near the presidio. From there they would steadily be absorbed into the community, undergoing a parallel process of "Hispanic-ization," making Janos as much a multi-ethnic community as Chiricahua.[47]

Janos too made its borderland community by incorporating the original Uto-Aztecan-speaking Indians, and the baptism of Indian children, adding their souls to the roster of the community of the faithful, was a strong pointer to this reality. In 1699, the year after the Janos and Jocomes asked for peace, baptismal records listed sixteen Janos, one Jocome, and nine Sumas. Yet Janos had had Indians in the community ever since records had been kept; in 1688, the first year, records noted fourteen Indians baptized, although their ethnicity was not given. Nearly twenty years after the peace of 1698 enough friendly Indians lived at Janos that when a hundred families of Jano and Jocome Indians moved from El Paso in 1717, orders went out to reestablish the Indian town of Nuestra Señora de la Soledad, destroyed in the 1684 uprising, by building a church and a public building three leagues from the presidio, although there is no evidence that the order was carried out. Ten years after that a large enough Indian presence remained at Janos so that 143 Sumas came to settle at the presidio, yet it is not known if they stayed. The parish records, however, show this sizeable Indian presence in the first decades of the eighteenth century steadily declining throughout the decades to midcentury. Janos, Sumas, and Jocomes, among others, increasingly became known simply as Indians, especially as they intermarried with one another. They also intermarried with the "Spanish" population of the community, evidenced by an increase in the recording of *casta* (caste) groups.[48]

Along with baptism into the Catholic Church, the process of Hispanic-ization also included assignment into the *sistema de castas* (caste system). *Españoles* (descendants of Spaniards or Europeans) sat atop this ethnic hierarchy, with *indios* (Indians) at the bottom. *Negros* (offspring of Africans), often although not always associated with *esclavo* (slave), occupied the lower rungs. In between lay a vast and bewildering array of *castas* (mixed ethnicities) that included *mestizo, coyote, lobo,* and *mulato,* the last occasionally associated with *esclavo*. The first hints of Janos as a multi-ethnic borderland community come from Bishop García de Legaspi y Velasco's visit to Janos presidio in the late seventeenth century, when he confirmed some 150 persons: 74 Spaniards, 61 Indians, and 15 *castas*. The mixed-ethnicity *castas* included seven *mestizos,* four *mulatos,* three *coyotes,* and one *negro*. All of these individuals increasingly intermarried with each other, producing mixed-ethnicity offspring.[49]

Mestizo soldier Pedro Padilla's family evidenced Janos as an ethnically mixed community. Parish books recorded his wife, Josefa Rosas, as an *"india"* and his two daughters, María de los Dolores born in 1729 and María Francisca born in 1733, as *"coyotas,"* signifying them as the offspring of a father of Indian and European descent and an Indian mother. As the number of Indians decreased in the first half of the century, the number of *mestizos* and other *castas* increased. María de los Reyes, the daughter of *coyota* María Victoria Solis and *mulato* Juan de Olguín, baptized in 1750, entered the community as a *"mestiza."* By midcentury this

was increasingly the default category at Janos, marking its genetically admixed nature. Nicolás de Lafora of the Royal Engineers
reported that the community consisted solely of *mestizo* and *mulato* families, "including those of the company." One final group,
however, added to the ethnic mélange of Janos: Apaches. Janos and
Chiricahua not only incorporated the original Indian inhabitants
of the region; each also added members of the other via captivity
as both made their borderland communities.[50]

In early April 1741 a patrol from Janos apparently surprised a
small group of Apache men and women. Most probably escaped,
several were likely killed, and at least one was captured, a woman.
The soldiers brought her back to the presidio, where she was given
to one of the community's leading citizens, the notary Lucas de Abecia. On April 24 Abecia stood as *padrino* (godfather) for the woman, who was baptized as María Antonia, her Apache name discard-
ed. María Antonia served in the household of Abecia and his wife,
María Antonia del Río. Yet even in this alien environment among a
new people, María Antonia found companionship and possibly even
love. She married José Miguel, a *mulato* slave of Abecia, and bore
him a daughter, baptized as María on April 2, 1743, with María
Antonia del Río standing as godmother. That the bonds of moth-
erhood now served as a method of bondage may have tempered the
joy María brought into her mother's captivity, but this ultimately proved short-lived. José Miguel died or was sold sometime after his daughter's birth, for when María Antonia died in July 1748,
the priest José Montaño recorded her burial in the old church as a
single Apache Indian, servant of Abecia. He also noted no sacraments had been administered "because I was absent." One suspects
María Antonia did not mind dying as she was born, as an Apache.[51]

The enforced addition of adult Apaches to the community of
Janos was not unknown, but it was uncommon. Adult male captives were dangerous and were often killed in the field. If they were
returned to the presidio, they would have found it far easier simply to run away and return to their people unless constrained in
some way; by a child if they were female or by force if male. The

community of Janos preferred to incorporate children taken as captives, but baptized and raised in households as servants, as evidenced by the results of one 1723 campaign.

Soldier José Lujan initially brought an Apache woman to the chapel to be baptized as "Rosa," but within a few weeks a steady stream of captors and captives crossed the dusty plaza to appear before the baptismal fount. Cayento Madrid, another soldier, brought a captured girl, baptized as Jasinta, an "infant Indian of the Apache nation," of "unknown parents," who entered his household as a servant, only to die a year later. *Cabo* (corporal) Juan Lopez de Ocanto stood as godfather for his infant Apache captive, baptized as Anna María, while Lujan and Rosa were the godparents for José Miguel, an infant male Apache of "unknown" parents. Don Antonio Bezerra Nieto, captain of the presidio, sent Apache Agustín Bezerra, who was all too likely himself a captive, raised in the Bezerra household as a servant, to claim his portion of the captives. Agustín served as godfather for Benito, who would have suffered the same fate as his *padrino* had his life not ended just over a year later. Finally, the wife of the probable campaign commander, Don Juan Bautista de Anza, stood as godmother for Ignacio, who too died in November 1724, as a *criado* (an Indian child reared as a Hispanic). In all, nine Apaches entered the community of Janos during that October of 1723.[52]

These were not isolated individuals. Parish records between the late seventeenth century and the middle of the eighteenth list some 134 baptisms of Apaches and individuals whose parents were not listed, and who therefore were likely Apaches. The numbers of baptisms did not stay steady but spiked during the 1690s, 1710s, early 1720s and 1740s, and later 1750s. At any one time during this period Janos held from ten to thirty Apaches in a population that rarely topped four hundred souls. Families raised these detribalized Apaches to follow Hispanic cultural norms as members of the community of Janos, albeit on the lower social rungs.[53]

Not only did Apache captives and *criados* become part of the community, so too did their children. María, daughter of Apache

Indian captive María Antonia mentioned earlier, entered the mixed-ethnicity population of Janos as a "*loba*." María de los Dolores was the daughter of Cayetana, "India Apache," who had likely been raised as a *criada* before her marriage to Domingo Conejo, a servant of Captain Bezerra. Female captives may well have had children with men from Janos. When the priest baptized Juan Francisco his mother, "Margarita, India Apache," was present, but the father was listed as "unknown." However, the godfather was known and was present, Francisco Gómez, a long-serving soldier and respected member of the community. Gómez may simply have been serving as *padrino*, something he often did, yet the lack of a godmother at Juan Francisco's christening, especially Gómez's wife Doña Antonia Granillo, suggests that Gómez could have been the father. Juan Francisco may have been the result of rape, or Margarita may have been coerced into or simply chosen a sexual liaison with Gómez, counting on his status to help provide for her.[54] However they did so, Apache captives at Janos, whether taken as adults or raised from childhood, had to make their way as best they could as members of a human community.

Chiricahua practices with Hispanic captives were not that different from those at Janos. Men, when taken, were usually interrogated and then killed. If Hispanic males were taken captive and returned to camp, it was so that women could take revenge for their dead relatives. This was not intended to be a fair fight; with bound hands the captive had to face women armed with knives and spears, or they were on foot with the women on horseback. It was intended as an execution to return a sense of moral balance to the community. "Grown men," a Chiricahua remembered, "are never kept alive to be married into the tribe or enslaved." This was because "a mature man is dangerous," and so "they kill him."[55]

Hispanic women too were "rarely taken," especially if the men were out for revenge. Late one spring near Janos a party of warriors killed two women and a child, who were buried as having "died at the hands of the enemy." When Apache warriors did seize women, "they didn't do anything with them," for fear of breaking the taboo against sex while on the raid. After they were returned to camp Chiricahuas insisted women captives were not sexually mistreated. They would be welcome into the community as wives, but only "if you can make her love you." Since Chiricahuas contrasted their behavior against that of the Hispanics, who "did it [raped] every time they got Indian women," it is possible some Apache men risked coercing Hispanic women captives, as a Coyote tale cautioned.[56]

One time Coyote found a very pretty woman to whom he wanted to make love. He got her away from camp, taking a walk in the woods. He was about to have intercourse with her when he saw that she had teeth in her vagina. Fearful of losing his penis, Coyote got a stick and a rock. He put the stick first into the woman's vagina, where it was ground up. Coyote then put the rock in, where it knocked out the teeth. He then had sex with the woman. Afterward the woman was valuable.[57] Coyote's experience points to the potential danger for a Chiricahua man taking a Hispanic woman as a captive but also to the potential rewards.

While neither men nor women were valued captives for Chiricahuas, children were, especially male children. Apache warriors "would try to catch a young boy" not bothering to take "women and older people" or female children; one Chiricahua remembered only boys being brought back to live in the community. These Hispanic captives' life paths among the Chiricahua were initially similar to those of Apache captives at Janos: acting as family servants. As time went on these decultured Hispanics came to be members of the community as the "feeling of captivity" wore off, although their roots would never be forgotten. Brought up by the man who captured him, the captive came to call the man father and the "woman who adopts him mother." Ultimately they would marry into the community, and their children were accepted as Chiricahuas. This would have been the ultimate fate of one José María, "a Spanish captive, an infant brought from among the unfaithful," had soldiers from Janos not recovered him. However, the shock of being taken from his Apache parents, having already lost his Hispanic family, may have proven too much for José; the priest José

Montaño buried him in June of 1749, an inadvertent member of both borderland communities.[58]

The initial encounters between Apaches and Hispanics in the Southwestern Borderlands engendered an armed wariness overlaid with the potential for violence. Acts after the conquest of New Mexico turned the mutual uncertainty into suspicion, giving rise to insecurity, preemption, and retaliation. Spanish attempts to control and benefit from the Apache-Pueblo trade threatened the survival strategy of the Apaches, who then struck back at Spanish livestock, for which they suffered retaliation. The inability of the Spanish crown to enforce laws on subjects at the margins of control resulted in raids on Apaches for the slave trade. This spurred increasing Apache revenge and Hispanic retaliation with violence.

The Pueblo Revolt did nothing to change this situation. Indeed for the New Mexican refugees, it only increased their general feeling of insecurity, a feeling that became all too real. The presence of so many more Hispanics among the Uto-Aztecan peoples in the Casas Grandes region sparked another Indian rebellion. This time the refugees had no place to go and held on, fighting back and ultimately forming a garrison community when the crown authorized a presidio initially at Casas Grandes and then Janos. Into this milieu migrated Chiricahua Apaches, seeking to reestablish the links in the horse trade with their Plains Apache cousins. With many of their adult males lost in the fighting the Jano, Suma, Chinarra, and Jocome peoples, among others, gravitated to the Apaches for protection and provision. Chiricahuas eagerly added these Indians, especially taking their women as wives. Perhaps because of this, added to a general fatigue, other rebellious Indians sought peace with the Spaniards, many settling at Janos. These Indians entered into the community on baptismal rolls and by the results of steady intermarriage. Chiricahua and Janos added to their communities by taking captives, especially children, from each other's communities during exchanges of violence. Both furthered their admixture by raising these decultured captives as members of their own communities, opposed to the community of their birth. Ultimately, Janeros and Chiricahuas were related, at least at the genetic level.

This, however, only increased the fear of both communities that they could be destroyed and incorporated into the other, something they witnessed on an individual level every day. The insecurity and endemic suspicion created by the fear of Janos and Chiricahua for each other remained. By the early eighteenth century Spanish officials recognized the need for Janos to be a community of violence, to "punish" those Apaches "who have been continually attacking their borders." Since attempts to convince the Apache Indians to be peaceful by other means had failed, "forays by the soldiers into their territory are needed to gain their respect."[59] Chiricahuas understood the situation differently, however.

As they told it, after Child of the Water killed all the monsters that killed with their eyes, he made two men out of mud and two women. To one man and women he said, "You two will be called Indians." To the others he said, "You two will be called white men." Child of the Water then decided he would choose which things the Indians got and Killer of Enemies would chose for the white men. Child of the Water then put down a bow and arrow and a gun. After quarreling among themselves over who would chose first, Child of the Water went first. He chose the bow and arrow for the Apaches, saying, "The making of these is understood." Killer of Enemies then took the gun for the white men. Next, Child of the Water put down two mountains. Heavy vegetation, food plants, turkeys, and deer—"Indian food"—covered one mountain. The other mountain was barren. Child of the Water chose the first mountain for the Chiricahua, and Killer of Enemies chose the barren mountain for the white men. Then the barren mountain opened up and from within it emerged horses, mules, cattle, sheep, pigs, chickens. Child of the Water declared the Chiricahuas would live on "wild growing things" while the white men "will live on cultivated plants." However, Child of the Water also declared Apaches and white men would live "very far apart" and "whenever you see one another, you will fight—Indian with the white man."[60] And fight they would.

| Chapter 3

Fierce Dancing and the Muster Roll
Campaigns, Raids, and Wives, 1750–1785

The men of both Chiricahua and Janos used violence to establish themselves as married adults. A round of campaigns, raids, and Apache requests for peace in the 1750s only led to temporary respites from the cycle of violence, which continued through the next decade. From the 1770s to 1785 Janos's muster roll steadily grew from around 50 men to nearly 150. Men were continually willing to join the garrison in the face of potential death, as enlistment was closely linked to marriage. Chiricahua used "fierce dancing" to mobilize its men for violence in raids or revenge. These raids turned boys into men via the novice complex. When raiders returned, the community welcomed them back with more dances. These allowed interaction between the newly adult men and unmarried women, often turning the celebration into "marrying time." This period climaxed with a late fall campaign in 1785 carried out by Janeros and other soldiers who sought Chiricahuas in their winter encampments on the lower slopes of the sierras. For two months both sides skirmished; they ambushed, fled, and pursued one another as the weather grew colder and the snows began. Men from both communities were willing to endure such misery and risk death since they used violence in campaigns and raids to secure their place in the community as adults in order to secure wives.

A Black Wooden Cross

An exhausted horse and rider stumbled into Janos early one February day in 1757, giving the alarm. The day prior, Apaches, probably from the loose confederation of families under the headman Chafalote, struck at the Valle de San Buenaventura, taking cattle and horses from the spread of Hispanic settlements along the river of the same name southeast of Janos. At the command of *Capitán* (Captain) Santiago Ruiz de Ael thirty-two soldiers saddled up, cut a spare horse out of the presidial herd, received bags of provisions from their wives or mothers at their doorsteps, and rode out of Janos, the setting sun illuminating the trail. Through the long winter night they traversed the path past the abandoned settlement at Casas Grandes, across the river, and down into the Valle de San Buenaventura. *Cabo* (Corporal) Marcelino Antonio de Herrero, a native of the Valle and a fifteen-year veteran of the war between Chiricahua and Janos in the Southwestern Borderlands, likely led the way. Pausing long enough to mount fresh horses, the soldiers pushed on into the rising sun. With the early morning light to guide them, the Janos troop found the raiders' trail and followed it south and east to the Corral de Piedra. At midmorning they caught up with the Apaches, initiating a day-long battle. As the fighting surged back and forth across the boulder-strewn slopes, costing Bacilio Pacheco his life, a few of the Apaches managed to drive off most of the pilfered herd before the rest escaped in the coming darkness. The soldiers returned to Janos apparently with only an emptied saddle to show for their efforts.[1]

The fight at the Corral de Piedra was the first of several seemingly fruitless operations carried out by Herrero and his fellow soldiers in the first months of 1757. A *campaña* (patrol) scoured the sierras of Doña María and La Laguna to the spring of Ojo Hediondo north of Janos in March and found nothing. Another patrol in April searched the Sierra del Carcay southwest of the presidio, where Apaches were reported, but came up empty-handed, as did a concurrent *campaña* that patrolled the Sierra de la Escondida

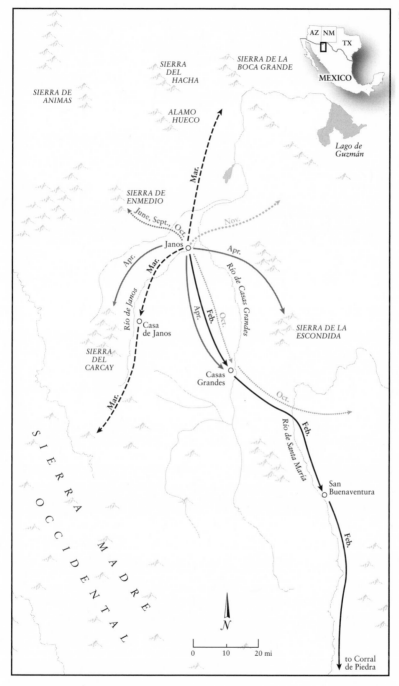

Map 8. Campaigns from Janos, 1757

and the valley of Casas Grandes to the south. A *corredurίa* (pursuit) in late March met with mixed results. Fifteen men set off after a party of Apaches who had run off some steers from the Casa de Janos, thirty miles southwest of the presidio. For forty-five miles the soldiers chased the Apaches, and upon being overtaken, the Apaches abandoned the cattle and escaped into the mountains. While all this effort appears unsuccessful, the Chiricahuas' actions suggest otherwise.[2]

Not "despite these hostilities" but precisely because of them Apaches sought to treat with Janos. With their raids met by pursuits and their respites challenged by patrols, Apaches sent envoys to the presidio. The first was an old woman carrying a black wooden cross. In the "diplomacy of gender" as practiced in the borderlands, she sought peace for her people. Obeying Article 193 of the Reglamento de 1729, which ordered that "any Indian from enemy rancherias who comes to a presidio and asks for peace will be granted it," the captain treated her kindly, presenting her with gifts of tobacco and corn as well as other gifts for her chief. She left the presidio in peace that day with an entreaty for the whole band to settle at Janos. A week later three Apache men, each bearing a black wooden cross, approached the presidio. They Apaches listened to reprimands from Captain Ruiz de Ael for their raiding and then received their gifts; they left the same day.[3]

Janos kept up the pressure behind these initial visits with a patrol in June into the Sierra de Enmedio to the northwest of the community. While the *campaña* found no sign of Apaches, it had an effect. Once again a woman led a delegation to Janos to ask for peace, this time the wife of the ranchería headman, accompanied by four other Apaches. She explained that the families were currently hunting, spread out in camps across the sierras, and once they finished they would come to Janos. Indeed, for the next few days Apache family groups arrived outside the presidial walls, where they presumably received gifts and traded the fruits of their hunting with the community of Janos. However, eight days after the initial delegation's arrival, the entire group left. While Ruiz de Ael termed the Apaches' actions an "uprising," he launched no pursuit, for the Apaches were at peace.

August found Janeros back in the saddle. A patrol took an Apache raid unawares at the Hacienda de Casas Grandes, recovering two horses. Yet September saw *Soldado* (Soldier) Ignacio Ruiz lose his life at "the hands of the enemy." Pursuit of another raiding party later the same month lost contact with the Apaches in the Sierra de Enmedio and failed to recover the herd of mares they had driven off. Apaches also drove off a herd of steers from Janos, and it took the garrison five days to round them up as the raiders escaped into the sierra. Again, however, after several months of violence, the Apaches decided to treat at Janos.[4]

On October 10, 1757, four Apache women arrived at the presidio carrying a message from their leader. He had four Spanish captives to trade, and Ruiz de Ael offered horses, cattle, clothing, or whatever the Apache leader wanted in exchange. Ruiz de Ael immediately sent a *campaña* to the Sierra de Enmedio, but it found nothing. Eleven days later a Spanish girl, a captive taken ten years earlier from the Hacienda del Carmen, walked into Janos. Shortly thereafter an Apache woman came looking for her, offering the four captives in exchange for the girl. After three days of receiving gifts from a skeptical Ruiz de Ael, the woman left, without the girl. The next day Apaches took their revenge, striking the Hacienda de Casas Grandes. Soldiers trailed them to the Valle de San Buenaventura before losing them in the hills. The Apaches struck again a few days later, and this time the pursuit followed them far to the east of Janos, where the Apaches' trail headed northward toward the Gila River.

As far as the people of Janos could tell, there the Chiricahuas stayed until winter forced them to lower elevations near the presidio. In January and March of 1758 groups of five to eight women, many nursing infants, came to Janos to receive gifts and provisions, including *pinole* (parched corn). In April one party of five women asked for someone at the fort to talk to their headman. Ten men escorted *Teniente* (Lieutenant) José Camilio Chacon, a native of Sonora who only wished to be a "good countryman" but knew the "Indios Bárbaros" well, to meet with the Apaches. Twenty-two warriors showed up for the parley, four of them chiefs. The fact that these men wore leather jackets for body armor and carried swords and lances impressed Chacon. For four hours Chacon and the four chiefs talked; Chacon agreed to provide land, oxen, and supplies so that the Apaches could farm, in return for which the Apaches pledged to live in peace. Ending the meeting with gifts of tobacco, Chacon and his escort returned to Janos. The Apaches departed immediately, and from their tracks, soldiers estimated their number the next day as 150.[5]

While the Apaches did not settle to farm, their women continued to visit the presidio throughout May, unmolested and often staying in rooms set aside for them in Ruiz de Ael's house on the north side of the presidial plaza. Women often came with specific requests: once for a hat, several times for a knife, and always for tobacco and corn. But by June Chiricahuas disappeared from around Janos. No women came to the presidio, and no men raided Hispanic settlements for several months. However, on August 12 a party of soldiers spotted the tracks of five Apaches at a ford on the San Antonio River near Casas Grandes. They set out in pursuit and managed to catch the Chiricahuas, killing one. After the rains Ruiz de Ael led a large *campaña*, likely including *Cabo* Herrero and *Teniente* Chacón, north of Janos. At the Alamo Hueco the soldiers discovered a ranchería and attacked, killing three Apaches and wounding others in the three-hour battle that followed. Ruiz de Ael continued to the Sierra del Hacha, but with Apache smoke signals warning of his progress rising from the sierras around him. Warned of the Hispanics' approach, the Apaches fled and Ruiz de Ael cut his patrol short, returning to Janos after only two weeks.

Yet this effort yielded a response a month and a half later. On January 4, 1759, an Apache woman approached Janos again carrying a black wooden cross. She asked for corn and tobacco and relayed a message from her headman that he wanted peace. Her band wished to camp at La Boca on the Casas Grandes River in order to harvest mescal. Good relations continued over the next few months, with another ranchería asking to settle near the presidio, followed by several more visits. However, in May violence returned with *Soldado* Antonio Misguia perishing "at the hands of the enemy Indians of the Apache nation." Misguia was clearly a popular man whose marriage six years earlier to María Rita Verdugo was witnessed by the leading lights of the community. The chaplain buried Misguia on May 25, noting he had died without the solace of holy sacraments.[6]

By the middle of the eighteenth century the community of Janos knew violence against the Chiricahuas would get a familiar result: the black wooden cross carried by Apaches seeking peace. They also knew this peace would not last, but combined with the violence, it did allow for relations with their Indian neighbors. Besides a respite, however brief, the violence also brought rewards for individual members of the community. On February 1, 1758, in the midst of the comings and goings by Chiricahua women, *Cabo* Herrero received a promotion to the rank of sergeant, increasing his status and position within the garrison community of Janos.[7] Yet Janeros were not the only ones to profit from the bloody borderland exchange.

The Sons of Chafalote

By 1760 Chafalote had grown old. Long the premier leader of the Chiricahuas to the extent that they were often called "Chafalotes," he now lived in semi-retirement in the Mimbres Mountains in the summer and along the Gila River during the winter, accompanied by a great herd of horses and many armed warriors. His sons, however, quickly took up the mantle of leadership. Two of them, likely the eldest, were soon leading their own camps and maintaining a violent coexistence with Janos.[8] So successful had these two become at leading raids deep into Hispanic lands that the Spanish organized a large expedition against them with more than two hundred soldiers and Indian auxiliaries. Sheltering with their rancherias on the lower slopes of the sierra during the colder winter months, the two brothers proved vulnerable. Surprised by their enemies, both men stood their ground and fought, allowing most of their people and warriors to escape. So important had these two sons of Chafalote become that the Spaniards considered killing them a great victory, although they captured only three men and sixty horses.[9]

Yet Chafalote had other sons. The next to lead his own group was Natanijú, and he proved more adept at coexisting via violence than his brothers. About a year after their deaths Natanijú and his settlement were living near Janos in the usual round of violence and peace. When his ranchería was suspected of having stolen horses, Natanijú assisted the commander of Janos in inspecting the brands of all the horses in his herd to see if any were the stolen animals. Natanijú's camp was soon joined by those of his two brothers: Asquelite and Brazo Quebrado. All three led their people through the sierras and valleys around Janos, especially during the winter when the bitter cold drove them from the mountains, hunting, gathering mescal, and joining with "less notable chiefs" to raid Hispanic settlements.[10]

Clad only in breechcloths, with their bodies and faces painted in many different colors, bonnets adorned with feathers on their heads, and armed with bows and arrows, the sons of Chafalote descended on the Spaniards. One Spanish observer wrote that the Apaches inflicted "every imaginable cruelty," including eating the living flesh of their victims after shooting arrows into them. He even accused them of killing pregnant mothers by cutting out their unborn children and beating them together. While this accusation was likely hyperbole, Chafalote's people undoubtedly found it easier to steal the herds of horses and mules than to hunt elusive deer. If the Apaches were "dangerous to their neighbors," Natanijú would have noted that their Spaniard neighbors were likewise dangerous to them.[11]

Within a few years of these accusations, a large force of soldiers and allied Opata Indians invaded the Mimbres Mountains during the summer. The Spaniards attacked and destroyed two of the rancherias led by the sons Chafalote, killing sixty Apaches, capturing fifteen, and freeing two Spanish captives. Possibly led by Natanijú, the Apaches dealt the invaders a sharp blow at the Corral de San Agustín. Other Apaches sidestepped the campaign and took the opportunity to raid deep into the Spanish settlements. One party struck the Pueblo of San Gerónimo five leagues from the Villa de Chihuahua and took revenge for their kinsmen and women, killing forty-nine men, women, and children and seizing eleven captives. Three days later the Chafalotes closed to within one league of the city, attacking the Mission of Nombre de Dios, killing eight more Spaniards.[12] It appears Chiricahuas took this all in stride. They were, after all, a community of violence, as was Janos. And it was by violence that the sons of Chafalote became leaders among their people, a position Natanijú would keep for the next two decades.

The Muster of Janos

On the first day of 1774 Capitán Don Juan Bautista Perú, the commander of Janos, mustered his company in the plaza before his house. Working from a roll listing all by rank and name, Perú marked each man as present. For those not physically present he noted in the margins where they were assigned, often on horse guard duty or to ancillary duties such as escorting official travelers or carrying messages. Perú mustered forty-seven men in all that raw winter day, including himself as captain, a lieutenant, one *alférez* (ensign), a chaplain, one sergeant, two corporals, and forty soldiers. His roll would have been short one soldier if not for his son Joaquín, who served as an unpaid volunteer. His son's presence in the ranks must have provided some sense of place to Perú. A native of Paris, France, he had come to the Southwestern Borderlands more than two decades earlier as a member of one of the ill-fated expeditions from New France to New Mexico between 1749 and 1751. The lieutenant governor of New Mexico held him captive in Santa Fe along with his compatriots. But when the lieutenant governor departed the province he took Perú along, enlisting him in the company of Guajoquilla in 1752. Perú steadily rose through the presidial ranks, becoming a captain and commander of Janos in May 1772.[13]

Two weeks after Perú's muster the new *comandante inspector* (chief inspector) of the presidios blew into Janos accompanied by a few exhausted Spanish dragoons. Lieutenant Colonel Don Hugo O'Conor, an Irish Catholic with long service in the Spanish Army, immediately set about inspecting Janos and was not pleased with what he found. Perú's company was only "adequately clothed," but "poorly equipped" with saddles, bridles, and spurs, although it was "well mounted." The men's *escopetas* (short muskets), lances, and pistols were in "poor condition," while their shields and leather body armor, the *cuera*, were "nearly useless." In its current condition the Janos company could not "launch an effective offensive."[14]

O'Conor also promulgated a new regulation, *The Regulation and Instruction for the Presidios*, signed in 1772. The Reglamento de 1772 established Perú's command at its current strength and authorized a further ten Opata Indian *exploradores* (scouts). Perú would soon have need for the extra manpower as the violence between Janeros and Chiricahuas continued. On October 4, 1774, "los Indios enemigos" killed Soldier José Antonio Griego, but Perú quickly made up the loss to his muster roll by recruiting José Antonio Montoya two days later. At the close of the year three soldiers chose to take their discharge, "usaron de licencia," on another wintery day, having served out their ten years. Again, Perú replaced these deletions from his muster with three new recruits the very next day.[15]

Perú looked to recruit healthy and hardy men from the borderlands since, as O'Conor noted, they were inured by their frontier upbringing "to the extraordinary hardships of this warfare." Training for Perú's new recruits consisted of shooting at targets, for which each received an extra three pounds of gunpowder during their first year; horse handling; and "those maneuvers that are useful and adapted to the type of war in which they will be engaged." The requirements for a trained soldier proved minimal, consisting of "being skillful" on horseback, knowing how to fire the *escopeta* and use a shield, "something which is quite natural with them," and an ability to travel great distances horseback in all weather, subsisting on little more than pinole mixed with water, with only a cloak for shelter. Perú's men were expected simply to "shoot with skill, to load quickly, to maintain formation, to break it and reunite in order to sustain each other," since, as the 1772 regulations noted, the borderland soldiers' battles were fought "with individual strength and valor."[16]

Joaquín Perú was certainly one who fought with strength and valor. In 1775 he took part in a pursuit led by his father that killed one Apache *gandule* (from the Arabic *gandur*, meaning "rogue, rascal, or vagabond," this referred to Indian warriors in the Southwestern Borderlands) and recovered seventy head of livestock. Joaquín chased another raiding party with Lieutenant Chacon, retaking seventy-six animals and seizing three Apache prisoners. He also served in a two-month campaign to the Río Gila under O'Conor, capturing fourteen Apaches and recovering some horses in September 1775. His steadfast service saw Joaquín promoted to the rank of an officer cadet on August 26, 1776. But steadfast service could apparently secure more than a promotion at Janos in 1775 for on the second day of June, O'Conor's chaplain, Fray Francisco Honrada, ministered marriage rites to eight soldiers and their brides, seven of them from the Janos muster.[17]

Along with Joaquín's promotion the summer of 1776 saw another wedding, that of José Tapia, the son of Janos *Alférez* Don Narcisco Tapia, and a native of nearby San Buenaventura. José enlisted on April 27, 1772, and, perhaps due to his father's rank and his own literacy, received a quick promotion to *cabo* in January, 1775, replacing the retiring José Francisco de la Garza. In June 1776 the twenty-two-year-old José requested permission from Perú to marry sixteen-year-old Juana Manuela García, an "originaria de este presidio," a native of Janos. José and Juana apparently attempted to raise a family outside of military service, for José departed the company in April 1777. However, he returned to the military in 1782, perhaps lured by the pay and semiregular supply to provide for his family.[18]

With the coming of the summer rains in 1777 to provide fodder

and water, Capitán Perú joined forces with Terrenate presidio, leading a 150-man force out on campaign. The force first scoured the
Sierra de Animas, attacking a ranchería, killing three Apaches and
taking thirty-eight horses. Perú then returned to Janos before setting out northward to the Mimbres and Florida mountains. There
his troops surprised a Chiricahua settlement defended by twenty warriors. Perú's men killed four of the warriors and seized six
as prisoners. They also rescued a Spanish captive and took twelve
horses and some saddles. It was likely during this attack that *Cadete* (Cadet) Perú received recognition for actions that would con-
tribute to his promotion during the next year. In the fall of 1777
his fellow cadet José Manuel Carrasco, too, proved his worth when
he rallied the *guardia de caballada* (horse herd guards) to drive off
a Chiricahua attack; an action recounted a decade later in his own
quest for promotion and presidial command.[19]

The winter of 1777–78 found the former *alférez* Narcisco Tapia,
now a lieutenant, negotiating with Apaches for the exchange of
captives while Perú was absent in Chihuahua. Of critical importance was the fate of one particular captive, *Soldado* Félix Guerra, seized by "los enemigos" on January 22, after he departed the
Presidio of San Bernardino in Sonora. Tapia managed to negotiate
an exchange of ten horses for Guerra in early February. Perú's absence did not cause the careers of his sons to suffer. Perú arranged
for his son José to enter the rolls as a cadet on February 11 and for
Joaquín to receive his promotion to the newly authorized second
alférez position on April 11. Joaquín burnished this honor by recovering twelve-year-old Juan José Misquis from Apaches in February 1778, likely during the negotiations that secured Guerra, and
returning the boy to his grateful mother Teresa.[20]

Joaquín's new rank was part of *Comandante general* (Commandant General) Teodoro de Croix's attempt to increase the presidial
muster. Croix authorized nineteen new *plazas* (positions) for each
presidio, including Janos, in April 1778: an *alférez*, a sergeant,
and seventeen soldiers. These were to be his new-style *tropa ligera* (light troop) who would be less expensive, lacking the heavy

defensive armaments and lengthy string of horses used by the traditional *tropa de cuera* (leather jacket troop). Croix's new light troops would carry just an *escopeta*, two pistols, and a sword and would be authorized only three horses. The Reglamento de 1772 earlier assigned a veritable armory to each soldier: *escopeta*, two pistols, sword, lance, and shield in addition to the *cuera*, a leather jacket of four to six thicknesses of hide. It was this armament Croix wished to simplify, but the realities of borderland warfare were already doing so. Despite the 92 firearms, 102 pairs of pistols, 86 swords, and 112 lances O'Conor sent to the presidio in 1774, most Janeros carried just the *escopeta* and lance, since pistols proved fragile and swords ineffective, but the men continued to carry the shield and wear their *cuera* for protection from Indian arrows.[21]

The Reglamento de 1772 also assigned a lengthy string of mounts to each soldier: six horses, one colt, and one mule. Croix wished to reduce this to just three horses as the supply of horses to the presidios was an ongoing concern. Regulations prohibited soldiers from gambling away their horses or mistreating them. Officers were specifically prohibited from taking serviceable horses away from their men. Captain Perú ran afoul of these strictures in 1778 when royal officials charged that he had allowed the officers at Janos first choice from a supply of remounts, although the charges were ultimately dropped. Horses proved a near-right for solders. While detached from Janos and serving at Carrizal in 1792, a party of men missed the resupply of horses and mules. The general command ordered another supply mission from Janos to procure horses for these men as it was considered "capricious to omit some individuals and does not [do] justice to those who served the king."[22]

Besides receiving horses from the king, Janeros also took them from Chiricahuas as spoils of war, along with mules and cattle. An owner could reclaim his animals if he could identify them, but until people showed up at the presidio to collect their stock, soldiers clearly felt they had a right to use the horses as their own. Notices in 1781 and 1784 reminded officers and men that all livestock taken from enemy Indians had to be returned to their owners.

Ultimately bowing to current practice, the commandant general authorized soldiers to use horses that were waiting to be recovered by their owners but ordered that the animals had to be relinquished when the owner appeared.[23]

Horses featured in the continuing recruitment for the *tropa ligera* at Janos during 1778. When José Montoya, who joined the company in October 1774, died in action on June 3, 1778, José Galaz enlisted in his place. Galaz, however, apparently refused to serve in the light troop, likely due to the seventy-four pesos per year less in his pay and four horses less in his string, and joined the *tropa de cuera* on the muster roll. Disaster struck the Janos company on October 16 when Apaches killed six soldiers and two civilian auxiliary scouts, men recruited two years earlier from the community after the effort to use Opatas failed; the Apaches also captured a soldier and a scout. Reacting to this decimation, Perú discharged the surviving seven scouts, but despite the fate of their comrades, four of them chose to enlist as regular soldiers, filling most of the holes in the muster. Thus by November 1778 Perú completed the recruitment of the *tropa ligera* he began with his son eight months earlier.[24]

During the next year, Perú entered Cornelio Delgado on his muster roll in the place of the deceased Antonio Luján on March 1, 1779. While Delgado had served for three years before coming to Janos, he secured a bride within six months of his arrival, marrying María Galindo of Janos on August 21, 1779, in one of five ceremonies conducted by Fray Blas Benites on that day. In addition to Delgado and his new bride, Perú had a new category to add to officials, *tropa de cuera*, and *tropa ligera* on the rolls: *inválido* (retiree), a man who had served out his twenty years and was authorized to stay at the presidio, continuing to muster, to receive pay, and to use the supply system.[25]

The Reglamento de 1772 paid close attention to the system of supply for the presidios. It began by removing captains from their previously lucrative position at the top of the supply chain and placed the payment and provision of each company into the hands of an officer elected by the soldiers, the *habilitado*, or quartermaster.

Soldiers placed their orders with the *habilitado*, who filled them on his biannual trips to the supply center in Chihuahua. The quartermaster then delivered the goods to the soldiers and deducted the expense from their supply account. Thus by the end of the 1770s the supply of the presidios was regular, if often corrupt and always inefficient because of the great distances material had to travel to reach the edges of the Spanish empire. It did, however, prove able to provision the soldiers of Janos and their families. Supply accounts and lists steadily accumulated in the Janos archive, recounting twice monthly issues of staples such as beans, corn, salt, and soap and semiannual issues of such items as blankets, shoes, or *sarapes* (cloaks). Men who survived the violence could thus retire and continue to make use of the quartermaster's stores and services. Perú discharged four men on March 1, 1779, and another four on April 1, moving them to the category of *inválidos* on his muster roll.[26]

Three of Perú's charges did not survive their twenty years and would never retire, dying "en manos de los enemigos" (at the hands of the enemies) in the Valle de San Buenaventura on September 23, 1779, including Félix Guerra. Guerra served for another year and a half after his release from Apache captivity and was possibly killed by the same men who held him prisoner. Like many others, Guerra's place did not remain vacant for long as José María Pacheco, a native of Janos, joined the company on September 26, along with Victoriano Ronquillo, another Janos son. An encounter on November 26 saw Roberto Rico killed outright and Francisco Javier wounded so severely that he succumbed on December 4. These two were not replaced as swiftly as Guerra; it was not until July 1780 that the two were replaced. One of the recruits, Manuel Lucero, was experienced, having served as a scout in 1778. By the end of 1780 Perú's muster roll listed sixty-nine men, including himself as captain, Tapia as lieutenant, two *alfereces*, a chaplain, an armorer to repair weapons, a sergeant, four corporals, and one cadet, his son José. The *tropa de cuera* counted twenty-eight soldiers, while the *tropa ligera* stood at twenty-two. Four *inválidos*, led by retired Capitán Don José Camilio Chacon, completed the muster. However, Perú's command was about to get larger and his muster roll longer.[27]

In 1782 Perú received orders for a "new footing" for his presidio that did away with Croix's two *tropas*. From July 1 the company would include a captain, two lieutenants, two *alfereces*, a chaplain, an armorer, four sergeants, a musician (*tambor*), eight corporals, eight *carabineros* (carabineers, senior soldiers), and 116 soldiers, all armed and equipped as *tropa de cuera* per the Reglamento de 1772, for a total 144 *plazas*, doubling Janos's current strength. Perú thus set about recruiting the more than seventy men he needed to fill out his roll throughout 1783, including luring back José Tapia from civilian life and recruiting extensively outside of Janos in the Valle de San Bartolome south of Chihuahua. He managed to recruit twenty soldiers that year but lost two—Bonifacio Reas and Bautista Duran—to his "enemies" on September 14. Perú filled their empty places a week later and extracted revenge while leading an attack on a ranchería on October 5, killing five *gandules* and five Apache women and capturing two boys and two girls. As the number of soldiers slowly grew at Janos, so did the number of families. Enlisting in another unit in 1778, Bernardo Sepúlveda transferred to Janos in January 1782 and married a year later in 1783. Fernando Grijalba, who married at the same time as Sepúlveda, enlisted in March 1783.[28]

Yet Perú still had not filled out his new muster roll by the start of 1784. To gather the needed men, recruiters—typically sergeants of the company—ranged farther afield, including south to the city of Querétaro, albeit with questionable results. There Vicente Santillon enlisted in May 1784. Santillon, a native of Mexico City, volunteered to serve eight years. However, he apparently grew tired of his service after only two, for he deserted from horse guard duty in 1786. Caught after two weeks, he tried again four years later, for which military authorities condemned him to work for another eight years in the far north, with one leg in a shackle, receiving no pay, only food.[29]

The recruiting effort continued over the following years. Perú's recruiters were able to bring in only nine men in 1785, but Apaches killed four and captured three, most of those in two separate engagements in October. Perhaps motivated by the deaths of his comrades, Agustín Guevara, who had earlier taken his discharge, returned on November 15 to serve for ten years. All the while Perú continued to lead his company out on campaigns; five in 1784, three more in 1785, killing six *gandules*. As the year ended with a miserable winter campaign, which Perú had been too sick to lead, 1786 began with a windfall of ten men enlisting in El Paso, and by September Perú mustered 141 men, just three shy of filling out his roll, having doubled his company in just over four years. That December, as he looked back over his thirty-four years of service, twenty campaigns, and seven wounds, with his sons firmly ensconced in the royal service, Perú must have felt some pride. All the violence, all the deaths had not been in vain for they provided him, like many of his soldiers, with the status to secure his and his family's place among the community of Janos.[30]

Fierce Dancing

Natanijú had a problem. Having migrated down from the mountains in midfall, the women of his ranchería now wanted to harvest mescal from the agave plants on the lower slopes of the Sierra Madre near the settlements of the white men. The women would dig several big pits, line them with rocks, and fill them with wood. As the wood burned, the women would gather the lower portion of the agave plant, the crown. With the wood reduced to ashes, the harvesters placed the mescal crowns into the pit and covered them with wet grass and dirt. The mescal would bake and smoke for two to four days, be allowed to cool, and be transported back to camp. The women would repeat this process several times over the next month to harvest enough of this important foodstuff for the coming winter.[31] However, spread out among the agaves, across the slopes and plains, with smoking pits to mark their presence, the women would be very vulnerable to attacks by soldiers, and this was Natanijú's problem.

To solve his problem he joined with two other Chiricahua leaders encamped nearby: Pachatijú and El Zurdo. These two, however, were not his brothers as in decades past. Pachatijú and El Zurdo were new men who arose from the cauldron of borderlands violence to lead their own local groups. Leadership of extended families and local groups was often hereditary among Apaches, as in the case of Natanijú. *Gò'tàh* in its exact meaning referred to the extended family encampment of parents, grandparents, children, unmarried sons, and married daughters and their husbands, all under the leadership of the father. Since extended families were not powerful enough to defend themselves alone, they "lent" their manpower to a local group for warfare. Chiricahuas also used *gò'tàh* to refer to these groupings of family encampments in a specific locality under a leader. The use of *gò'tàh* for these local groups, camps, or rancherias in the Spanish rendering, suggests that their leadership too had been hereditary, as had been the case with Chafalote's sons, but by this time camps increasingly consisted of families who chose to live together under a headman who relied upon his influence and prestige, not his kinship ties. Loyalty to a leader depended upon his successes in war, and if a man became dissatisfied with his current leader, he would move his family away and join another local group, often under a more prestigious leader. The leader of a ranchería was the most powerful leader of the families who comprised it. His power depended upon his ability and willingness to use violence against the group's enemies, along with the wealth and generosity that flowed from this, and his capability to keep the peace within camp. Violence often proved the most direct way to gain prestige and influence, allowing men the means to start their own families, leave hereditary local groups to join others, or rise to lead their own *gò'tàh*, as was the case for Pachatijú and El Zurdo.[32]

For this reason Natanijú and his new allies decided to attack the horse herd at the place they called Kaskiyeh, or Janos. Depriving the soldiers of their horses would not only reduce their ability to interfere with the mescal harvest, Natanijú, Pachatijú, and El

Zurdo must have reasoned; it would also increase the prestige of the three leaders and provide their warriors with a useful commodity. Since an action of this size required more participation and cooperation than a simple raid for supplies, the community needed to be mobilized and organized. Natanijú, Pachatijú, and El Zurdo thus held a war dance or "Fierce Dance."

The three leaders let it be known in their rancherias that they were going to hold a war dance. At night all the men assembled at a fire, dressed for war with their hair tied back and breechcloths tucked in, many with weapons. Drummers and singers sat on the west side of the fire, while four dancers, likely including Natanijú, Pachatijú, and El Zurdo, came in from the east, shoulder to shoulder. They danced around the fire four times before splitting, with two dancers on the north side and two on the south, and exchanging positions four times. Then all the men who agreed to go and attack Kaskiyeh danced; some went around the fire only once to announce their intentions, while others danced and sang softly. Those men who did not dance were then called by name, likely by their leaders, saying, "You many times have talked bravely. Now brave people at Kaskiyeh are calling to you." When all who agreed to go on the war party had danced, Natanijú, Pachatijú, and El Zurdo led all the men around the fire four more times. Then it was over.[33]

The next day Natanijú, Pachatijú, and El Zurdo led the war party out, armed with bows and arrows, lances, and shields. Their first attack on the horse herd proved less than successful. Although the warriors crept in close to the herd, then rose up yelling and shouting to spook the horses, the guards managed to rally and drive off the Apaches. With this affront to avenge, a few days later Natanijú led most of the men from all three camps, more than sixty in all, to attack the herd again. This large force meant that as the warriors approached the herd, the soldiers were able to detect them, opening fire, catching the Apaches by surprise, and wounding several. A pursuit force tore out of Kaskiyeh after the Chiricahuas.

The three leaders led their men in a desperate rush to the south, attempting to gain the sanctuary of the mountains, but they were burdened with wounded and the soldiers were able to overtake them, forcing the warriors to deploy for a fight. Before a battle broke out, however, Natanijú, Pachatijú, and El Zurdo all rode out to the Spaniards to request a truce in order to harvest mescal.[34]

Unable to chase off the presidio's horses, the Apache leaders decided to negotiate instead, since this would also accomplish their goal. Granted their request by Lieutenant Tapia, and with members of their rancherias busily harvesting mescal along the slopes of the Sierra de la Boca Grande and envoys regularly visiting Janos, Natanijú, Pachatijú and El Zurdo went among the Apache camps below the Mimbres Mountains to inform them of the truce. Pachatijú and El Zurdo, perhaps wishing to burnish their reputations even more, sent messengers all the way to the Rio Grande to tell Apaches there to come to the sierras around Janos to harvest mescal in peace. While envoys from Chiricahua rancherias went to Janos, parties of warriors also set out to raid other Hispanic settlements, especially those in the Valle de San Buenaventura.[35]

Chiricahuas considered raiding a necessity due to their relative deprivation in times before. They raided for supplies when they were "in need," for they remembered when Chiricahuas "lived poorly," sleeping in the dirt without blankets, working without steel implements, without luxuries such as tobacco. A recognized leader organized a raid, announcing his intent and calling for men to join him. Typically only men in need of prestige goods, such as horses, or whose families lacked supplies volunteered. Since raiding was considered an economic activity, refusal to participate was not seen as cowardice, although some men were considered to be too lazy to go on a raid. A raiding party normally had only a few men, five or six; no more than ten, according to one Chiricahua. A raid did not seek combat, preferring to take unguarded possessions, especially horses, although raiders would use violence to waylay unwary persons. Upon return to camp, the raiders divided the booty, often giving some to poor families or trading it to richer families, who functioned as middlemen in the larger trade networks in the borderlands. However, a raid not only supplied goods for Chiricahuas; it also added to the community's stock of adult male warriors.[36]

Chiricahuas made boys into men via the *dikohe* (novice complex, or "novice on the raid"). The training for a *dikohe* included running, wrestling, and fighting with sticks and rocks. Starting at the age of fourteen the novice volunteered to accompany four raids. Since the novice was to be kept out of danger, often escorted by an elder warrior to observe the action from a distance, it was unlikely he would be allowed to accompany a full-blown war party. The *dikohe* was to be respectful, observant, and carry out camp chores for the raiding party. He could not eat hot food or entrails as this would "destroy his luck with horses." A novice could only scratch himself with a stick from a berry or fruit tree and had to drink through a length of hollow carrizo wood. He might have to wear a hat or other distinct item of clothing. The *dikohe* also had to use a special war path language consisting of indirect words for items of importance. A rope, used to capture horses, had to be called a *bènàdóó'ó*—"that by means of which it (the horse) would be tied"—while a horse was to be referred to as *císnìzé*, a "nose to the ground." After the *dikohe* successfully accompanied four expeditions, the community accepted him as a warrior and an adult male with little fanfare.[37]

Raids, however, not only made new men; they also made new political groupings among the Chiricahuas. These divisions became apparent in the ongoing negotiations at Janos. Originally undertaken to allow for the mescal harvest, the negotiations by Natanijú, Pachatijú, and El Zurdo were kept going through the first month of winter to allow for trade and the exchange of captives. Chiricahuas from these leaders' camps traded captured weapons for knives, awls, and blankets at Janos on one occasion, and on another they asked for the return of two small girls taken by the Spaniards. In exchange the Apaches promised to release all their captives and assist Janos against all its enemies, particularly the Chiricaguis, another Chiricahua band.[38]

Bands possessed a "political consciousness" and consisted of those local groups who lived closed enough to each other to come together and cooperate in times of crisis or for social interchange in ceremonies. The primary role of the band was warfare, especially for mobilizing, organizing, and leading larger war parties via the war dance. Fierce dancing lay at the heart of the band. Janos had long encountered the Chiricahuas as one band, typically called Gila Apaches, or Gileños, or by the name of the primary leader; recently they had been called Chafalotes, after Natanijú's father. By this time, however, violence had fractured and reordered the Chiricahuas into at least three separate bands, which the Spaniards named Gileños, Mimbreños, and Chiricaguis for prominent mountain ranges in their areas.[39]

At this time Natanijú, along with Pachatijú and El Zurdo, led the Gileños, and while the latter two were apparently jockeying for influence among the Mimbreño camps, all opposed the Chiricaguis. This was clear during the negotiations surrounding the release of Félix Guerra. Natanijú, Pachatijú, and El Zurdo informed Janos that Chiricaguis held Guerra for the release of prisoners at Encinillas and Chihuahua. However, the Gileño leaders cautioned the presidio that any Chiricagui request for peace was false and should be refused. While this attempt to sow dissension caused some suspicion of the Chiricaguis on the part of the Spaniards, the exchange of Guerra for ten horses did eventually take place.[40]

Natanijú, Pachatijú, and El Zurdo continued negotiations with Janos. Their goal was simply to continue to negotiate as their camps hunkered down in the hills around Janos, riding out the winter weather and waiting for spring. Likely to buy time for their people, Natanijú and his fellow leaders declared they would wait for one year to see if the Spaniards were serious about wanting peace, before entering into any agreement. Besides, they complained, Spaniards had earlier taken captives and put them to work in their fields. The return of such captives remained a prime node of exchange. As their leaders negotiated, Apache parents went to Janos, where they were often able to recover their captive children. They were unable, however, to recover one child, perhaps a daughter of one of the leaders, who was held by a priest in Sonora.[41]

This failure clearly rankled with the Apaches, as did the capture and imprisonment at Janos of twelve more kinsmen. With the coming of spring, the camps of Natanijú, Pachatijú, and El Zurdo began their migration back to the higher country for the summer months. Forced to move away from the hills around Janos in order to exploit fully the limited food sources available, they would be unable to continue the regular visits to the presidio seeking exchanges and the release of prisoners. Learning that Perú was returning to Janos from Chihuahua, a number of Chiricahuas "accosted" him along the way, seeking the release of Apache prisoners. Perú refused them.[42]

Those Apaches with kin imprisoned by the Spaniards also accosted their leaders. With their rancherias ensconced in the mountains Natanijú, Pachatijú, and El Zurdo led another fierce dance followed by a desperate attack on Janos. Knowing the soldiers guarded their horses closely, the Apaches avoided the horse herd and approached the presidio itself in the middle of a late summer night. As Chiricahuas typically did not attack settlements directly or fight at night, they were apparently incensed at the lack of exchange and clearly trusted their leaders. The warriors slipped up on the presidio and assaulted the postern, or back gate, by the captain's house, a weak spot they would have identified on their numerous earlier visits to Perú. They almost broke through, but the few soldiers still present climbed to the wall of the fort, actually the roofs of their houses, and in a chaotic exchange of gunfire and arrows, shouts and screams, they managed to drive off the Chiricahuas.[43]

The Apaches were not beaten. A month and a half later they managed to ambush a patrol from Janos, killing eight and capturing two, adding to two they had previously seized. Among their four captives, the Gileños realized they had one of Perú's sons. Attempting to capitalize on this, two Apache men visited the presidio, but they found Perú in no mood to negotiate. He seized the two men, holding them hostage until they were traded for his soldiers and his son. These events made Janos less inclined to negotiate or exchange. When an Apache *gò'tàh* attempted to open negotiations in the time-honored tradition by sending a woman to approach the presidio, Perú also seized her.[44] Hence, for the rest of that year and into the next, Chiricahuas continued their raiding, striking far north of Janos into New Mexico near Albuquerque and far to the south near the Parral mining district. Natanijú's people also avoided Spanish retaliation when several columns of soldiers penetrated their territory, although the troops did kill thirty-one, imprison twenty-five, and rescue four captives. And so it went; Chiricahuas raided and retaliated while Janos patrolled and pursued, and the space for negotiations and exchanges steadily decreased.[45]

For several years Natanijú's ranchería, along with the rest of the Chiricahuas, continued their fierce dancing, motivated by a need for resources and revenge. The violence continued to throw up new leaders and create new camps; Francisquillo joined the ranks of Gileño leadership with his *gò'tàh*. Apaches learned that they could not approach Janos unless they had captives to exchange. This too eventually changed; all those who came near the presidio risked being taken prisoner, as Pachatijú and his people learned.[46]

That winter a party of Chiricahuas, likely from Pachatijú's camp, entered Janos. The Hispanic community attacked them, killing twenty-one men and two women and seizing three people. Probably acting on information from their prisoners, the Janeros surprised and captured Pachatijú. A large party of warriors assembled several months later and attempted to free the Gileño leader, but they withdrew after eight hours of desultory skirmishing. This was the start of a bad season. Francisquillo and many of his men died at the hands of the Spaniards, due to treachery and deceit, the Chiricahuas believed. Natanijú lost a number of his people killed and captured, while Pachatijú remained imprisoned.[47]

The next year began with Chiricahuas suffering another Spanish campaign consisting of multiple columns and several hundred soldiers crossing their spring ranges for several weeks. The soldiers killed more than sixty Apaches and captured seventeen. They also took many horses and looted buffalo and deer hides. Undeterred,

seeking revenge, and needing to replace the material lost, especially the horses, Apaches attacked the area around Janos throughout the spring and summer. With the coming of winter Nataniju
and El Zurdo once again led their camps down to the hills above
Janos to wait out the months of severe weather. They again held a
fierce dance to collect men and led them in yet another attack on
the horse herd at Janos. This time they crept in at midnight and
were able to drive off 225 horses, despite being discovered by the
horse guards who fired "many shots."[48]

As Nataniju and El Zurdo, driving their loot before them, came
within sight of their camps, the women came out, cheering and ap-
plauding. The warriors divided the horses among those who had
gone on the raid and then the two rancherias held a victory dance,
lasting up to four days and nights, paralleling the war dance. First,
the warriors danced the fierce dance again, but this time to recognize those who had gone on the raid. As a man danced around the
fire the singers sang what he had done. With all the warriors recognized, the Gileños held a round dance. All the men danced around
the fire while the women danced in a circle around the men, facing
them. A partner dance followed in which the women were free to
choose their partners. The final dance took place with two facing
lines of men and women, approaching and separating. For many
young warriors and young women this victory celebration turned
into "marrying time."[49]

Four raids not only turned a young man from a novice to a warrior; four raids also showed that he could provide for and defend
a family, making him eligible to marry. As evidence of this ability,
a man gave gifts to his desired bride's relatives. Horses were the
main gift, always specifically mentioned. Chiricahuas explained
this practice with the tale of how Coyote made women valuable.
Once he had done so, the woman exclaimed, "Hereafter I shall be
worth a lot. I am worth horses and many things now." Chiricahuas figured "that is why men give horses and different things when
they marry women." Possibly due to the liaisons made earlier that
year, another raid set off in the fall, driving off another 280 Janos

horses, many likely to serve as bridal gifts. Then Natanijú and El Zurdo, along with the new married couples among their people, settled into their camps in the canyons and sierras fifty miles northwest of Janos to wait out the winter months.[50]

"Their triumph is limited"

In early November 1785 Perú witnessed a muster of over 350 soldiers at Janos from presidios all across northern Nueva Vizcaya. He was to lead 60 of his own Janeros and 50 from other presidios, including 20 Opatas from Sonora, as the "Second Division of the Campaign." In conjunction with the Third Division, led by Capitán Don Antonio Cordero of San Buenaventura, Perú was to march north-northwest searching out Apache camps, rendezvousing with the other two divisions at the water hole of Santa Lucía near the Río Gila. After combing the area between the water hole and river, the divisions were to return to their presidios; the first to Carrizal, the third and Perú's to Janos. The instructions for the campaign were quite clear concerning anything taken from the Apaches. Horses were to be handled in accordance with current regulations, while cattle could be distributed among all the men. Any other goods seized were to be the property of the Opata Indian auxiliaries accompanying each division.[51]

Perú, however, did not ride out of Janos on campaign, having fallen sick. Command of his division passed to Captain Cordero. Natanijú did not know this, but he did learn from a returning raiding party that several hundred soldiers were heading his way. As the soldiers scoured the sierras to the south of his winter encampment, Natanijú scattered the Gileño Apaches, some three hundred families in all, north and northeast toward hoped for refuges along the Río Gila and the lower slopes of the Mimbres Mountains. There fleeing Apaches ran into the first division of the campaign. One group had to abandon nineteen horses and mules in order to escape, while another lost twelve animals and a young warrior who died covering his family's retreat. As the soldiers closed in, a larger party of

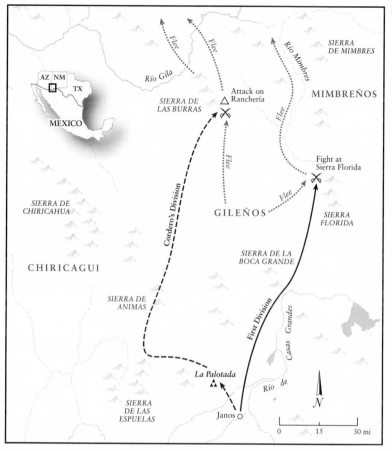

Map 9. Cordero's campaign, 1785

young warriors ambushed more than sixty soldiers in a narrow canyon in the sierra. Attacking with arrows, guns, and war clubs, they managed to kill one soldier and one horse, seriously wounded four men with arrows, and struck many with their clubs. But this rearguard action cost the Apaches three of their warriors.[52]

Chiricahuas in the Mimbres attempted to warn their fellows along the Río Gila of this new force by sending up large columns of smoke. Cordero's forces spotted the response from the Sierra de las Burras on the south side of the Gila drainage. Cordero concealed his men until midnight and then moved through the frigid late fall night into the sierra. Spotting campfires, Cordero split his force into three groups, two mounted to attack, and one on foot to climb to the high ground and cut off any escape. At daybreak Cordero attacked, but the site proved abandoned, much to his "frustration." Again the Gileños, possibly still under Natanijú's leadership, managed to evade the campaign by moving ahead of any attack. Yet one family gò'tàh for some reason—perhaps a disagreement between this group and the camp leader—did not accompany the rest of the escaping ranchería. Instead they moved into the heights above the abandoned camp, perhaps hoping to rely upon concealment. This proved a fatal error, for the soldiers afoot discovered the family encampment, surprising them and killing all five women and one male child. All the two men could do was grab their horses and flee.[53]

Cordero continued to the Río Gila, dispatching two patrols along the way to search for the Apaches. The first patrol discovered yet another abandoned campsite, the ranchería having fled in the night. But again one warrior chose not to accompany them with his family, again perhaps voting with his inaction against the current leader. All—the man, his wife, and their daughter—died at the hands of the soldiers. Despite finding many more tracks of Apache families scattering into the sierras north of the Gila, the soldiers could not pursue them. An early snowstorm covered the Apaches' tracks and weakened the Spaniards' horse herd, forcing the withdrawal of the ill and frostbitten soldiers. "Their triumph is limited," Cordero

would later wryly note. Meanwhile, Natanijú's exhausted people
settled into their snow-covered camps, simply glad to have survived
another year.[54]

But why? Why did Janeros starve, freeze, fall sick, and watch their
horses die of exposure and exhaustion? Why were Chiricahuas prepared to keep fleeing northward, into a snowstorm, abandoning
their campsites, their herds, and in some cases their kin? In short,
why were so many willing to be full-fledged members of their communities of violence? And they were violent. From the middle of the
eighteenth century the violence between the two steadily escalated. Campaigns from Janos and Apache raiding parties that counted their members in the tens during the 1750s were numbering in
the hundreds thirty years later. Spanish actions killed hundreds of
Apaches and captured hundreds more. Apaches killed thousands
of Spaniards, captured hundreds, and ran off livestock numbering
easily in the hundreds of thousands.[55]

However, both communities not only engaged in violence and
suffered its consequences—they also used it. Despite their losses,
presidial forces steadily grew. Janos tripled its strength, proving
able to recruit enough men even during a smallpox epidemic, a "de-
mographically catastrophic period" in the borderlands.[56] Chiricahuas too, despite their losses and likely affected by the same demographic collapse, increased their numbers of leaders, local groups,
and possibly even bands. Such increases were not despite the violence; they were because of it. Both Janos and Chiricahua men used
their participation in the violence as warriors or soldiers to secure
a place in the community and to enlarge it via marriage.

To marry in both communities a man first had to show he was
an adult, capable of providing for a wife. Chiricahua males accom-
plished this by serving out their novice period to be accepted as a
warrior, a period that could last several years, and by providing
gifts taken on raids or the war path to show that they could take
care of a woman. At Janos the path was more complex. By enlisting
on the muster roll as a soldier, a young male could show he was an

adult. Being a soldier also gave him access to the presidial supply system, one of the few steady sources of goods in the community. Once he had shown himself to be a good soldier, a man sought to wed. This took some time; as best this can be determined, most soldiers waited up to a year, sometimes longer, from the time of their enlistment to marry. Some of this time could be due to the fact that there were not many women to marry on the frontier of Spanish society. In general men always outnumbered women in and around Janos; some years there may have been no eligible women at all. In view of this, men undoubtedly sought some edge in marriage competition, and being a soldier clearly provided an advantage, given that most soldiers were married. Chiricahuas had to face the practice of polygyny, especially sororal polygyny, whereby a man married his wife's sister, often upon her death. Leading men or experienced warriors often had multiple wives, upward of five, further reducing the number of available women. So Chiricahua males too sought an edge and found it in doing violence.[57]

Once a man was accepted as an adult and located a marriageable woman, he had to go before the whole community to complete the marriage. Marriages made families, the building blocks of communities among both Hispanics and Apaches. For Chiricahuas marriage was a straightforward "economic arrangement" binding men into affinities, although love matches were not unknown. Because of this, parents and close relatives oversaw marriage choices, with young people expressing their preferences when asked. Typically the man's family took the initiative to request consent from the girl's kin, often via a go-between, a friend, relative, or well-known figure. This could take time and convincing, often dwelling on the character and abilities of the young man. Once it was done, and the appropriate gifts were delivered, the man would move to his new bride's family camp. This was sometimes done without ritual; sometimes it was accompanied by games, feasting, and social dancing.[58]

At Janos a *soldado* who wished to marry needed the permission of his commanding officer for the chaplain to perform the ceremony. A soldier usually sought permission in a request to the captain in which the soldier identified himself and his intended and requested the chaplain to perform the marriage ceremony. The chaplain typically wrote this request, as most soldiers were illiterate and could make only a crude cross on the paper in place of a signature. With permission secured, usually just a marginal note on the request, the chaplain interviewed the groom, the bride, and three witnesses drawn from among the community. These witnesses would testify to their knowledge of the groom, his status, his occupation, and how long they had known him. They would also testify about the bride, that she was old enough to marry and had not been coerced by violence. Once the chaplain determined from these testimonies that no reason existed not to marry the couple, he completed the ceremony in the chapel, with the witnesses and, one imagines, friends and family in attendance.[59]

As all stages of marriage required at least the tacit consent of the whole community, marriage would be made far more likely if the man was in good standing as a member of the community of violence. Becoming an adult and acceptable marriage partner, locating a marriageable woman, demonstrating the ability to care for and protect her, and having the woman's family and the community as a whole accept the marriage all hinged upon the man's ability to do violence. Thus it should be no surprise that Chiricahua and Janos men were willing to suffer and to risk death. Doing so, they likely believed, gave them their chance to marry and have a family. But the violent coexistence between the communities did not end with marriage, for marriage led to families, and violence was necessary to keep a family in the Southwestern Borderlands.

| Chapter 4

A Vigilant Peace
Families, Rations, and Status, 1786–1830

.

A willingness to do violence secured and supported status and families in both communities. After 1786 Spanish strategy was to grant peace immediately to all Apaches who asked for it and to wage unceasing war on those who did not. This accepted that any peace was likely temporary and would require more violence to ensure. By 1789 this strategy bore fruit, and many Apache leaders and their extended families began to settle at Janos. The return of captive family members was a primary inducement for peace, to which a regular issue of rations was added. Men in both communities depended upon their families, and especially their wives, to be fed, clothed, and cared for. Since men were often away from their families for weeks or months at a time, even a suspicion of improper behavior could have serious consequences. As a result men continued to position for status within their community, now tied into rations as much as violence. Janos nearly disintegrated in the decade after Mexican independence; rations all but ended for both communities, troop strength declined precipitously, and Chiricahuas stayed away from the presidio. As both communities felt their ability to influence the other weakening, they became more suspicious, wary, and fearful, dredging up memories of hurt and hate.

"Allowing them to possess their homes"

Change rode into Janos in December 1786, embodied in the figure stiffly dismounting in the plaza after his ride from San Buenaventura. As Captain Antonio Cordero rubbed his hands for warmth and walked into the captain's house that was now his, perhaps he reflected on how far he had come from his native Cadiz on the southern coast of Spain. Now aged thirty-three, he had first enlisted as cadet in the Regiment of Zamora at the age of fourteen and had served for two years. After a three-year hiatus Cordero joined the Dragoons of Spain and Mexico in New Spain as a cadet in 1771. He served for three years and won promotion to the rank of *portaguion* (guidon bearer). In August 1774 Cordero transferred to the northern frontier as an ensign in one of the new *compañías volantes* (mobile companies). Promoted to lieutenant in 1781, he joined the San Buenaventura presidio and became its captain in 1783. Three years later Cordero found himself at Janos as its new commander.[1]

The commander's quarters at Janos were not quite vacant, however. The previous captain, Juan Perú, a serving soldier when Cordero was born, was still at the presidio. His fifty-nine years of age and seven wounds suffered on nearly thirty campaigns were taking their toll, as Perú was increasingly ill, missing a critical campaign the previous year. He attempted to claim his health had improved, citing it as "robust" on his service record in 1786, but to no avail. After nearly forty years of service, including fifteen years as the captain of Janos, Perú retired. He left the presidio, leaving two of his sons serving in the company and Cordero in charge.[2]

The change Cordero brought lay in a newly articulated strategy. This new Indian policy flowed from the pen of Viceroy Bernardo de Gálvez several months before in the form of an instruction to his frontier commanders. Gálvez's *Instrucción* of 1786 was not altogether new. It was a "synthesis" of two decades' worth of past policies, including recommendations from 1768, the Reglamento de 1772, a 1776 instruction, council of war resolutions in 1777 and 1778, and a royal order in 1779. The *Instrucción* of 1786 was extraordinary "in its clarity of statement and detail in specification." It was the first time that policy had been stated in its entirety, had the force of a royal ordinance, and was accepted by presidial commanders as a practical prescription, in large part because Gálvez had served as a commander on the frontier back in the late 1760s and early 1770s.[3]

The *Instrucción* of 1786 called for unceasing war everywhere and at all times against the Apaches. However, should any sue for peace, it was to be conceded to them immediately. To assist in the negotiations for a lasting peace, gifts were to be provided to the leader—goods, tobacco, and provisions worth fifteen to twenty pesos—and one to two pesos' worth of goods to each Apache warrior "for himself and his family." Once peace was established, and the Apaches were showing good faith, regular rations of food were to be provided. Whatever the costs or irritants of relentlessly pursuing peace, Gálvez held that "a bad peace with all the tribes which ask for it would be more fruitful than the gains of a successful war."[4]

Peace with the Apaches, Gálvez held, would be "founded, as everything else, on private interest." The private interest of the Apaches was to survive. They attempted to live by hunting, but there was not enough to sustain their life, so they turned to warfare because "if they do not, they perish of hunger." Apaches suffered great risks to take horses and mules for warfare, hunting, and to eat "because they are their favorite food." They also sought guns, powder, and munitions for "pleasure and security" and wished for adornments that Gálvez believed made them appear "ridiculous." But Hispanics would "benefit by satisfying their desires" via "limited" gifts and a "miserable barter of skins, seeds, and wild fruit." Gálvez admitted such a peace would not always be peaceful. Even when Apaches were at peace at a presidio or a town, they never ceased raiding other Spanish settlements "to acquire the things they desire," but they did refrain from attacking those places where they lived at peace so as to protect the families they left behind. Thus, while his peace would "be broken many times," Gálvez insisted that if it were followed by vigorous war, the Apaches would soon seek a return to a safer and more secure peace.[5]

Cordero not only brought this new strategy to Janos; he also brought his own experiences and insights. During his first years on the frontier, Cordero had served in four campaigns, killing or capturing fifty-three Indians, or *piezas* (pieces), in the slang of the time. He had been the commander in all the *funciones* (engagements) in which he had participated. Over the four years prior to his arrival at Janos, he led another eight campaigns attacking rancherias, killing or capturing more than thirty Indians and restoring a Spanish captive to his family. Cordero had also seen many pursuits of Apache raiders recovering innumerable horses and other livestock.[6] All his action led to an understanding of Apaches, especially the men.

Although he did not write down his insights until nearly a decade later, Cordero did exhibit many of its tenets while at Janos. He realized the central role each Apache man played as the head of his own family and that "every family head in his own camp considers himself a sovereign in his district." Because of this, Cordero knew Apache family leaders did not suffer other leaders lightly, as "there are some so jealous and proud that they prefer to live completely separated from others with their wives and children, because thus no one disputes their leadership." Apaches were thus quite prickly and cautious in their dealings with others. "The Apache," Cordero would later write with some exaggeration, "does not even approach his own brother without weapons in hand, always on guard against an attack or always ready to commit one." So, Cordero believed, the only way to bring peace would be by "allowing them to possess their homes," families, wives, and children in safety.[7]

Despite this new strategy and his own insights, things did not immediately change at Janos. Literally days before Cordero's arrival a war party of Apaches attacked the Janos horse herd. The Janeros rallied, killing seven Apaches in the ensuing pursuit, and recovered most of the horses scattered in the melee. However, in mid-March 1787, El Zurdo took the opportunity of a visit to Janos by Commandant General Jacobo Ugarte to approach the presidio seeking peace for his and Natanijú's people. Ugarte met with

El Zurdo and Natanijú—now entering their second and third decades respectively of leadership among the Mimbreños—and tasked
Cordero to see to the peace, with the stipulation that all those who
wanted to live in peace were to camp near the presidio of San Buenaventura and refrain from hostile actions. He also sent five Chiricagui from those at peace near Bacoachi in Sonora to assist Cordero, who rode to San Buenaventura to oversee the arrangements.
Within two months Cordero settled eight to nine hundred Apaches, under eight different leaders, near the presidio and "went alone
among" them to recover four Spanish captives.[8]

At the end of April the peace began to unravel when troops
from Sonora attacked a Chiricagui camp that included a number
of Mimbreños. In this attack the Chiricagui leader El Chiquito lost
one of his wives and four daughters, and he sent emissaries among
the Apaches at San Buenaventura to tell of the death of their kin.
El Zurdo and another leader, Nayelel, complained to Cordero of
the attack, but many of the Mimbreños decided to abandon the
peace. El Zurdo and Natanijú used their standing to restrain others for several days, but the arrival of Manta Negra, an obstinate
enemy of the Spaniards, overcame the influence of the aging leaders. On May 21 the Mimbreños rose, attacking the five Chiricagui,
the interpreter, and ten soldiers who had just arrived with horses
for the Indians. The interpreter, one soldier, and three Chiricagui
died in the fracas, one Chiricagui was captured, and one escaped
to report the news to Cordero.[9]

Following the tenets of the *Instrucción* of 1786, Cordero immediately ordered more than three hundred men into the field in pursuit of the Mimbreños. One detachment from Sonora, guided by
Chiricaguis seeking revenge, killed or captured more than one hundred Apaches in four engagements, while another from El Paso with
Navajo and Comanche auxiliaries took twenty more. He himself
led three campaigns during the rest of 1787. The first, in July, attacked a ranchería in the Sierra de los Metates led by Manta Negra
the Younger, Manta Negra's brother, a group that included some
of El Zurdo's people. The second campaign trailed Apaches to the

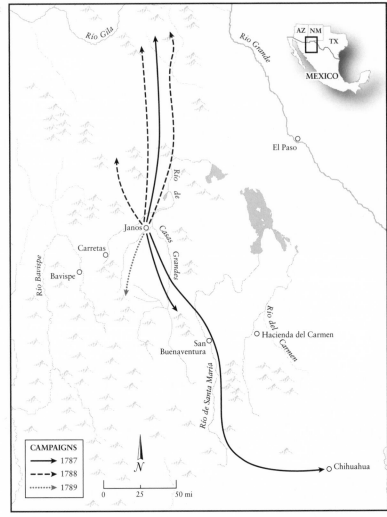

Map 10. Cordero's campaigns, 1787–89

south of Chihuahua City during the month of August. Cordero's last campaign for the year scoured the mountains above San Buenaventura during December and assaulted a settlement of Mimbreños under Ojos Colorados, before the cold and snow forced him back to Janos. Likely warming himself before the fire in the captain's house at the presidio, Cordero recorded that these three campaigns resulted in six engagements that killed or captured forty-five Apaches, including nineteen warriors.[10]

Cordero kept up the pressure on the Mimbreños during the next year, leading four campaigns, attacking six rancherias, and killing or capturing twenty-five "enemies," warriors, women, and children. The first campaign early in the year went to the Mogollon Mountains and the San Francisco River. Cordero set out again in March, trailing Apaches to the Sierra de las Mulas, then through the El Gallego and Barrigón sierras, before surprising a camp in the Sierra de los Arparejos. He attacked another ranchería and scoured two more sierras before ending the campaign after forty-three days in the field. A few weeks later Cordero pursued Apaches into the Animas and El Hacha mountains.[11] But not all the violence of 1788 involved large campaigns.

On August 18, 1788, Justo Mesa, accompanied by Fermín González and Bartolomé Galaviz, left the presidio of Bavispe in Sonora carrying messages back to Janos. At three in the afternoon, as the men neared the mouth of Carretas pass between Bavispe and Janos, twenty to twenty-five Apaches attacked them. The three Janeros opened fire, killing one Apache and wounding several others. With the way toward Janos now blocked, they turned back toward Bavispe, with the Apaches in pursuit. When the Apaches caught them, Mesa and his compatriots halted and fired at their attackers, who shot arrows and guns in return. One arrow struck Mesa, who would later admit that he feared for his life. Their gunfire allowed the soldiers to break away, but the Apaches continued the pursuit and again attacked the increasingly desperate men. In this third attack Galaviz took a musket ball to the head, killing him instantly, but Mesa and González held off the Indians until nightfall, when the Apaches quit the fight. Mesa and González then placed rocks over Galaviz's body and led his horse back to Bavispe.[12]

A reconnaissance party from Bavispe scouted the route a few days later and confirmed the men's account. They found the body of an Apache, whose ears they cut off, and evidence of several wounded men at the first site; many arrows and spent musket balls at the second; and Galaviz's body at the place of the third attack. Surveying the carnage, the party's commander congratulated Mesa and González on escaping with their lives. Cordero relayed the story—and the ears—to the commandant general, who ultimately rewarded Mesa and González, and Galaviz's heirs, with fifty pesos each. The plight of the men had been so desperate that González remembered it over twenty years later on his service record. Even though he had served for forty-one years by that time and had seen thirty-seven campaigns and pursuits, it was this long, hot, and fear-filled afternoon that dominated his memories.[13] Nor would Mesa soon forget.

By 1789 Natanijú's sons, now leaders of their own rancherias, and both Mantas Negras occupied the Sierra Madre to the south of Janos, striking out to Chihuahua City and beyond. Soldiers searched the region, but the Apaches managed to elude them. At the end of the year Cordero led another long campaign that stayed in the field for forty days and killed or captured 241 Apaches, also recovering a few Hispanic captives. And it was after the end of this campaign that the change Cordero brought to Janos finally began to bear fruit. The Mimbreño leader Squelnoctero brought his family to the presidio and sought to make a peace.[14] Squelnoctero, also recorded as Esquielnoctén or Jasquienelté, would be the first of many Chiricahua leaders who would seek to live with their families in a violent peace at Janos.

El Compá

As winter lessened its grip on the borderlands the Chiricagui leader El Compá and his *gò'tàh*, numbering some fifty to sixty persons, joined Jasquienelté/Squelnoctero at Janos. It was not El Compá's

first brush with living at peace with Hispanics. Several years earlier he had settled at Bacoachi, across the mountains from Janos,
but had abandoned the presidio after several months. Nearly a year
later troops captured El Compá's wife. In order to redeem his wife
from her captors El Compá surrendered, along with some twenty
warriors, many of them his close kin, to a Spanish campaign. A year
after his capitulation, El Compá led his people to settle at Janos.[15]

El Compá's deliberate submission proved a wily move. By this
time Spanish authorities regularly deported Apache prisoners of
war far from their native lands across the sea to Havana, Cuba,
but allowed those who surrendered voluntarily to stay in the region. The campaign to which El Compá surrendered also seized
125 Apaches in other engagements. The commandant general decided that these captives, since they were taken in war, would be
deported via Chihuahua and to Mexico City. However, El Compá's
people would not be exiled and could settle again at Bacoachi, as
he had willingly yielded.[16] Perhaps bad blood with the relatives of
those exiled prompted El Compá's decision to relocate over the Sierra Madre to Janos.

Not long after he arrived at the presidio El Compá set out to find
the ranchería of Ojos Colorados and convince him to make peace
at Janos. He found Ojos Colorados in a receptive mood, as a few
days earlier soldiers from San Buenaventura had seized three wom-
en of his *gò'tàh*. Accompanied by El Compá, Ojos Colorados went
to Janos with nine warriors to ask for peace. He also asked Cordero for one of the women taken, the wife of one of his warriors,
currently held at San Buenaventura, exchanging two captive Spanish children for her. Ojos Colorados asked further that his brother's son, Tagaquechoe, be returned. Spanish officials scrambled,
as the youth, captured in January 1788, was to have been exiled
to Havana. A search failed to turn him up in Cuba, although he
may still have been in Veracruz. Apparently satisfied, Ojos Colorados completed his treaty to live in peace at Janos, agreeing to
settle near the presidio, to keep the peace, not to attack any other
Hispanic settlements, to participate in campaigns against Apaches

still at war, and to "harbor no malefactors." Ojos Colorados convinced his kinsman Jasquenachi and even old Natanijú to settle at
Janos, joining El Compá.[17]

Besides serving as a go-between with various Chiricahua leaders to convince them to settle in peace, El Compá also participated
in a number of campaigns against recalcitrant Apaches. In the fall
of his first year at Janos, while scouting for a Spanish force near
the Hacienda del Carmen, El Compá apprehended two of Manta Negra the Elder's warriors, who were also serving as scouts, as
they warned an Apache ranchería of the impending attack. While
one of the men escaped, El Compá seized the other and presented him to a befuddled Spanish official at El Carmen. This incident
only added to El Compá's stock at Janos, where his wives were receiving an extra ration of mutton and a Spanish-style house was
constructed for him and his growing household within the bounds
of the presidio.[18]

The household grew from captives given to its members for their
service. That first summer, at El Compá's suggestion, Cordero ordered that an Apache woman taken captive on campaign be turned
over to a member of El Compá's ranchería, a young man known
as Nac-cogé, called El Güero by Spaniards due to his light-colored
hair. The gift to El Güero, Cordero noted, was in appreciation for
his "good services." A year later El Compá asked the new commandant general to free a number of his relatives taken captive in a recent campaign. The commandant general did remove El Compá's
kinsmen from the contingent of prisoners bound for Mexico City
and exile from the borderlands, but he released only one to Juan
Diego, El Compá's son. He held the rest as prisoners in Chihuahua as inducement for the five warriors "they belong to" to reside
in peace at Janos. Then he would return their families to them.[19]

El Compá was not the only Apache man to have his family and
kin used as leverage to get him to settle in peace at Janos. The warrior known as Gimiguisen saw his wife, sons, and relatives taken
captive in a campaign at the end of 1790. Cordero fully expected
that this "disgrace" would make Gimiguisen seek peace and then

seek to redeem himself by serving with the next campaign. Whether Gimiguisen surrendered is unknown, but such tactics did appear to have some success, as many more Chiricahuas came in to settle at Janos, joining El Compá.[20]

Manta Negra the Elder negotiated a peace to recover kinsmen, his wife, and three children captured by Spaniards, settling first at Janos and then moving to Carrizal to make way for more Apaches at Janos. The Mimbreño chief Vívora settled at the presidio with his go'tàh of twenty warriors and their families, totaling more than one hundred persons, where he was joined by the sons of Pisago with twenty-two Chiricahuas in their group, although their father stayed away. Cal-lo settled in peace and joined a campaign with ten of his warriors the next month. Cal-lo's party, along with twenty soldiers and twenty Opatas, attacked a ranchería near San Buenaventura, capturing seven relatives of Tetsegoslán. Accompanied by his brother, El Padre, Tetsegoslán then went to Janos and settled in peace in exchange for the return of his kin. So many Chiricahuas came to Janos during the summer after El Compá's arrival that Ojos Colorados and Jasquenachi, and their rancherias, joined Manta Negra in moving to other presidios.[21]

Overcrowding may not have been the only reason some Apache leaders left. El Compá found himself appointed the "Gefe Principal de la Apacheria Pacifica" (principal chief of the Apaches at peace) over the protestations of other Apache leaders, who warned that such an appointment was "un-Apache." Some of those may have chosen to leave Janos in honored Apache political practice rather than deal with El Compá in his new role as "El Capitán Compá." El Compá, along with the other Apache leaders (capitancillos), was to meet regularly with the presidial commander in council with all the warriors and women present. Only a capitancillo such as El Compá who had proven his loyalty could request the return of a woman or child captured on campaign. Recognized leaders received more rations. Each week a married warrior received two measures of wheat or maize, four boxes of cigarettes, one piloncillo (issue of sugar), half a measure of salt, and a ration of meat when available, along with another half ration for each additional adult and a quarter ration for each child, although those under the age of seven did not receive cigarettes. A *capitancillo* like El Compá received another *piloncillo* and two more boxes of cigarettes. Further, *capitancillos* and their favorite wives received clothing and tack, as did those who distinguished themselves in battle. However, whenever El Compá or any warrior left Janos to go hunting or visit friends and relatives at other presidios, he had to leave his family behind.[22]

Two years after his arrival at Janos El Compá's family included three wives and one child. His twenty-year-old son Nayulchi, known to the Spaniards as Juan Diego, was married and likely lived with his wife's family, one of the ten to twenty families regularly associated with El Compá's ranchería at any time. He also had living with him the kinsman Juscaye, who soon married into one of the families in the *gò'tàh*. By late spring El Compá had another wife living with him, and in late summer one of his wives added another child to his family. His *gò'tàh* added the family of El Tadiya from Bacoachi, but El Güero split off from El Compá to create his own local group, joined by four families.[23]

The next year, his third at Janos, El Compá's family had four wives and three children, one of whom, called Juan José by the Spaniards, attended the presidial school with the sons of the soldiers. El Compá was also a grandfather for a short time as Juan Diego's wife gave birth in the spring, but the child died by the fall. Juscaye was now a father as well and had a nephew living with him and his wife. A year later El Compá might have seen Juan Diego's second child, but he died a month too soon, aged fifty or fifty-one years, the Spanish record keepers thought. El Compá apparently died from natural causes after a lifetime of violence to get a family and violence to keep a family, a family he needed to ensure his own survival.[24]

Wives and Households

Every morning one of El Compá's women, likely the junior wife once listed as a *cocinera* (cook) in Spanish records, rose before dawn, built up the fire, and prepared breakfast for the rest of the family. Afterward the others, under the direction of María, El Compá's primary wife, left their children with one woman and set out to gather, prepare, and store fruits and vegetables in the seasonal round of women's labor. In the spring they harvested the stalks, roots, and flowers of the yucca and the mescal. In early summer María sent her sister Canslude and El Compá's other wife, Guadalupe, to pick the blossoms of the locust tree and gather wild onions. From midsummer they gathered juniper berries, seeds, wild fruits in the mountains, and pitahaya cactus. Come fall, El Compá's household foraged for screw beans, the fruit of the giant cactus, suma berries, datil fruit, prickly-pear cactus, mesquite beans, and walnuts. The women also collected piñon nuts, greens, and sunflower seeds. Wherever she went María kept an experienced eye out for beehives and their honey. While living at Janos the women also received the weekly ration issues of wheat, maize, sugar, salt, and meat. All this food had to be prepared—ground, roasted, parched—and cooked to feed El Compá and his family.[25]

If El Compá killed a deer, he butchered it, but it was up to María, Canslude, Guadalupe, and their sister-wife to cook the meat or dry it out, "jerking" it for later consumption. The wives also prepared beverages, from herbal and plant teas to the all-important alcoholic beverages made from mescal, sotol, and mesquite, and the favored drink *tizwin*, "grey water," a weak maize beer. And if they had gathered and prepared a large amount of dried food—meat, yucca fruit, mescal, berries—the women then cached what could not be carried. They located a cave or cleft in a rocky place, first putting down a layer of rocks, then oak brush, then the cached goods, which were covered with grass. The women then sealed up the entrance with rocks, plastered them over with mud, and camouflaged the cache with grass and dirt.[26]

Besides food gathering and preparation, María also oversaw the labor necessary for the upkeep of the household. She and the other wives brought water back to camp from a spring or stream in a pitch-covered basket and carried in firewood with a special rawhide rope the women made themselves. The consummate woman's work was the preparing of hides, scraping them with a bone or stone tool and then tanning with the animal's brains. From these skins the women made robes, saddlebags, moccasins, and parfleches (flat hide containers) and sewed together quivers and bow covers from pieces cut out by El Compá. To make baskets the women drew upon their labor and their knowledge of materials and techniques. María made coiled tray baskets for food storage from sumac stems with yucca leaves for decoration; wove large burden baskets from twined sumac and mulberry with bands of color; and made her water jar of twined sumac, covering the inside with pitch and attaching wooden or rawhide handles. She and El Compá's other wives made simple pottery plates and bowls, and made their cups, dippers, and spoons from gourds and wood. They also had to build, maintain, and repair the home itself, the brush-constructed, hide-covered wickiup.[27]

All of El Compá's extended family contributed to the well-being of the household. Boys hunted small game, girls assisted in gathering and domestic chores, including watching younger siblings, and the elderly kept watch, repaired articles, and contributed as they could. Yet it was women who anchored the family while overseeing and ensuring its household economic activities. Given her future importance, a girl underwent an elaborate four-day puberty rite when she first menstruated. The rite, one of the few purely joyous and festive Chiricahua ceremonies, began with a feast, accompanied by masked dancers, followed by singing for the girl, and then social round and face-to-face dances. During the ceremony the girl was identified with White Painted Woman, mother of the cultural hero Child of the Water. Before the rite a female was called a girl and was not eligible for marriage, but afterward she was a marriageable woman. However, women were so valuable to their families that no family wanted to lose its daughters when they married, resulting in the matrilocal residence pattern. María and her sister-wives, secure in their social place, attached to their family, carrying on familiar activities for familiar family members, working with women whose habits they knew, functioned efficiently and productively, making them very valuable to El Compá.[28]

Hence it was important that El Compá protect his women. Cordero admiringly noted the "valor or temerity" Chiricahua warriors displayed when they were attacked. The men stayed calm, fought to the "last breath," and preferred to die "rather than surrender." When a ranchería moved, often to avoid a Spanish campaign, parties of men at the front, rear, and flanks guarded the women and children in the center. Yet men also protected their women by accepting peace, especially when they feared the women would be deported. El Compá settled in peace, the second time, to ensure that María would not be sent away. Peace and settlement near the presidio, however, brought another set of potential threats to El Compá's women: other Chiricahua men. Cordero noted that some Apache men preferred "to live completely separate from the others with their wives and children" for, as one Chiricahua later recounted, they were jealous of their wives and did not want anyone else around.[29]

El Compá likely told his sons the tales of how Coyote lost his wife and family to another male and then got them back. Coyote was married to a "pretty wife" and had a young boy. Another coyote tricked Coyote to get on a rock that went up out of sight. Then the other coyote got Coyote's wife and abused his son, giving him only the toughest meat to eat. Coyote convinced some bats to help him get down from the rock and set out to find his family. After ten days Coyote found his wife's camp, but the other coyote was out hunting, so he hid in a quiver. When the other coyote returned, Coyote got out of the quiver and shot the other coyote with several arrows, killing him. But when his wife returned from dragging the other coyote's body out, he saw that she had been crying. In another tale, Coyote's pretty wife "was unfaithful to him all the time." When Coyote caught his wife and her lover loudly having sex, he killed the other coyote, this time by making him swallow stones heated in the fire. Chiricahuas had other tales of women's — and it was always women's — unfaithfulness. Some concerned women who pretended to be sick or even pretended to have died to be with their lovers. When a husband caught his unfaithful wife with her lover, he killed them both for, as one Chiricahua later said, "it was their law then." In one tale a husband beat his wife with a club when he learned of her infidelity and told her if she danced naked before all the camp he would let her marry her lover. If she did not, he would kill her.[30]

Since the relations between a Chiricahua man and his wives were primarily of economic necessity, there was often little sentiment or display of affection between the two. A man who was too warm to his wife would be ridiculed by other men as his wife's "slave." Typically husbands and wives referred to each other simply as "one with whom I go about," and respect and affection were expected to grow across the years. Not unsurprisingly, affairs were thus common after marriage, when women were not closely watched by their family. While a man was allowed to take drastic action upon discovering infidelity, including killing the woman or cutting her nose, leaders did attempt to dissuade the man from violence. Men and women could dissolve their marriage by common assent, although the women kept the critical camp goods necessary for survival. If abused, a woman could take refuge with a strong leader for protection. However, nothing led to trouble between Chiricahua men more readily than suspicion of wife seduction.[31]

The men of Janos could not have agreed more, especially Justo Mesa. Mesa returned to Janos after an October 1793 campaign and discovered his wife of fourteen years, Josefa Padilla, under arrest and imprisoned in the calabozo (jail) by the order of Captain Manuel de Casanova. Mesa made himself enough of a nuisance to the captain over Josefa's incarceration that Casanova assigned him to guard the horse herd some distance from the presidio, even though he had just returned from the physical hardship of a campaign. Mesa thus decided to take matters into his own hands. Cutting one of his horses out of the herd, Mesa saddled up, deserted his post, and rode the 95 leagues, approximately 250 miles, to Chihuahua.[32]

Mesa was no young soldier shocked into desertion by the demands of military life. He was instead one of the most senior soldiers in the company, a calm and capable veteran who had won commendation for his combat skill five years before. Nor was Mesa homesick, as he was a native of Janos who began his service in October 1776 as a civilian auxiliary replacement for the failed attempt to use Opata Indians as scouts. In 1779, the same year he married Josefa, Mesa enlisted in the company, and he served with distinction for the next fourteen years.[33] Mesa thus knew what he was doing when he rode into Chihuahua, where he sought and received an audience with Pedro de Nava, the *comandante general* of the northern frontier.

Mesa decided that honesty was the best policy in dealing with Nava and admitted at the start of his interview that he had deserted his post, "impelled by the fact that his wife" was jailed. Mesa's story won the sympathy of Nava, who absolved him of desertion due to his "good record and service" and sent him back to Janos, preceded by a letter to Casanova. Nava ordered Josefa released and instructed Casanova not to arrest or detain the wives of soldiers unless they committed a "grave crime." If they did commit some indiscretion, they should be notified discreetly, allowing them to correct their actions. If chastisement was necessary, it should be done with prudence and, if their husbands were not present, women were to be placed not in jail but in "homes of recognized honor" among their husbands' companions. Above all, Casanova was to avoid "incidents among married couples that might be to the perdition of good soldiers."[34]

Mesa, like El Compá, relied upon his household as the central node of survival. His married and family life consisted mostly of trying to get along, run a household, make a living, raise children, and maintain the economic and social links necessary for survival in the borderlands. Given this large requirement, Mesa's household was actually quite small, consisting only of Josefa and one young son in 1791 and 1792. The son died young, for the household in 1796 consisted of Justo, Josefa, a new daughter, and a servant, but the servant was no longer with them in 1799.[35] To Josefa fell all of the necessary household chores, especially during Justo's regular absences.

Justo was often gone as the company of Janos sent smaller *partidas* (detachments) of soldiers to serve with detachments drawn from other units when ordered, as had occurred in the month prior to Josefa's incarceration. Such *partidas*, of five to fifty men, lasted anywhere from a few weeks to several months. At any given time, however, only some of the company were available for assignment to detachments since a sizeable portion of them were guarding the presidio, watching the horse herd, carrying dispatches, and providing escorts to official travelers, duties that kept them away from their homes for several days, if not weeks.[36] Josefa could easily expect Justo to be absent for two or three weeks out of every month.

Thus Josefa and the other women of the company had to draw their men's supplies and keep their households functioning, arriving "every Saturday to receive the weekly ration which their respective husbands are assigned, consisting of an appropriate measure of corn, flour, vegetables, salt, soap, and cigars." Despite their acquiring food and clothing from the military supply system, there is little evidence that women's activities at the presidio differed from the regular run of women's work in the Mexican north. At daybreak Josefa was the first to rise to prepare chocolate, followed by the morning meal of beef seasoned with red chile, beans, and tortillas. The midday and evening meals consisted of much the same. Josefa drew water, washed clothes with the regular issue of soap, raised her children, and kept other wives company during their men's long absences. Women also nursed sick and wounded men.[37] Justo thus needed Josefa in order to be fed, clothed, and cared for when sick or wounded.

Justo Mesa was not alone in his reliance upon his wife; all the men of Janos were in the same situation. As among Chiricahuas, their relations to their wives were overwhelmingly economic in nature. When Cordero sent Mariano Sandoval to the San Pablo jail for rape of another woman, he also ordered Sandoval's wife, Juana

Leiba, to accompany her husband so that she could continue to see to her husband's needs. Yet, however reliant upon—and thus jealous and protective of—their wives soldiers were, they were not given full scope to harm them. In September 1795 Antonio Adame attacked and wounded his wife, Antonia Montañez, possibly for some infidelity. *Comandante General* Nava sentenced Adame to four years of labor in shackles, receiving rations but no pay. Adame's greatest punishment, however, came days earlier when Nava notified Montañez that she had been granted a divorce from Adame. Having brutally harmed his wife, Adame lost all rights to her and her household labor and was now apparently expected to draw his own water and cook his own food.[38]

A Vigilant Peace

By the spring after his father's death Nayulchi, better known as Juan Diego, assumed leadership of the *gò'tàh*. His ability to do violence may well have contributed to his rise, for he had earlier served as an auxiliary for Janos, receiving a captive for his service. Apaches at peace pursued those at war, reconnoitering their encampments before guiding troops to the attack, although they preferred to fight Apaches from other bands. One observer, Lieutenant José Cortés of the Royal Engineers, noted the pride of those Indians chosen to accompany an expedition, who would get to keep any goods they took in battle, and the sorrow of those excluded. These Apache auxiliaries fought "as lions," dying in combat against their kinsmen with "gallantry and loyalty." Another noted in the early nineteenth century that they boasted of nothing other than their bravery. A man about whom no exploits were known was held in contempt by the community. When a warrior did accomplish some feat of courage he would place "Jasquie," meaning valiant, before his name. This custom prevailed among the Gileños and Mimbreños, many of whom resided near Janos, "who were truly among the boldest."[39]

Juan Diego, however, primarily secured his status and power through his relations with and rations drawn at Janos. That same summer he led three of his warriors and seven women together with a delegation of Apaches from Janos to meet the commandant general. While he and his *gò'tàh* drew monthly rations at Janos, they did not stay there all the time. Juan Diego often traveled, south to San Buenaventura, east to Sonora, and west to Carrizal, hunting, gathering, visiting relatives, and undoubtedly politicking, seeking alliances and support to bolster his own position among the Chiricahuas, albeit one dependent upon his relations with the Spaniards. To strengthen this connection Juan Diego, realizing the importance the Spaniards attached to settled life, asked to settle at Casas Grandes south of Janos, a new agricultural community, stating that he wished to take up farming and wanted two oxen. The commandant general denied his request, but Juan Diego did receive the two oxen, which his ranchería happily butchered. He lived for a while at Janos, receiving rations and serving with troops in campaigns against other Apaches, before visiting other presidios and returning to the sierras to harvest mescal and hunt. For his loyalty Juan Diego received gifts, especially for his ill mother, likely María, including clothing, cloaks, sugar, and cash to pay for a local *curandera* (folk healer). He continued to lead his local group around the borderlands, on one occasion going to Sonora to avoid a smallpox outbreak at Janos.[40]

Other Chiricahua leaders at Janos during these years were Pisago, Jasquienelté, Tetsegoslán, Targarlán, Vívora, and Coyote, who all came regularly with their people. Jasquienelté, one who appended the appellation of valor to his name, was often camped at or near Janos and visited regularly for rations. When his brother El Padre died, Tetsegoslán incorporated his brother's group and moved to San Buenaventura, perhaps to avoid the discord this action might have caused. Dissension and disagreement continued to exist in the Apache community, as in all communities. Another Apache, probably a competitor, killed Targarlán in the Sierra de Enmedio. Vívora, who lived at Janos until his death, when Coyote assumed his leadership role, was often in competition with Juan Diego.[41]

Juan Diego regularly visited the encampment of Vívora, who was

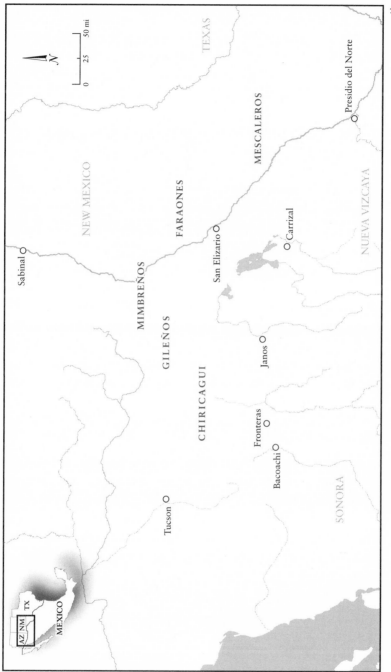

Map 11. Apaches de Paz, ca. 1790

likely his kin, apparently seeking out warriors to join his ranchería. A number of families moved between the two leaders' camps, and when several young men misbehaved one summer at Janos, Vívora disciplined them, as it was his right to do as a recognized leader. When Juan Diego found out that Vívora had chastised some of his people, he angrily confronted the other leader. Clearly he felt Vívora was challenging his status. A few years later Juan Diego's continuous attempts to parlay his preferential position with the Spanish authorities at Janos into a higher social standing among Chiricahuas proved disruptive. He regularly announced to his peers that he would be appointed the principal chief of all Apaches at Janos, the title his father held. This jockeying for status proved so rancorous, as other Apache leaders vigorously opposed such a move, that the commandant general ordered him away from Janos for a while.[42]

Juan Diego soon returned to Janos and the good graces of its officers, working hard to maintain his links with the community. He received rations and gifts, including blankets and on one more than one occasion seed corn, hoes, and axes to encourage agriculture. While Juan Diego had little interest in agriculture at Janos—likely because his people already included it in their seasonal resource migration—he did offer to help the Spaniards explore for copper ore. He had his brother Juan José, a recent graduate of the presidial school, draft a petition asking for ten horses to assist in his search. Further, Juan Diego cultivated a friendship with a leading citizen of Janos, Don Mariano Varela, once passing on to Don Varela a rumor that the Apaches at peace planned an uprising within four to six days. Nothing came of this, but it did serve to cement Juan Diego's affiliation with Janos. And so in the last month of the year the Spaniards called 1810, he and the forty-three men, women, and children in his ranchería settled near Janos to wait out the winter.[43] While Juan Diego had experienced the peace as rations and a search for status, Janos knew mainly vigilance.

The peace between the two communities proved vigilant because Chiricahua men did not give up raiding even when settled in peace at Janos, although they limited their assaults to other Spanish communities in Sonora and the San Buenaventura valley. Nor did soldiers cease to set out on campaigns or patrols, as not all Apaches had settled in peace. Therefore soldiers regularly discovered tracks of raiding parties, stolen horses, and pilfered livestock near or at Janos; Chiricahua men from rancherias at peace would quietly coalesce into a raiding party and set off, acting of their own accord. They were able to trade much of their loot with their relatives who still roamed the hinterland. Because of this Nava instructed Janeros to use "caution . . . when dealing with the Apaches." They were to be watchful, with weapons loaded at all times, "remain distrustful," and "ever vigilant" of the Apaches at peace.[44]

Raiding continued, forcing Commandant General Nava to take action. He ordered Chiricahuas currently living at designated sites near Janos move away from the presidio, back into the hinterlands, some thirty leagues (ninety miles) away, but still keep the peace. Nava intended to separate Apache and Spanish communities to limit the opportunities for violence and make it easier for patrols to spot raiding parties as they approached Hispanic settlements or pursue them afterward. Thus any Apache discovered within the thirty-league limit would be considered an enemy. While Chiricahuas could visit Janos to gather their rations or make exchanges, they could only do so once a week, and only in small parties of four or fewer. However, these parties were to receive fewer rations and gifts than before. These changes, initiated in 1794, ultimately did have an effect. In 1795 over more than eight hundred Chiricahuas in fifteen rancherias lived in, around, or near Janos. By the next year some seven hundred remained, but that number soon dropped to around two hundred, where it would stay for the next three decades as Chiricahuas came to Janos to receive rations before moving back into the hinterland from where they could gather, hunt, and raid.[45]

Soldiers from Janos therefore continued to be members of a community of violence. Manual Albino Rodriguez started 1800 with a *función de guerra* (skirmish) capturing five Apache men, four women, and four children on January 30. Albino Parra took part in a campaign in April 1800, four months after joining the company, which killed nine Apache warriors and recovered thirty horses, while José García died "at the hands of the enemies" on October 16, 1800, during another campaign. José Olguin fell at the hands of the enemies while on campaign on December 1, 1800. Over the next five years Rodriguez served in five "actions of war" or battles and three functions, along with Parra, killing and capturing 159 Apaches, including 51 warriors. After his 1805 reenlistment Rodriguez took part in a campaign that killed eight warriors, and Parra served in a July 1810 campaign that killed and captured fifteen Apaches.[46]

Officers at Janos recorded the actions of these soldiers due to an increasing emphasis on "merit." Commanders were to enter all "actions of war" and other "functions of service" on each soldier's *filiación*, or enlistment paper. A soldier's *filiación* listed his "war and other services," noting all "promotions, rewards, campaigns, skirmishes, and defects." Merit, and subsequent promotion, depended upon these "campaigns and actions of war." Promotions overwhelmingly went to those men who had the most years served, participated in the most campaigns, and fought in the most skirmishes, and such service brought status to soldiers. Zebulon Pike, on his thwarted reconnaissance of the borderlands in the early nineteenth century, noted somewhat incredulously that not only did men want to marry the daughters of sergeants but that a soldier "considers himself upon an equality with most of the citizens and infinitely superior to the lower class."[47]

One result of the vigilant peace was that more and more soldiers survived their enlistments and retired at Janos to enjoy their hard-won status and continued access to the supply system. The list of *inválidos*, retirees, grew steadily on the muster rolls and by 1801 counted more than twenty men, including Justo Mesa. He retired honorably from the company a few years after his encounter with Nava, and for the next decade he lived with his wife and daughter at Janos. Much like El Compá, whom he had undoubtedly known, Mesa died peacefully of natural causes, on December 30, 1808, having kept the vigilant peace for much of his life.[48]

Ronquillos and Compás

The year after Mesa's death a new commander rode into Janos, Captain José Ronquillo. A robust fifty-nine-year-old from San Bartolome south of Chihuahua, Ronquillo claimed a *calidad* (status) among the upper stratum of borderland society, *calidad noble*, and the honorific of "Don." He enlisted in 1772 and steadily rose through the ranks, serving in the mobile companies created at that time and at the presidios of Carrizal and San Buenaventura. His fourteen campaigns, "various" pursuits, and eight combat actions earned him his promotion to the captain of Janos in 1807, although he did not arrive until 1809, household in tow. His family in 1810 consisted of his wife, possibly María de la Luz Chacon of Janos, one male and two female adults, and a boy and two girls. Don Ronquillo, however, did not record whether these six were his children, servants, or Indian captives.[49]

Ronquillo also brought with him to Janos his eldest son, José Valentín. Valentín, as he was listed on the company's rolls, was born sometime in 1772 to Ronquillo and María. He enlisted in the presidio of San Buenaventura in 1791, where his father served as an *alférez*, although he claimed his mother's home of Janos as his own. His literacy—he was one of the few enlistees who signed his enlistment papers—and eighteen campaigns earned a promotion to *carabinero* in 1803 and the right to carry the sword as a symbol of his rank, as doing so was "required to create respect." By the time he transferred to Janos with his wife and her widowed mother in 1809, Valentín had added five more campaigns to his service record. In July 1810 he served on a campaign from Janos that killed and captured fifteen Indians "of both sexes." This service won him a promotion to *cabo* in his father's company in October 1812, for he had fought in more skirmishes and served in more campaigns than the other two nominees, although he did not have as many years of service.[50]

Ronquillo completed the collection of his family at Janos in 1815, bringing his second son, José Ignacio, to the presidio to fill

a vacant ensign's billet. José Ignacio was born ten years after Valentín, when Ronquillo was more secure in his social status as an
officer. When José Ignacio enlisted in 1800 in the Third *Compañía Volante* (Mobile Company), where Ronquillo served as a lieutenant, he ensured that José Ignacio was carried on the rolls as a
"distinguished soldier" with the right to have "Don" before his
name. Transferred with his father to the First Mobile Company in
1804, Don José Ignacio served with it until his promotion to *alférez* in 1815. His father's status undoubtedly helped Don José Ignacio win this promotion, for he only had three campaigns to his
name, in which he captured a Mescalero warrior, two women,
and a boy. This was likely because he had spent most of his time
detached to the staff of the subinspector of the Eastern Provincias
Internas, serving as the secretary and participating in the "reconquest" of Texas from insurgent forces.[51]

Yet Ronquillo did not get to spend much time with his son, for
in 1816 Don José Ignacio set off with a detachment for New Mexico. Upon his return to Janos, he received command of another detachment from the presidio, this one bound for Coahuila. Before
he set out, Don José Ignacio married Doña Josefa Varela, daughter of Don Mariano Varela, leading citizen of Janos, friend of the
Compás, and now related by marriage to the Ronquillos. In Coahuila for over a year José Ignacio served as the *comandante de
armas* (military commander) in the Villa de Palafox, leading several campaigns against Comanches and Lipan Apaches, recovering more than eight hundred head of stock before returning to his
bride in 1817.[52]

Besides assembling his family, Ronquillo had to ensure that all
the other families in the community were supplied, often personally signing supply receipts. In 1811 he authorized an issue of beef
to the *mujer* (woman) of José Vizcarra, another to Doña Manuela Perú of the Perú military clan, and sugar to another soldier's
woman. Ronquillo further approved the requests by the wife of
Torobio Mendoza to draw meat, sugar, and wheat and by the wife
of a corporal to receive gaiters from the quartermaster's stores. In

1812 he gave Merced la Montes thirty pesos and issued eleven pesos to Romana Acorta for her husband, Francisco, for which she made her mark on the receipt. In one instance three mothers received their sons' rations, in addition to rations going to fifty-seven wives. Women remained so important to maintain soldiers' households that José Marrufo sought and received permission to marry María Antonia Lucero, the daughter of a settler at Janos, five weeks after his enlistment on January 1, 1814.[53]

Peace clearly sat well with Juan Diego, who was entering his third decade of leadership among Chiricahuas, relying in large part upon his access to rations at Janos to maintain his status. He continued to visit the presidio regularly and receive rations, sometimes staying for months, other times days, accompanied variously by just one woman or upward of twenty-five warriors and their families. Juan José soon joined the ranks of adult males in his brother's ranchería, with two women and a child in his household. Juan Diego was not the only Apache leader who anchored his status in the peace with Janos. Jasquienelté and Pisago were both also entering their third decade of leading their rancherias in peace with Janos, coming to the presidio to collect rations with anywhere from a handful of people to nearly one hundred people. They were joined in their longevity by Feroz, who assumed the leadership of Cayetano's group, and by Chirimi. Other leaders came to Janos with their people to visit and draw rations: Prieto, Nanegí, Asquiedenchul, Molote Pinto, Mayá, Yescas, Compañé, and El Güero, himself kin of the Compás.[54] However, the rations they received, and the supplies Ronquillo issued, steadily declined.

Alberto Maynez, who commanded the presidio while Ronquillo was detached to San Buenaventura, found the supply situation critical at Janos by 1818, primarily because the costs of fighting the insurgency in central Mexico took funds away from the northern provinces. Maynez was running short of money or supplies to give the women of the community. In January 1818 he despaired of having enough supplies for the 130 soldiers' families or rations for the more than four hundred Apaches who regularly came to the presidio, "without which they cannot survive." Maynez needed lead for musket balls, cigars for Apaches and soldiers, and clothing for soldiers and their families. The soldiers had no hats or shoes, and their wives and families were "in such nakedness" that they could not "leave their homes nor go to mass." While Maynez may have been engaging in some hyperbole, by October he was issuing only corn to Apaches, having suspended rations of cigars, salt, and beef.[55]

Problems with supply were not the only indicator that the old colonial order in the borderlands was drawing to a close. In the fall of 1820 the Opata Indians of Sonora, who served in their own presidios, broke into open revolt. Orders two years prior to transfer the Opatas to Baja California had resulted in an open mutiny and general dissatisfaction that ultimately broke out into warfare in 1820. Royalist troops from Durango, Sonora, and Chihuahua, including Janos, gathered to engage the "rebellious Opatas." Both Ronquillo brothers, along with almost all of the presidio, fought in the Battle of Arivechi on November 16 and 17. Valentín recorded his experience as another campaign in which he killed some and captured the rest. José Ignacio recounted service with a mounted force that entered the pueblo on the first day, killing thirty-seven men and forcing the women to flee to the church. On the second day his command killed more Opata fighters, captured eighty-two, and took three hundred women and children prisoner.[56]

José Ronquillo, however, did not serve in this strange campaign, a twisted mirror image of those from his youth. By the summer of 1820, now almost in his seventh decade, he decided he had had enough and retired on August 23, 1820. His retirement left his sons as the only Ronquillos at Janos, where they, along with the two Compá brothers, were soon to face the coming of a new era in the borderlands.[57] Fittingly it was José Ignacio who would bring the tidings.

A New World

José Ignacio reined up his lathered horse in the plaza of Janos on September 1, 1821. Detached to Chihuahua, and likely seeking to parlay his service fighting the Opatas into a promotion, he learned of the proclamation of independence and the end of Spanish rule. It was his honor, he later stated, to proclaim the independence of Mexico to all the presidios in northern Chihuahua, carrying the commandant general's order of August 26, 1821, relaying the news. Ronquillo's information was not a bolt from the blue, for as early as July rumors of independence had circulated in the borderlands. Yet "independence in this America," as Maynez referred to it, would fundamentally alter both communities' coexistence as communities of violence.[58]

Ronquillo received his promotion to lieutenant, but a transfer never came through, and he remained at Janos in his ensign's billet, part of a slowly disintegrating company. Still calling itself a "Royal Presidio" at the end of 1821, Janos carried 126 men and officers on its rolls. As an "Imperial Presidio" just over a year later, Janos still totaled 119 men, but by the end of 1823 it had only 58 men on its roster and no "Imperial" in its title. For José Ignacio his brother's experience was symptomatic of the company's larger problems. Valentín, still a corporal, along with Sergeant Ignacio Arneros, deserted the horse guards on January 8, 1823, taking a horse and mule. Having been imprisoned for a month for desertion and having lost or sold the horse and mule, Valentín took his discharge on June 16, ending twenty-two years of service. He left behind his brother, who now, in the more republican spirit of things, no longer claimed "noble" status but simply insisted he was of "honorable" quality.[59]

Ronquillo was soon the only ensign in a company with just fifty-six men, yet he persevered; but when he transferred to San Carlos presidio in October 1825, Janos could muster only forty-seven troops. However, as Ronquillo rode out of Janos, after ten years and many changes, relief was on the way. In September of that year the state of Chihuahua, now solely responsible for all the forces within its boundaries, disbanded the four colonial-era mobile companies and reassigned their members to the state's presidios. Further, the nation of Mexico returned its interest to the northern

defenses, reissuing the 1772 regulations and continuing the existence of Janos as a presidio, along with six others in Chihuahua,
and assigning it a new strength of ninety-six *plazas*: six officers
and ninety men. By May 1826 these two measures allowed the
commander of Janos, Lieutenant Colonel José Antonio Vizcarra,
to muster ninety-one men.[60]

Juan Diego watched this disintegration with some concern, as
did the other Chiricahua leaders who had been coming to Janos
for almost two decades: Jasquienelté, Feroz, Sidé, Chirimi, and
Pisago. They did so because it soon impacted their status. Mexican authorities ordered Janos to cease issuing rations *in absentia*.
Apaches could no longer pick up supplies for their entire family
or family group at the weekly issues but were now able to draw
only their individual portions. All those out hunting or gathering
would thus lose their share of supplies, albeit an ever-diminishing
supply of corn. This decision weakened the power of Juan Diego
and the other leaders over their warriors. Unable to ensure an adequate supply of rations from Janos, they had to allow more rustling and raiding so that men could feed their families.[61] For Juan
Diego it was a new world.

Juan Diego was finding it hard to coexist with Janos. He was
now joined by his brother, Juan José, who led his own local group.
Juan José typically camped in the Sierra Madre west of Janos and
regularly visited Casas Grandes, although he was officially required
to draw his rations at the presidio of Galeana, as San Buenaventura was now renamed. He did visit Janos on occasion but, like the
rest of the Chiricahuas, received fewer and fewer rations, leading
to more and more raiding. Like his brother, Juan José relied upon
relations with the Mexicans to bolster his leadership, and he tried
to identify the guilty individuals. When he learned that Calabazas,
Yayame, and Andrés had pilfered horses from Sonora and hidden
them on the Río Temehuaque west of Casas Grandes, he informed
Janos of the herd's location and the robbers' names. However as
rations continued to decrease in amount and diversity, rustling increased, and Mexican authorities grew increasingly sharp with

Apaches they suspected of raiding, further decreasing the power of leaders like Juan José. When the commander of Janos seized the Chiricahua Quidé on the suspicion of theft, he placed Quidé head-down in the stocks for two hours. Quidé, his status and honor sundered, attempted to kill himself. While he apparently failed in his attempt at suicide, Quidé, his kin, and his group, were now more suspicious of the Mexicans.[62]

Suspicions between Chiricahuas and Mexicans had only grown over the preceding ten years. When Chiricahuas encountered a party of American trappers on the Río Gila the initial skirmish resulted in a stand-off. Then the Apaches "begin to banter us in Spanish," as James O. Pattie of Kentucky later recalled. They asked who these newcomers were, and when the answer was "Americans," the Apaches "stood in apparent surprise and astonishment." Several years later Pattie and the other Americans were serving as guards at El Cobre when they managed to convince the four Apache leaders besieging the mines to negotiate a peace. While these four were willing to make peace with the Americans, Pattie recalled, they would "never make one with the Spaniards." When asked why, these Chiricahuas explained that "they had long been at war with the Spaniards and that a great many murders had been mutually inflicted." As Pattie recounted, the Apaches "indignantly alleged" that once a large party came to an unstated place to make peace and the Spaniards, now Mexicans, had "decoyed" them within the walls and "commenced butchering them like a flock of sheep." Thus they resolved never to make peace.[63]

Juan Diego may have been concerned with just such a scenario at Janos by this time. He was certainly concerned about the rations he was receiving. For years, sometimes accompanied by just one of his women and other times with all the members of his ranchería, up to ninety-eight in total, he had been coming to Janos for rations, as had Chirimi, Feroz, Jasquienelté, Pluma, and Sidé. Over the thirty-five preceding years the rations Juan Diego and the other leaders received at the presidial gates were fewer in quantity and lesser in quality, now just a measure of corn versus the corn, meat, cigarettes, blankets, and cash of earlier years. While he did not know the numbers, Juan Diego's experience told him the Spaniards spent far more on gifts and rations than the Mexicans—at least ten times more. Becoming desperate, he had asked for two hoes to begin farming near Janos, versus his people's usual mountainside gardens. The actions of the ever-weakening Janos garrison, now about half the size it had been in his youth, also concerned Juan Diego. Whenever Apaches gathered to receive their rations outside the presidial gate, the outnumbered soldiers gathered in the guard house by the gate and closed the door. Juan Diego, along with the other Chiricahua leaders at Janos, asked the soldiers to cease this practice. Possibly the Apaches were concerned that the soldiers would attack them. Chiricahuas were experiencing the new world of the borderlands, although they still kept a vigilant peace.[64]

Chiricahuas and Janeros accepted a peace starting around 1790 and lasting until at least 1830 because of families, rations or supplies, and status.[65] Members of each community saw peace as an opportunity to protect their families from the other; from being killed or, potentially worse, being captured and suffering the physical separation of deportation or the cultural dislocation of incorporation. El Compá's decision to settle in peace, albeit for the second time, to ensure that his wife María would not be deported to central Mexico or to Cuba, and then to keep the peace until his death, is the most obvious example of this calculation in action. María, as the heart of El Compá's family, was invaluable to him for it was his family who fed, clothed, and supported El Compá. And it was not much different at Janos. Soldiers like Justo Mesa depended upon their wives for all the services and support needed to keep them healthy and prepared. To keep the support of women and a family, both El Compá and Mesa in turn had to provide for them.

Such provisions came in the form of weekly rations or supply issues. Given the reams of paper left in the Janos archive about supplies for soldiers and rationing for Indians, it was an ongoing struggle to do both. While supplies were never excessive and the supply chain was accompanied by a large amount of graft and in-efficiency, rations and supplies were generally accessible and ad-equate during the period, although steadily declining for the last decade or so.[66] Yet Mesa and El Compá realized that provisioning a family meant little if they could not ensure solitary access to the results of their families' labors. Men of both communities knew they had to protect their women not only against men from out-side the community but also against men within it. Consider Me-sa's willingness to desert in the face of his wife's treatment by the Janos commander, and the Coyote tales El Compá likely told his sons about the dangers of other men wanting their women.

Men of both communities knew that the best way to protect their women from other men and help provide for them was to en-sure their status. Mesa clearly felt, and his commanding general agreed, that simply being a soldier was enough of a social position that no one, not even his captain, could interfere with his wife. Among Chiricahuas men of known valor and proven bravery ap-pended "Jasquie" to their name, advertising this fact and making it less likely anyone would challenge them by attempting to seduce their wives. And this quest for status did pay off materially. Heads of Apache households got more rations than single men, and rec-ognized leaders received even more, along with gifts, especially in the case of the Compás. Promotion up the ranks at Janos also in-creased a man's access to resources, as higher rank brought more pay and consequently more supplies. As a captain José Ronquillo was able to acquire fifteen times more than when he was a soldier.[67]

The struggle for status, however, was firmly grounded in the ability to do violence as martial skill carried not only material but also social benefits. As both communities continued to attach pos-itive connotations to harming members of the other, this made the peace between them a wary one at best. Chiricahua raiding con-tinued, as it was the primary way a young man could become an adult. Yet assaults also continued because at any given time a size-able minority of Chiricahuas were not at peace. They stayed off in the hinterlands, from where they continued to attack settlements

and traffic with their kin in the peace establishments, before returning at some point to receive rations and then setting off for the
backcountry once again. At Janos the dictates of military service
continued, for campaigns decreased around 1810 as detachments
were assigned to other presidios and other duties, including fighting insurgents, a "new class of enemies," in the *tierra afuera* (far
away land) during the Mexican War for Independence.[68]

Since it was ultimately based on violence, status formed the
linchpin of the peace between the two communities. As long as
peace enhanced and maintained the status of leaders and followers
in both communities, especially allowing them to dominate their
women and families, it proved attractive. Although the struggle
for status did involve violence, the power of leaders derived from
the status bequeathed by the peace and symbolized by rations and
supplies; for several decades this style of peace proved able to limit
the impact of violence. At Janos commanders—Cordero, Gálvez,
Nava—regularly instructed the soldiers to maintain their vigilance
and be wary of the Apaches, fully expecting peace to break down
at times, before it would be restored, often via violence. This was
certainly the experience of the Ronquillos. Among Chiricahuas,
leaders such as El Compá and Juan Diego undoubtedly redistribut-
ed rations within their local group in such a way as to enhance not
only their own status and control but also that the status of their
warriors. Further, leaders did arrange for men to go on the war
path with the soldiers, as allies and auxiliaries, for which they were
often rewarded. Finally, leaders cooperated with Spanish and then
Mexican officials, identifying individuals guilty of thefts and tres-
passes to ensure that the entire community would not be punished.

By the 1820s, as the availability of rations and supplies declined,
so too did the status and control of those who had kept the peace.
For Chiricahuas this resulted in and was reinforced by an increase
in rustling and raiding, despite attempts by some to stop it, including Juan José, who ceased to visit Janos after 1827. At the same time
the garrison of Janos all but disintegrated, losing three-fourths of its
strength at the lowest point, before recovering to barely two-thirds

of its earlier numbers. Valentín Ronquillo did not wait for the recovery, taking a horse and mule, deserting, and then taking his
discharge rather than continue to serve. Both communities felt
their control over the peace weakening. They thus became more
suspicious, wary, and fearful, dredging up old memories of hurt
and hate, reinforced by recent acts of treachery and deceit. Their
thoughts now turned to retaliation and revenge.

| Chapter 5

War, Peace, War
Revenge and Retaliation, 1831–1850

Revenge and retaliation dominated relations between the two communities after 1831. An end to rations led to an increase in Chiricahua raiding, resulting in increased hostility from Mexicans. For most of the 1830s many Chiricahuas attempted to reestablish a peace with the Mexicans, but these efforts fell victim to the desires for revenge and retaliation. By the 1840s Janos had to restore a declining garrison, deal with outside scalp hunters, and then pursue and persecute Indians for ongoing raids. Only then could Janos cobble together peace deals, which rarely lasted as rations typically did not come, and troops kept leaving for other assignments. By the last years of the 1840s Mexicans returned to the scalp hunt, Chiricahuas continued to raid, and both sides exchanged treacheries whenever able. Yet this hostility was tempered by ongoing exchanges of goods and continuing negotiations for peace at Janos. The seemingly irrational cycle of revenge and retaliation, negotiation and exchange was quite rational as both Janos and Chiricahua were weak, unwilling to trust the other community, and unable to enforce any settlement, leaving revenge as their primary option.

"A Terrible Hatred"

Death stalked Janos in 1831. *Viruelas*, smallpox, swept through both Mexican and Apache homes, targeting their most vulnerable

members, infants and children, ultimately killing forty. The epidemic spared neither community, killing an Apache child, "un apachi-
to," before moving on to kill the infant daughter of Captain Juan
José Zozaya and Doña Petra Varela. To escape this outbreak of
smallpox both Compá brothers and their groups, and those of other Chiricahua leaders, fled at the beginning of summer to the higher, cooler, and decidedly less deadly ground of the Sierra Madre.
There they continued the seasonal round of hunting and gathering, with a few young men likely slipping off for some raiding. As
the smallpox burned itself out at the start of winter Juan José grew
concerned with his and his people's standing among the Mexicans.[1]

In January 1832 he sent a letter to Mariano Varela at the Hacienda
de Ramos, a long-time friend of the Compás, father-in-law to Captain Zozaya and José Ignacio Ronquillo, and likely Juan José's godfather. Juan José dispatched the letter in the hands of several women
who carried it to Janos, the means of customary communication between the two communities. In the letter Juan José insisted to Varela
that he and the Apaches just wished for peace. The women added to
Juan José's message, saying the Apaches were gathered together for
defense if no peace was forthcoming. While Mexicans accepted that
Juan José and the Chiricahuas were at peace, they could not extend
the Indians any rations. No rations guaranteed continued raiding.
Chiricahuas ran off horses from a ranch west of Janos in mid-Feb-
ruary, killing the *vaquero* who attempted to stop them, and stampeded livestock away from ranches near an intermittent lake to the
north, the Lago de Guzmán, and the Corral de Piedra to the east.
Two months later they attacked a favorite target, the Janos horse
herd, and haciendas all around the presidio. In retaliation José Ignacio Ronquillo led a combined campaign deep into Chiricahua territory. For three days on the Río Gila in May Ronquillo's forces, including men from Janos, fought Apaches, killing 22, wounding 51,
and recovering 141 horses. They took only two prisoners. Ronquillo
then returned to Janos and opened negotiations. For the next several months Apache envoys came and went from El Cobre and Janos,
until twenty-nine leaders signed a peace treaty on August 21, 1832.[2]

Chiricahuas agreed to end their raids, to return all livestock recently taken, and not to enter the interior of Chihuahua without permission. For his role in the negotiations Juan José Compá was appointed one of three principal chiefs and called "general," a position his father had held and his brother had longed for. General Juan José would oversee Chiricahuas living northwest of Janos. Fuerte, also named a general and later better known as Mangas Coloradas, was paramount chief of the rancherias around El Cobre, and General Matías headed those Apaches living along the Río Gila north of Sonora. But without rations or any reciprocity, the peace proved defunct almost from the moment it was signed, and Chiricahuas resumed raiding all across northwestern Chihuahua.[3]

This placed Juan José in something of a quandary. When he asked Mariano Ponce de León for permission to go to San Buenaventura to recover a captive Apache boy, long the prerogative of Chiricahua leaders who kept the peace, the Mexican officer responded that Juan José should not come, for the Mexicans now held "a terrible hate" for the Apaches because of all the "evil" they had done. Again uncertain of what the Mexicans were up to, Juan José wrote to Mariano Varela from his camp in the Sierra del Carcay west and south of Janos. He told Varela he had heard of Mexicans killing Apaches, sometimes without provocation and even in front of José Ignacio Ronquillo, Varela's son-in-law. Apache rancherias fled west and north to escape unprovoked attacks, but Juan José promised to try and stop them, telling them "not to believe stories and lies." However, Juan José asked for some gunpowder to defend himself from those Apaches who thought he was an informer for the Mexicans.[4]

A week later Juan José again wrote to Varela, telling him he had been unsuccessful and the other Apaches had left the area. He now wished to go to Varela's hacienda or Janos, for he feared if he stayed away the Mexicans would think he was acting in bad faith. Varela replied the same day. He encouraged Juan José to go to Janos with his wife and his children for he would be safe there from "bad Apaches." Varela reminded him that his father had not cared what other Apaches thought of him, and neither should he. Juan José, however, did not go to Janos. He wrote to Varela again, apparently several weeks later, saying he had joined with the other Apaches and was still exhorting them to keep the peace and not to believe stories of Mexican attacks and atrocities. But he was growing increasingly apprehensive of the Mexicans, and rightfully so, for in August 1833 a Mexican campaign set out against "the Indian Juan José Compá," although to no avail.[5]

As winter deepened its grip, Juan José tried again to ensure security for his people. Now uncertain of the situation at Janos, he chose to approach the copper mining town of Santa Rita del Cobre (present-day Silver City, New Mexico), established to the northwest of Janos some thirty years prior but still administered and often garrisoned by the presidio.[6] There Juan José, "full of joy," met with Mexican officials, accompanied by eight other leaders and thirty warriors. Juan José told the Mexicans that Apaches had been mistreated, even murdered, and desired justice. Since he could find no security among the Mexicans he had led his people away from their settlements, "since all men value their lives." Juan José did admit that Chiricahuas had done "many evils," but it was only because the Mexicans had harmed them. Yet Juan José was willing to forgive the Mexicans, if the Mexicans forgave the Apaches and let them correct their "faults."[7] However, Chiricahuas continued their "faults," raiding widely and deeply across northern Mexico.

In late summer Juan José visited the ranchería of Pescas, a large encampment north of the Río Gila with much livestock and ten Mexican captives; nine boys and one woman. While there Juan José took part in card games by the fire late into the night and joined in the dances accompanying the return of a successful raiding party. One of these attacked Carrizal, taking José Madrid, a twelve-year-old Mexican captive, who stole a horse and escaped two months later. While in Pescas ranchería, Juan José learned that many of the older Apaches wished to make peace, but the young men and women opposed them. With the winter months looming again Juan José was able to convince twenty-five other Chiricahua

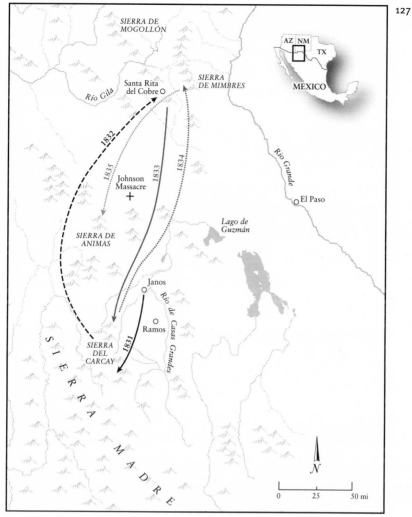

Map 12. Juan José's wanderings, 1831–35

leaders, although not Pescas, to propose a peace with the Mexicans again in exchange for returning stolen livestock and captives.[8]

After several weeks of wintertime negotiations, Chiricahuas agreed to practice agriculture but refused to return any livestock taken on raids. There was not that much, they told the Mexicans, and besides, the stock were legitimate spoils of war. Several months later Juan José managed to convince sixteen leaders to ratify the peace with the Mexicans. All received the title of *capitancillo* and a monthly salary of twenty pesos; Juan José received thirty for his part. Hard feelings remained, however. When Juan José entered El Cobre one early spring day, he had an altercation with soldier Pedro Betancourt. Betancourt—who later claimed that Juan José had threatened the exposed town—told the Chiricahua leader that the Mexicans considered the treaty false and were only keeping the peace for three months, just long enough for Apaches to help them fight the Comanches, who were currently ravaging the northeastern portions of Chihuahua. Then over a thousand soldiers would descend upon the Apaches.[9]

While Juan José confronted Mexican officials over Betancourt's threats, he did have other concerns. Juan José objected to the restrictions placed upon trade between Mexicans and Chiricahuas in the recent peace. Mexicans could not sell weapons, lead for ammunition, gunpowder, alcohol, or playing cards to Apaches. Juan José especially protested the ban on playing cards since games of chance were an important part of Chiricahua entertainment. Gunpowder was his main worry, however. Since many Chiricahuas used firearms by this time, gunpowder was a "primary resource," not only for hunting, as Juan José protested, but also for war. Access to gunpowder, with its mysterious qualities, took on some aspects of the supernatural. In a tale one Chiricahua killed another and fled to a mountain cave to escape the vengeance of the murdered man's family. There he encountered a Mountain Spirit, a *Gahe*, who took pity upon him. The *Gahe* told him to take four handfuls of fine sand, tie it up in a skin, wait four days, and then give it to the father or brother of the man he had killed, for the sand would have turned into gunpowder. The man did as he was told, and when he gave the powder to the father of the man he had killed, the father said, "You did wrong to me, but the powder is worth more."[10]

Having shown himself as a leader to Mexicans by negotiating a peace, Juan José now had to show himself as a leader to Chiricahuas by leading a raid. Dressed in his best red clothes, wearing a silver necklace, and riding in a silver-decorated saddle with *armas* (saddle-mounted leg protectors) of hide, Juan José led thirty of his warriors and nearly sixty more from other rancherias to the hacienda of Tomás Carbajal. Watched by the other warriors, Juan José's men drove off 270 mares, colts, stallions, mules, and burros, assaulting a herder and a servant. As one of his warriors was about to kill the servant with his lance, Juan José intervened, yelling, "Don't kill him. The blow he got was enough. Get his shirt and let's get going."[11]

Given his desire both to have peace and to raid, Juan José was understandably cautious when he once again approached El Cobre in his annual peace negotiations in the spring of the following year. This time he joined Pisago Cabezón as they moved northward to avoid a Mexican campaign. Both approached the town but refused to enter, fearing treachery, as captives told them the Mexicans wanted to exterminate the Apaches. However, in the discussions that followed, Juan José contributed little, for it was now Pisago Cabezón who spoke for peace, agreeing to bring other chiefs back to El Cobre to talk.[12]

When Juan José returned twenty days later he functioned only as a messenger for Pisago Cabezón and with "false courtesies" asked for the release of two other leaders, Chato and San Juan. Juan José visited both men, who were being held until Chiricahuas turned over Santana, who had taken a young sheepherder, and El Advino, a known horse thief. Juan José led the Mexicans through a day of fruitless and frustrating negotiations, buying time for his brother Juan Diego to bring in El Advino. With El Advino in custody, the Mexicans did release San Juan, but they continued to hold Chato. When Juan José again approached El Cobre twenty days afterward, he did not enter the town for fear of being taken prisoner. But he was negotiating a peace for Pisago Cabezón and his allies to be ratified in Chihuahua City. For himself Juan José finally agreed to settle in El Cobre, in a house with rations, to be free of both Mexican and Chiricahua suspicion.[13]

Juan José never did settle in the Mexican town, instead leaving Pisago Cabezón and retreating to the high country for the summer. He likely viewed this decision with some relief when he heard a tale of horror later that year. Five women, including two of Pisago Cabezón's wives and two women from Sidé's *gò'tàh*, accompanied by two of Pisago Cabezón's sons-in-law and one other man, approached El Cobre in early fall with fifteen steers to trade. Ponce de León, the commander at El Cobre who several years earlier had warned Juan José of the "terrible hatred" Mexicans held for his people, allowed only the women to enter the town. Other Mexicans then induced the men to enter, where they fell upon the Apaches, killing two men and one woman, likely one of Pisago Cabezón's wives, in a paroxysm of violence; beating, stabbing, spearing, and shooting. The Mexican commander rescued four women, and one man managed to escape. While the commander did seize two Mexicans for the murders, he had to let them go when the townspeople—accompanied by his soldiers, including some from Janos—turned on him "with their weapons in their hands." The women escaped only when Ponce de León personally escorted them three miles beyond the town.[14]

For the rest of the winter Juan José and his ranchería hunkered down along the slopes of the Sierra de Animas, northwest of Janos. With the coming of spring he joined his brother Juan Diego, Marcelo, and Vívora and their people along a *playa* (dry lake bed) near a flowing spring, from where some fifty warriors departed for a raid against mule trains resupplying El Cobre. One day lookouts spotted a party of some twenty men, soon revealed to be seventeen *extranjeros* (Americans living in Mexico) and five Mexican muleteers, trailing into the encampment. Warned of their approach by smoke signals, Juan José suspiciously questioned the party's leader,

John Johnson of Sonora. Why was he not on the main road, Juan José asked? To get to his own country quickly, Johnson replied, since Mexico was at war with his countrymen in Texas. Juan José knew from captured dispatches of the war in Texas—he had in his possession the Mexican plan of operations—so when Johnson offered to trade flour, sugar, and the all-important gunpowder for a guide and safe passage to El Cobre, Juan José agreed.[15]

That evening Juan José accepted Johnson's invitation to dine with his party, where the Apache told tales of Juan Diego's and his cousin El Güero's exploits and prowess. However, Juan José and his fellow leaders were taking precautions. With the raiding party away, they sent messengers to nearby rancherías asking for assistance. After a day of wary stand-off, Johnson finally delivered the trade goods to the encampment. As Juan José, Juan Diego, Marcelo, and their leading men began to go through the sacks of goods, Johnson's party opened fired on them. Observing "acts of mistrust and treachery" the previous day and outnumbered by the remaining warriors four to one, Johnson concealed a small cannon or swivel gun loaded with bits of chain and musket balls under a tarp near the trade goods. Throwing back the tarp, Johnson fired the swivel gun into the gathered Chiricahuas, and his men added their rifle fire. The force of the shot from the gun struck Juan Diego in the torso, almost ripping his body in half. Juan José and Marcelo also fell to the fire, along with another seventeen men. Stopping only long enough to retake a female Mexican captive and then scalp the fallen Apaches, Johnson quickly beat a fighting retreat to Janos.[16]

With the loss of so many leaders and leading men, the Chiricahuas were slow to take their revenge, but retaliate they did. As Janos brought in its harvest that fall, a large Apache party attacked, killing two men, robbing two women, and stealing a string of horses. Two months later another raiding party fell upon the Hacienda de Ramos, nearly killing Juan María Varela, kin to the Compás' friend Don Varela. The avengers also killed seven or eight *vaqueros* coming from Corralitos, before driving off a herd of four hundred steers.[17] While these raids did not bring either Juan Diego or

Juan José back from the dead, they did serve to assuage their people's grief and take a slight measure of revenge. After nearly four
decades of violent coexistence with Spaniards and then Mexicans,
the sons of El Compá finally fell at the hands of Americans, who
took their scalps. Neither development boded well for either Chiricahua or Janos.

Misdeeds and Outrages

In October 1840 José Baltasar Padilla had a problem; several problems, actually. The thirty-five-year-old native of San Elizario had
enlisted in his local company twelve years prior and had served
in Chihuahua and New Mexico before transferring to Janos that
fall. He now faced the fact that Chiricahua raids continued in the
Janos area. In September Apaches took eighteen head of livestock
and a large amount of corn from the fields near the community.
Although emissaries from Pisago Cabezón arrived the next day to
ask for peace, within a few weeks Casas Grandes suffered a loss of
sixty steers, and a party of Janeros on their way to Sonora to buy
cattle came under attack. Padilla's problem was that these raids
were motivated by revenge for a pair of attacks by mercenary scalp
hunters, albeit with the approval of the Chihuahuan government.[18]

At the end of the previous year Governor Angel Trías of Chihuahua had signed a contract with James Kirker, an American with
a shady background in the borderlands. Santiago Kirker, as the
Mexicans knew him, agreed to raise a force of two hundred men,
including at least fifty Mexicans in addition to Shawnee Indians
and Americans, to campaign against the state's "barbarian" enemies. Along with a salary of four pesos a day Kirker would also
receive fifty pesos for each warrior killed or captured and twenty-five for each female or child captive. Since Kirker had to collect
his bounty in Chihuahua City, Mexican authorities agreed to accept scalps, referred to as *piezas*, a term previously applied only to
captives, as proof for payment.[19]

Upon entering the area in January 1840 at Casas Grandes, Kirker learned of a large party of Chiricahuas under Pisago Cabezón

encamped northeast of Janos while negotiating a peace at the presidio. Although told to delay while negotiations continued, Kirker left his Shawnees at Casas Grandes and proceeded, guided by the local *juez de paz* (justice of the peace) José Morales and twenty-three men from Casas Grandes. On the morning of January 9 Kirker's force attacked a ranchería near the Laguna de Ascensión, killing ten men, capturing twenty women and children, and recovering seventy head of livestock. Kirker then proceeded to Janos, where he discovered Pisago Cabezón's son, Marcelo, within the walls of the presidio, likely negotiating for his aging father. Seizing Marcelo—who was worth fifty pesos—Kirker returned to Chihuahua City. Kirker further attacked several Apache camps in March and April. However disruptive to negotiations he may have been, Kirker had the only force in the field at this time.[20]

This was Padilla's other main problem: he had few men. When Kirker took Marcelo from within the presidio's walls, the garrison mustered only eighteen men, of whom just a handful were actually present. The Janos muster roll had shrunk precipitously over the past few years as the population in the district scattered southward to the new mining settlements at Corralitos and El Barranco on the slopes of the Sierra de Escondido, to the reborn agricultural hub of Casas Grandes, and to cattle haciendas such as Ramos. By the time Padilla arrived at Janos the community had fewer than fifty adult men, many of whom were "lazy" and "addicted to vice."[21]

The unwillingness of men from the now spread-out community to serve at the presidio drew upon a sense of betrayal. Five years earlier the governor of Chihuahua had transferred the company of Janos to El Cobre, but without their families. Soldiers immediately began to desert and return to Janos to look after their households and have their households look after them. After nearly a year at El Cobre, sixty-one of the ninety-seven Janeros refused to stand guard. Although officers and sergeants quickly quelled the mutiny, most of the men were discharged from service, dropping Janos to barely forty men, from which it only declined further. The distrust of service was still strong when, in 1841, the commandant

general queried how many men would be willing to serve voluntarily; local officials reported only three in Barranco, one in Casas Grandes, and none in Corralitos.[22]

However, Padilla did have some good news. As of October 15,
1840, he was promoted to *alférez* at Janos and was now an officer with the status to place "Don" before his name. And while he
had a few men, they would fight. On January 3, 1841, Padilla led
five of Janos's fifteen men, including two militiamen transferred
to the garrison two days prior, out in pursuit of Apaches who had
just taken livestock near Ramos, likely Pisago Cabezón's warriors
seeking revenge for the imprisonment of Marcelo. He caught and
attacked the Indians at the Punto de Parrito, forcing the raiders to
flee and recovering seventy-six horses. In December Padilla took
twelve men from the growing company to join a campaign under
Comandante General José María Elías González at El Paso. This
force of over three hundred, the largest campaign in years, scoured
the areas around the Lagos de Guzmán, Santa María, and Putos
north and east of Janos. Padilla later recounted that this campaign
took three hundred horses and three *piezas;* whether this meant
scalps or prisoners or both is unknown.[23]

Padilla's aggressive actions in 1841 restored some of the community's faith in the garrison, allowing him to add more men to
the muster roll. In July and August he enlisted nine men, all voluntarily and all for ten years. However, such enlistments would not
be enough. On November 24 Padilla enlisted another eleven men,
all for six years and all but one having been sentenced to military
service by political authorities in Janos, Casas Grandes, Barranco, and Corralitos. With these convict conscripts Janos mustered
sixty-seven men by the end of the year, more good news for Padilla. But the best news he received in 1841 was the decision by the
commandant general to return Marcelo to Janos to be turned back
over to his father, Pisago Cabezón.[24]

The return of Marcelo cleared the road for a return to peace at
Janos. Vicente, Pisago Cabezón's spokesman, trod this path, passing
through Janos in April to negotiate a treaty with the *comandante*

general in Chihuahua City. Vicente returned in late May with another delegation to await the official ratification of the peace, but it was not easy for either community to put the violence of the previous decade behind them. Padilla was especially suspicious, as Vicente arrived after fifty-six of the now eighty-six men of the garrison left on campaign. When the Apaches traded for liquor with residents of Janos, he grew infuriated, as all trade with Indians was illegal until the peace was accepted. Padilla's suspicion of bad faith peaked when Vicente and his companions kept a constant guard the night they spent in the presidio. And when the Chiricahuas saddled up at first light the next morning and rode a short distance from the presidio, Padilla expected some sort of treachery.[25]

No treachery came from Vicente, but the usual round of raids, hostilities, and disorders continued while arrangements for another peace settlement at Janos came to fruition. On July 4, 1842, Padilla watched as Pisago Cabezón, Manuel, Vicente, and Ponce, who also represented Jasquedegá, Jasquiatil, and Nachindo, ratified a peace treaty. These Chiricahuas chose Janos as the site of their peace establishment and accepted Manuel as their "general," as Pisago Cabezón was now too old. They agreed to help the Mexicans against hostile Apaches, request permission to travel, return all captives, and get their livestock branded. In exchange these rancherias could trade at Janos and would receive rations, as stipulated in colonial ordinances from 1791. This meant each family head would receive three *almudes* (measures) of corn, two packets of cigarettes, one *piloncillo* (issue of sugar), half a handful of salt, and a ration of meat every two weeks.[26]

For the rest of the summer and into the fall of 1842 Padilla observed Apache families and local groups making their way to Janos, and soon he had several hundred Apaches living in and around the presidio. Fortunately, he had more men to keep an eye on his former enemies. By September Janos had seventy-four men on its rolls keeping the peace, assisted by forty-three men from Padilla's old presidio of San Elizario, although Janos's herd of fifty horses and eighteen mules was in bad shape, with two horses dying the month prior. However, this close proximity between the two antagonistic communities caused problems. In December one Chiricahua, Chato, entered a garden along the Río de Janos, ate some watermelon, and trampled the vines. When confronted by the garden's owner Chato insulted and threatened the Mexican, mounted his horse, and trampled the neighboring garden. The local justice of the peace, a member of the Varela clan, attempted to apprehend the Apache, and Chato insulted and swore at him. Upon learning of this incident Padilla apparently decided the peace was worth more than some watermelon vines, but it was another injury to be added to the psychic damage of both communities.[27]

For Padilla, 1843 began with the settling of another five Apache leaders, all previous residents of the Janos peace establishment, and their followers. One of these leaders voiced a special concern to the Janos commander. Naperú complained of the sale of alcohol to Apaches, for Chiricahuas were liable to trade all they had in order to get liquor. Naperú, along with General Manuel, got a prohibition on the "sale of liquor to the Apaches." It is unlikely that Padilla was ever able to enforce this proscription, and alcohol-laced encounters continued between the two communities, often to the detriment of Chiricahuas and again adding to the grudges they already bore.[28]

By the spring only one major Chiricahua leader had not come to Janos in search of peace: Mangas Coloradas, previously known at the presidio as Fuerte. Yet he too arrived at Janos at the end of March, along with the gò'tàh of Itán. Padilla's satisfaction at seeing Mangas Coloradas settle in peace was tempered by the strain of trying to provide rations for several hundred Apaches. Within a month Janos had exhausted most of its resources for the "indispensable" rations, increasingly money, sugar, and cigarettes. When the commander was slow to distribute rations, Chiricahuas would pound on his door to demand their goods. Yet, with a slowdown in rations came a predictable increase in raiding, especially among the younger Apaches who had to make a name.[29]

In early May Padilla learned from Mangas Coloradas, via Manuel,

that eight Apaches from Fronteras and four from Janos planned
to raid the community. The warning came too late to stop the attack, and Padilla assembled a force of soldiers, citizens, and some
friendly Apaches to pursue the thieves. Padilla tracked them some
ninety miles to the Agua Hueca north of Janos, where he discovered the rancherias of Mangas Coloradas, Pisago Cabezón, and
Teboca. Padilla led his men into the large Chiricahua encampment.
But when some of his men, nine citizens and a soldier, spotted their
livestock, they broke ranks and attempted to reclaim the animals.
The Chiricahua raiders, including one of Pisago Cabezón's sons,
seized their weapons to stop the Mexicans, clearly expecting the
rest of the camp would support them. Padilla's seven Apache scouts
then joined the Mexicans, letting the thieves know that they would
die before they left without the animals. As the two sides scowled
and gestured at each other over their weapons, Mangas Coloradas entered the fray. He, much to the surprise of the raiders, sid-
ed with Padilla, admonishing the thieves, telling them he would
not go back on his promises. Pisago Cabezón then expressed his
anger and shame at his son, calling him a *pícaro* (rogue). After all
the other leaders present spoke out against the culprits, Padilla's
force returned to Janos, with the livestock.[30]

Yet the next month brought Padilla tidings of Chiricahua discontent. Reyes, an Apache leader who settled near Ramos, told the
Mexicans that stories of an Apache murdered at Fronteras made the
rest wary; those at Corralitos had taken to carrying their weapons
with them at all times. Also, a Mexican from Casas Grandes regularly visited Ramos and spread lies and rumors of Apache raids and
killings among the citizens, making them nervous. This was only
exacerbated by the Apaches failing to show up for their rations, but
Reyes reported that the amounts were so small it was not worth
the trip. Those who did go to receive supplies were frightened by
the sight of soldiers shooting at targets. Padilla did not have time
to deal with these concerns, for he was preparing to lead a contingent of troops from Janos to New Mexico to face a reported Texan invasion, hence the target practice.[31]

Although absent for only two months, July to August, Padilla returned to a steadily deteriorating situation. In July the political chief of the district, José María Zuloaga, reported raids around Janos. While the invasion of New Mexico failed to materialize, the possibility persisted, forcing Janos to keep a sizeable detachment, often the vast majority of available soldiers, at El Paso. Five soldiers deserted this duty in August and September, and Comanches killed one soldier, Romero Maesa, on September 23 at Doña Ana to the north. By November 1843 the situation was so bad that Apaches were "daily" committing "misdeeds" and "outrages" at Janos. With few rations and fewer soldiers present in the town, Apaches assaulted soldiers and stole from citizens.[32]

The lack of soldiers continued into the next year as Padilla with most of the Janos troop served at El Paso. Rumored Texan invasions gave way to very real Comanche assaults. After over a year of fruitless patrols and pursuits the Janeros under Padilla caught a Comanche party at the Hacienda de la Ramada on November 14, killing 50, recovering 264 horses, and rescuing 4 Mexican captives. When Padilla returned to Janos at the end of 1844 he discovered the Chiricahuas had abandoned the peace in February, driven away by another smallpox epidemic, which they blamed on the Mexicans. Even if they had wanted to stop the Apaches from leaving the soldiers at Janos could not have done so, never mustering more than five men under arms throughout the entire year, with most away at El Paso with Padilla or in Chihuahua City.[33]

Padilla now had to make up for lost time. In the winter of 1845 he led a *correría*, a running chase that killed two Apache raiders and recovered some animals. Early spring saw two more dogged pursuits of raiders by Padilla, one that recovered some mules and another that forced Chiricahuas to abandon the 117 animals they had taken from Corralitos. When Padilla received word on May 29 that Indians had taken all the mules from El Barranco, he saddled up a sergeant, a corporal, the troop's trumpeter, and twenty-four soldiers and rode out on yet another *correría*. Padilla and his small command arrived at El Barranco that evening and left at first

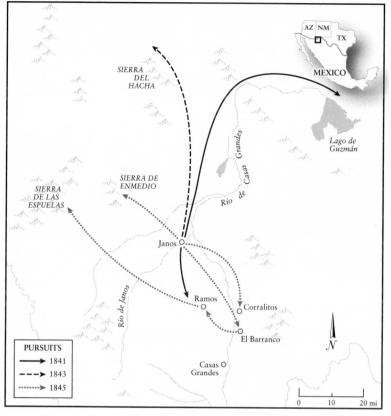

Map 13. Padilla's pursuits, 1841–45

light the next day, reinforced by twenty-seven *vecinos* (citizens). He tracked the raiders northwest toward Ramos and beyond for thirty miles before allowing his party to drop into an exhausted sleep alongside their mounts. Rousing them at four in the morning, Padilla continued to follow the trail, crossing west of Janos, continuing northwest, covering another fifty miles.

By the first of June Padilla was in the foothills of the Sierra de los Espuelas, after three days and more than one hundred miles of hard riding, when he located a ranchería and attacked. The encampment proved to be a large one, likely several local groups combined for a raid or ceremony, with over a hundred warriors. For the rest of that day and over the next two days, Padilla and his men fought for their lives in a series of skirmishes across the canyons, arroyos, and mesas. Padilla was finally able to extract his force on June 3, but at a loss of four soldiers killed, another four wounded, and five of his civilian auxiliaries wounded. In the confused cauldron of battle Padilla's men also lost four of the newly issued English-surplus Baker rifles, twelve horses, and thirteen sets of tack. Despite their also killing twelve warriors, capturing a woman and a boy, and recovering eight horses, the commandant general was less than pleased with Padilla's force. Padilla and his men, however, were likely glad to have escaped with their lives and looking forward for the chance to avenge their losses.[34]

At first it appeared to Padilla that peace might return, as parties of Apaches came into Janos throughout June, including three women on June 28 representing a number of leaders who wished for peace, among them General Manuel. But their chances were slim, for nine days earlier Apaches had killed four Mexicans at a Corralitos silver mine. During the next month a raiding party of six Apaches attacked two Mexicans outside Janos, killing one, and two days after that, four Apaches ran off an unknown number of cattle from the town. Padilla launched fruitless pursuits of all these assaults, but it was not until October that Padilla was finally able to catch two Apache rustlers in the Sierra de Enmedio, killing one and recovering the horses they had taken. But at the end of the year, things were not too bad at Janos. While the garrison of 62 men was short a second ensign, a chaplain, and 30 soldiers, and the presidial school had been closed for lack of a teacher, the *caballada* of 93 horses and 41 mules was in good shape for once and the troop had received an issue of clothing and blankets for the cold weather.[35]

However, Padilla learned in December 1845 that Santiago Kirker was back in the region and back in the employ of the state of Chihuahua. Kirker took part in an expedition at the end of the year and returned to Namiquipa to the south of Janos in March 1846. With a force of Delawares, Shawnees, Tarahumara, Americans, and Mexicans, Kirker attacked the rancherias of Chato and Maturan but only killed one Apache as his troops stopped to loot the encampment. Much to Padilla's consternation Chiricahuas took their revenge on May 19, virtually laying siege to Janos, killing one Mexican, taking two captives, and running off more than three hundred head of livestock. But Padilla heard in late June that Reyes was settling in peace at Galeana, with over a hundred of his people. Yet Padilla did not give it much thought, as he left Janos in early July to take up the billet of second lieutenant in the company of Chihuahua. A few days after his departure José María Zuloaga, the *jefe político* of the Cantón de Galeana, the political district that included Janos, rode into town from his headquarters in Corralitos to recruit men to join Kirker's assault on the Chiricahuas at Galeana.[36]

"Beat out their brains"

Baishan, known as Cuchillo Negro to the Mexicans, listened in growing anger to a tale of treachery. He was encamped near the hot springs west of the Rio Grande one summer when a few Apaches straggled into his ranchería. They were from the local groups led by Reyes, Irigóllen, Carro, Francisquillo, and Láceres, who had entered into a peace with Galeana, southeast of Janos. In early summer the Mexicans of the town invited the Apaches, over a hundred in all, to a feast. They spent the day dancing and drinking newly distilled mescal. Sadly, the survivors admitted, they could not drink in moderation; by midnight "nearly everyone was lying in a drunken stupor." Just before first light the Mexicans of Galeana, joined by some from Casas Grandes and Janos, fell upon the Apaches, sparing "neither age or sex" and "glutting their long pent-up revenge of many years of persecution." After a "ragged volley" the Mexicans proceeded to stab, hack, and club the recumbent Apaches. One pregnant Apache woman managed to escape into the church, where the Mexicans killed her at the altar and tore her unborn child from her still-warm body. After plunging the baby into holy water by way of baptism, the Mexicans dashed the child's brains out against a wall. A few Apaches managed "to steal away in the semidarkness" and straggled into Baishan's camp several days later. For the next few days each dawn was accompanied by wailing as Chiricahuas mourned for their dead. Almost every family group had lost a member.[37]

For days and weeks the desire for vengeance burned among the Apaches. But Baishan knew the matter of revenge was too important to be decided without deliberation and consultation, so he called a council of Chiricahua leaders in the late fall. Mangas Coloradas attended this gathering as, having lived over fifty summers, he was the preeminent leader among Chiricahuas. The leaders listened to the survivors' tales, and Mangas Coloradas would always remember the Galeana Massacre as when Mexicans attacked his people and "beat out their brains." For days the council discussed and deliberated what they should do to "pay back" the Mexicans, before deciding to attack Galeana.[38]

With the decision made, Mangas Coloradas, Baishan, and the other leaders held a "great war dance" to induce men to volunteer for the war party and to "stir up a fighting spirit." That night four or five singers and drummers sat ten paces west of a bonfire. Mangas Coloradas and Baishan danced first around the fire, calling on prominent warriors, who joined in the dancing. These eminent men were then joined by other, less well-known men who wished to go on the warpath. Once all the "brave and eligible fighters" danced,

Mangas Coloradas and Baishan formed the men into a skirmish line east of the fire, then led them as if in a real assault, leaping and zigzagging, stopping just short of the singers, and firing arrows or their guns over their heads.[39]

Afterward Mangas Coloradas returned to his band's territory, to hold his own war dance and make preparations for the expedition. The women of the band made extra moccasins and gathered food supplies, while the men assembled what ammunition they could and made new bows, arrows, and lances. The warriors tipped their sotol or spruce lances with knife blades taken in raids or received in trade and filed bits of steel and iron from the same source to make arrowheads, as stone arrowheads had not been made for several generations. Men fashioned their bows from mulberry wood, dried and then worked to the thickness of a wrist at the center and tapering to the ends. They fashioned spare bowstrings from twined sinew, made arrow shafts from carrizo wood or reed, and fletched them with turkey feathers. The local groups then joined together in rough terrain for safety as Mangas Coloradas led the newly equipped warriors to rendezvous with the rest of the Chiricahuas.[40]

In council months beforehand, the leaders decided that Baishan would lead the attack on Galeana, since it was his people who had suffered the most and their need for vengeance was greatest. When Mangas Coloradas arrived with his fighters, Baishan led the 175 warriors southward, accompanied by a number of young apprentices to cook the food and watch after the horses. The whole expedition set out early on a late fall morning, reaching a water hole north of Galeana in several days. Scouts watched the town, searching for soldiers, but saw none. Shamans consulted their power and found the signs favorable. Baishan divided his force into groups based around their bands and leaders, telling each where they would attack and on what signal. As a blood-red sky heralded the approaching dawn, the Chiricahuas stripped down to their breech cloths and moccasins and, on Baishan's word, advanced silently and rapidly.[41]

As they came bursting out of the morning mists, shouting their battle cries, the desire for revenge proved stronger than Baishan's plan, and the warriors poured into Galeana from all directions, streaming into the plaza. There they encountered thirty or forty Mexicans who, alerted by the battle cry, were struggling to form a line in front of the church. The first Mexican volley, practically at point blank range, killed a number of Apaches, but the warriors fell upon the Mexicans, forcing a hand to hand fight. The Mexican line melted under this assault, and small groups of Mexicans fell back into alleys and courtyards with the Chiricahuas "after them like tigers." Gunsmoke, arrows, and cries filled the air as the Mexicans at last gave way, seeking to flee, but mounted warriors chased them down and "impaled them in the back with lances." After hunting down the Mexican men, women, and children through the houses, Chiricahuas took what loot they could and headed back north, revenge taken, vengeance sated. A number of Chiricahuas distinguished themselves in the battle, adding to their reputation, including Mangas Coloradas, his son-in-law Cochise, who had married his daughter Dos-teh-seh nearly two decades earlier, and a man called Goyahkla, who would be known as Geronimo.[42] The future of all these men, however, would be entwined those currently invading the borderlands.

While preparing for the expedition against Galeana, Mangas Coloradas learned that Americans were once again passing through Chiricahua lands, camping just west of El Cobre. With one warrior Mangas Coloradas entered the American camp. The men he met, however, were not rag-tag trappers and mercenaries, but a hundred American soldiers, dragoons under General Stephen Watts Kearny, fresh from the conquest of New Mexico and on their way to California. What Mangas Coloradas saw in the camp impressed him. With the coming battle against the Mexicans on his mind he could not help but compare these soldiers to the Mexicans, finding them better armed, better disciplined, and more determined. Consequently Mangas was quite friendly, pledging good faith and friendship to the Americans, before departing their camp. He visited the Americans several days later and more miles to the west with thirty of his people and with mules to trade. Mangas again pledged friendship and safety for the Americans as they passed through the Gila country, as the Apaches drove hard bargains with the Americans for the mules. One Apache leader, perhaps Mangas, told the Americans that his people would help them take Chihuahua for "the Mexicans are rascals, we hate them and will kill them all."[43]

Padilla too met the Americans, but several months after Mangas Coloradas, at the Battle of Sacramento north of Chihuahua on February 28, 1847. Serving as lieutenant of the Chihuahua Company, Padilla and the rest of the Mexican cavalry charged the Americans in the opening phases of the battle but were driven back by artillery fire. Competent and capable as his troops were in ambush and personal combat, neither he nor they had ever faced concentrated artillery and rifle fire from an enemy who advanced remorselessly. Scattered along with the rest of the Mexican army after the battle, Padilla probably accompanied the Chihuahuan government as it retreated to the southern part of the state, before returning to Chihuahua in May, after the Americans abandoned the city. Still a member of the Chihuahua Company, Padilla was likely one of the officers captured and paroled by the Americans after the Battle of Santa Cruz de Rosales on March 16, 1848. With the end of the war, Padilla returned to Janos late in 1848 or early 1849.[44]

"War to the Knife"

Padilla's first task was to assist in the reconstitution of the company after its dispersal following the Battle of Sacramento. He assisted the company's senior officer, *Alférez* Don Mariano Cordero, in mustering and inspecting the garrison on the first of February, finding thirty men on the rolls, but with a sizeable detachment of twelve soldiers assigned to Zuloaga, the political chief of the district in Corralitos. But as the senior officer present, Padilla also returned to the usual round of Chiricahua raiding, albeit primarily into neighboring Sonora, and rapprochement. At the end of February he parleyed with a Chiricahua leader, possibly Cochise, who requested peace and ransomed a Mexican captive to show his good faith.[45]

Throughout the next month Padilla received messengers from more Chiricahua headmen asking for peace, but he soon learned that any peace with Apaches would face a formidable obstacle: Mangas Coloradas. El Negrito, an Apache who often lived at Janos and served as an informant, told Padilla that Mangas consistently opposed any peace and would thus have to be killed for any settlement to last. The Chiricahua leader Manuel had tried to kill Mangas previously, but would not try again, El Negrito said, until the garrison was increased to one hundred men to protect Manuel and his people from the wrath of Mangas Coloradas, in case he should fail. Padilla soon heard more about Mangas from Coletto Amarillo, who arrived at Janos on March 29, stating that a force of Americans was joining with Mangas and coming "to kill."[46]

Padilla pursued peace with Chiricahuas, however fleeting it might be, for he was well aware of how dependent Janos was upon interactions with Apaches and equally aware of the psychological price the community paid. In May Padilla allowed six warriors to trade mules for alcohol, and the six then promptly became intoxicated and roamed Janos, riding from house to house, demanding more liquor and other items. Yet Padilla still hoped to finish a treaty with a number of Chiricahua leaders at the end of the month. The state legislature's passage of the "Fifth Law" on May 25, 1849, dashed Padilla's hopes. By this law the first concern of the state was to be the war against the "barbarous Indians," for which the governor could enter into contracts with Mexicans and foreign volunteers, these contracts to be based upon a set price for each Indian killed or captured. The government was authorized to pay 200 pesos for each warrior killed, 250 for each warrior captured, and 150 for a female prisoner or a prisoner under the age of 14. Proof of warriors killed, typically their scalps, and the prisoners were to be presented to the council of a municipality or political chief of a district for certification, and the state would then pay the holder of the certificate.[47]

Mangas Coloradas knew nothing of the machinations of the Chihuahuan state legislature when he moved into the mountains northwest of Janos to continue raiding Sonora. A number of Chiricahuas, including the warriors Negrito (apparently a different man than El Negrito), Ratón, and Gervacio, the son of Juan José Compá, went into Janos to trade, to drink, and to gamble, secure in the knowledge that they would be safe since discussions of peace were taking place at the presidio. Padilla, however, was now in receipt of orders from Zuloaga who, following the Fifth Law, instructed him to seize any Apaches who came to Janos. Yet Padilla did not immediately seize the three Chiricahuas who visited him on June 15. Instead, he talked with them. Negrito, Ratón, and Gervacio told Padilla of their recent raids into Sonora, including a battle only three days prior in which four Apaches died. Gervacio declared that his brother, Candelario, had been so enraged by these deaths that he killed a recently taken captive, a youth from Bavispe, in revenge. The three, warming to their tale and still unaware of the relationship between Mexican towns even after decades of living in and near them, went on to announce that a war party would soon set out to raid Galeana, Casas Grandes, and Corralitos. As they had no plans to raid Janos, the three must have been befuddled when Padilla ordered them arrested. Padilla likely took the three men reluctantly, realizing all the trouble it would cause.[48]

Mangas Coloradas did not hear of the three captives for several days. Negrito's family first went to Janos to find him, followed several days later by Bartolo, the leader of Negrito's *gò'tàh*. Bartolo then went to Láceres, his band leader, who sought Mangas's support. With Mangas's backing Láceres, "sullen and morose," rode to Janos with twenty-five warriors, "well mounted, well armed, suspicious, prepared for war if necessary." He confronted Padilla, saying he was going to raid Casas Grandes and all the settlements to the south unless he saw Negrito. He refused to believe that the men had been sent south to Corralitos. Láceres insisted that Padilla had killed the men, but agreed to give him one day to produce Negrito. He then returned to the hills above Janos, where he likely met with Mangas, who, believing that the Mexicans had killed the three, was plotting vengeance.[49]

Padilla had sent the three prisoners south to Corralitos, to where he quickly sent a message asking for their return. Zuloaga, motivated by the Fifth Law, saw a chance for treachery and profit. Recruiting seventy men, including John Johnson who had massacred Juan José Compá twelve years before, and half of a party of Americans on their way to California, Zuloaga reached Janos before daylight on June 21. Padilla was aghast at the political chief's motley Mexican-American force, calling them "vagabonds," and shocked at the treachery he proposed. Outnumbering the garrison and overruling Padilla, Zuloaga hid his men in houses facing the plaza, waiting to ambush the Apaches. There they watched as small groups of Chiricahuas made their way into Janos, stopping at houses for a drink before gathering in the plaza, nearly one hundred in all. Unbeknownst to Padilla and Zuloaga, Mangas Coloradas was planning his own treachery, intending to attack the Mexicans while they negotiated the return of the prisoners. Mangas was in the hills near Janos with a force of warriors to sweep in when the fighting began. However, the approach of the other half of the American party caused the Chiricahuas to flee, thinking they were Mexican reinforcements, spoiling both communities' intended treacheries.[50]

Padilla, as he undoubtedly knew, was in for a busy summer and fall. Soquilla, an ally of Mangas Coloradas, struck back on August 31, driving off the community's horse herd. Padilla led thirty-six soldiers, nearly all the garrison, in pursuit on foot, joined by sixteen civilians led by Pedro Zozaya. For eight days Padilla pushed his men along, likely succored by the monsoonal rains, following the stolen horses' increasingly faint trail northward. Finally, on September 9, he surprised Soquilla's ranchería at the Laguna de Palomas near the Sierra de Florida, killing five warriors, four women, and a boy. Soquilla was later found among the dead, causing his captive daughter so much grief that she attacked the soldiers, who killed her. Padilla also captured nineteen Chiricahuas and recovered fifty-four horses, seven steers, and "all the spoils" in the encampment.[51]

But he was to have no rest. Two days after his return to Janos on September 12, Irigóllen with thirty warriors stole some cattle at Janos and then moved northward to pilfer a cornfield, where Padilla caught him, leading sixty soldiers and civilians. Outnumbered, Irigóllen waved a white flag, asking to talk of peace. He and Padilla conferred for many hours, and Irigóllen agreed to drive his stolen animals back to Janos as proof of his sincerity. But the Apaches, after initially moving the stock toward town, raced suddenly away, and Padilla, probably swearing, charged after them with the only mounted force he had, twelve men in all. He caught the fleeing rustlers and recovered the livestock, but Irigóllen immediately counterattacked with his thirty warriors. In the ensuing *acción de armas* Apaches killed six soldiers and wounded another, but the remaining soldiers under Padilla, outnumbered five to one, managed to kill four Apaches and take a saddle horse.[52]

For nearly a month Padilla braced for the revenge he knew must come, as it did on a foggy October morning. Summoned to the presidial walls early on October 11, Padilla saw small parties of Chiricahuas, totaling over one hundred in all, chasing the garrison's horses through the fog. As the clouds lifted one Apache waved a white flag and called for a parley, claiming to represent seven leaders. Padilla replied that they must all come to the plaza to discuss peace, but only two showed at the northern wall, refusing to enter the town. They asked for the return of the prisoners from Soquilla's group, held at Janos, and those at Corralitos, but Padilla told them they would first have to release all the captives, horses, and other livestock they had taken. Although Padilla sensed that most Chiricahuas wanted to take back their people by force, he thought he was convincing some. But a party of Americans bound for California appeared on the road into town and the Apaches seized them. Padilla reluctantly agreed to exchange his prisoners for the Americans, but before the swap could be made, Apaches seeking revenge for recent losses killed seven of them. The rest of the

Americans, naked and bruised, escaped to Janos during the night, and when the Chiricahuas departed the next day Padilla oversaw the burial of the dead.[53]

In retaliation the new "Sub-inspector of Military Colonies in Chihuahua," Colonel Emilio Langberg, a Dane in the service of Mexico, led out a force of soldiers, civilians, and scalp hunters in retaliation well into November. However, as Padilla remembered, this pursuit only killed one Apache woman, captured six more, and recovered ten horses and four steers. But his services were impressive enough to Langberg that the colonel transferred Padilla to Janos permanently on November 22. Soon after this Padilla led his own force, which captured one Chiricahua woman, rescued a Mexican captive, and recovered 270 head of livestock in the Sierra de Florida. Padilla's revenge was vigorous enough that from the end of November 1849 through March 1850, no Chiricahuas appeared at Janos or the nearby towns, giving the community a much-needed respite.[54]

On April 29 a Chiricahua woman approached Janos with petitions for peace, claiming to represent ten chiefs. Padilla knew her as Gertrudis, one of the prisoners he had taken the previous September but who had escaped in January. Gertrudis said the chiefs were now seeking peace for they had heard Zuloaga was no longer political chief of the district and thus no longer in a position to enforce the Fifth Law. The Chiricahuas were mistaken; Zuloaga was still at his stronghold of Corralitos, but the Chihuahuan government had effectively abandoned the scalp hunt as their primary tool. When informed by Padilla of Gertrudis's overtures, Chihuahua's governor accepted the proposal for peace, as it would cost less to ration Apaches than to campaign against them, and he appointed peace commissioners to proceed to Janos.[55]

Padilla welcomed seven Chiricahua leaders accompanied by fifty warriors and nearly fifty women and children to Janos on May 22 and waited for the peace commissioners. For two days the Apaches drank and gambled, becoming ever more apprehensive and remembering Zuloaga's attempted treachery of the previous year. So when the commissioners arrived, escorted by fifty soldiers, most of the Apaches fled, leaving only Arvizo, who had kin among the prisoners at Janos, to meet them. After several days more leaders began to trickle back into Janos, and over the next three weeks the commissioners negotiated, joined by Padilla and Juan José Zozaya of Janos. On June 24, 1850, six Chiricahua headmen accepted a peace, received rations, and settled near Janos. In return for the Chiricahua agreeing to aid the Mexicans in pursuit of hostile Apaches and branding their livestock, the Mexicans released their Apache prisoners.[56]

Mangas Coloradas observed the negotiations at Janos with some interest, and in December he sent an emissary to Zozaya, now the sole commissioner at Janos, to see about making his own peace. Zozaya, warned about Mangas's continuing raids into Sonora, told the messenger—perhaps Teboca, well-known as Mangas's *segundo* (second)—that Mangas would have to make peace with Sonora first, before he could come in peace to Janos. Mangas had no intention of doing either; Sonora was his primary target, and his desire for peace at Janos was likely with an eye toward receiving security and rations during the winter months. Besides, as the American Captain Enoch Steen who visited Mangas in August reported, Mangas swore "eternal hatred to the Mexicans" and that "with the Mexicans it was and ever would be 'War to the Knife.'" As the winter came to the borderlands, Mangas set out to make good on his threat.[57]

From 1832 to midcentury Chiricahua and Janos waged war, made peace, returned to war, and then repeated the cycle anew. The sequence of revenge and retaliation arose from the fact that both communities made ready use of violence to avenge injuries to their honor, property, women, and kin. Janeros and Chiricahuas took revenge in order to destroy the other or at least foster deterrence, fearing that failure to take revenge could signal weakness and invite further assaults. This murderous mix of anger and alarm underlay the violence in the borderlands, most spectacularly at the killings at El Cobre in 1836, the massacre of the Compás by Johnson the next year, and Zuloaga's and Mangas Coloradas's failed attempts at paired treacheries in 1849. However retaliation was rarely successful, for it failed to destroy the enemy and the surviving community hit back. Baishan's assault on Galeana in retaliation for Kirker's massacre there in 1846 evidenced this calculus. Revenge fed retaliation and retaliation led to escalation, not annihilation or deterrence. Janeros turned to scalp hunting and Chiricahuas raided more and more, with both communities taking captives either to ransom for their own held by the other or to kill them in revenge. Mexicans saw Apaches as "barbarians" and "savages" who only lived for war and robbery, while Apaches came to believe that "all Mexicans in their hearts simply 'wanted' to kill Apaches."[58]

This seemingly irrational acceptance of the cycle of retaliation was actually quite rational, given the absence of strong polities on either side. The Chiricahuas were never a unified people under one leader; not even Mangas Coloradas with his immense status and respect could make all Chiricahuas obey him. Politically they were weak and fractured, with some factions favoring violence, other factions favoring peace, and more in between. The membership of these factions changed regularly, as did band membership, since family heads shifted their allegiance between leaders as necessary. The fact that Manuel openly admitted he had tried to kill Mangas Coloradas speaks volumes about the amorphousness of Chiricahua political structures. And as these structures shifted, the Chiricahua population may well have dropped drastically. There are strong suggestions that violence and epidemics — smallpox and cholera — took a terrible toll on Chiricahuas during this time, destroying whole local groups.[59] No Chiricahua leader, local group, or band was able to deal with Janos or the Mexicans from a position of strength, and they thus accepted that they would have to continue to raid for subsistence and status, while compelling acceptance with assaults, realizing that both these would only invite revenge and necessitate retaliation.

Janos was not much better off. The Mexican nation was weak

in its north in these decades. The best it was able to do was to suggest that Indians were Mexican citizens, "unfortunates" to be encouraged with "kindness and consideration" to live in settled peace. Only when this failed was violence to be used.[60] Needless to say the northern states, Chihuahua included, ignored this advice. The state of Chihuahua was not much stronger and at crucial times often found its limited attention and resources diverted away from the Indian problem. In 1832, at the start of a new peace, all the state's forces had to be oriented southward to ward against rebellious states. Janos, and the rest of the presidios, became part of the "rearguard" and a number of soldiers went south to defend the state along the Río Florido.[61] The 1842 peace failed as the state ran out of rations to distribute and had no troops to contain the discontent, as they had been sent to New Mexico to counter the threat of Texan invasions, and any hopes for peace in 1845 foundered on the U.S. invasion.

The community of Janos was itself quite weak, with its population spread out among mining and ranching enterprises and suffering from the same epidemics. The garrison was never able to fill all 90 authorized soldier's billets; it never had more than 60 and more often than not only 20 or so, of whom only 5 or 10 would be available at any one time. The decrease in volunteers meant an increased use of conscripts—one-third of all soldiers by 1850—and a resulting increase in desertions.[62] A new regulation in 1848, which rebranded the colonial presidios as republican military colonies to preserve territorial integrity and guard against Indian incursions, did nothing to change this situation.[63] So Janos could not count on Chihuahua for help, nor could Chihuahua call on Mexico City. Left to its own defenses, Janos sent out pursuits in retaliation for raids or took revenge on unsuspecting Apaches for previous assaults, knowing both would only beget more raids and assaults but having no other alternatives.

Chiricahua and Janos, however, did not spend all their time at war, but made regular attempts at peace, some of which were successful for several months or even several years. They were able to do so via go-betweens who helped bridge the gap and get both sides to accept a truce. Such individuals as Padilla and Juan José Compá were able to arrange a peace for they realized and accepted the extent to which the two communities were dependent upon each other for critical resources. Chiricahuas had to trade stolen livestock for the strong liquor they craved, along with the cloth they needed for clothes, the all-important camp goods such as knives and hatchets, and gunpowder. Janeros willingly traded cloth and liquor for the horses and mules on which their agropastoral society depended, even if their trading partners became intoxicated, loud, and abusive. Those who had grain could sell it to the peace commissioners for distribution to the Apaches and then buy it back from the Indians with a "little liquor and some cotton goods."[64] Yet this was not enough for the go-betweens to maintain the peace, as the fundamental state of competition and old grudges led to a return to violence. For Padilla the weakness of his garrison limited his ability to keep any peace as civilian volunteers outside his jurisdiction benefited from violence. Juan José, despite his desires, was just "one among many" Chiricahua leaders. It was only in conferences with Mexican officials, where his linguistic abilities were crucial, that other leaders paid him any attention. Juan José never wished to cease being an Apache; he did not wish to assimilate. Mexican authorities realized that they never gave him enough support to make himself respected.[65] Peace no longer gave status; leaders and their warriors turned to violence, which begat revenge and retaliation. This dilemma, added to the national border now separating the two, would eventually bring the communities to an end.

Chapter 6

Border Dilemmas
Security and Survival, 1850–1875

The delineation of the border between the United States and Mexico not only began the separation of Chiricahua and Janos. It also created a dilemma of security and survival for both communities. Americans said Chiricahuas were not to do violence in Mexico, but violence was how Chiricahuas related with Mexicans, including Janeros. Yet the Americans were unable to stop Apache raiding and Janos did not have enough soldiers to defend itself. This forced the community to rely increasingly upon armed civilian volunteers, who could not provide a continual defense. Armed civilians and their leaders were willing to campaign against Chiricahuas when organized and ready but would trade for Apache plunder when they were not. The border dilemma for Chiricahua was that it feared treachery on the Mexican side, but the Americans would not let them raid or keep their captives. For Janos the dilemma was that being responsible for their own defense, they would eventually become a threat to the Mexican state.

"Why did you take our captives?"

In the late fall after his declaration of "war to the knife," Mangas Coloradas assembled the leaders of his band—Ponce, Teboca, Miguel Narbona, Esquinaline, Cochise—for an attack into

Sonora. Mangas instructed them to leave their families together in the mountains under a guard of older men and boys, designating several rendezvous sites should they be attacked and have to scatter. He then led the warriors southward into Mexico along mountain ridges and down drainages. A number of warriors left their families in peace at Janos, including Geronimo, and joined Mangas on his trek. Guided by Geronimo the warriors, now totaling over 150, penetrated ever deeper into Sonora. On the outskirts of a large town the Mexicans called Hermosillo, Chiricahuas killed eight men and seized a supply train. Having deceived his enemies Mangas struck back northward, attacking ranches and villages from the south, not the north as expected. Several days of raiding accumulated several hundred head of cattle and one thousand horses.[1]

As the cattle herd moved more slowly than the horses, Mangas Coloradas sent them on ahead with fifty warriors, while he and the rest of the warriors brought the herd of horses. One midmorning as the Apaches followed a river valley northward, a number of warriors from the vanguard rushed back to tell Mangas they had been ambushed by Mexican soldiers, who were now in pursuit. Mangas quickly and calmly led his warriors into the timber along the river, organizing them into a hollow circle to resist an assault from any direction. The pursuing Mexicans formed up into two lines of infantry, with cavalry in reserve, and advanced on the Apaches. Coming within range, the soldiers stopped and opened fire. Mangas kept his warriors under control, waiting until the Mexicans' guns were empty and becoming too hot to hold, and then unleashed his warriors in a direct attack while sending more to encircle the soldiers.[2]

The Mexicans broke ranks in the face of Mangas's attack and scrambled up a nearby hill to gain a defensible position. Chiricahua warriors swarmed up the slopes from all sides, taking the soldiers into fierce hand to hand fighting with bow, spear, and knife, negating their firearms. The Mexicans fell back to another hill under this assault, then another, and another, as Chiricahuas attacked again and again, reinforced by more warriors under Irigóllen and

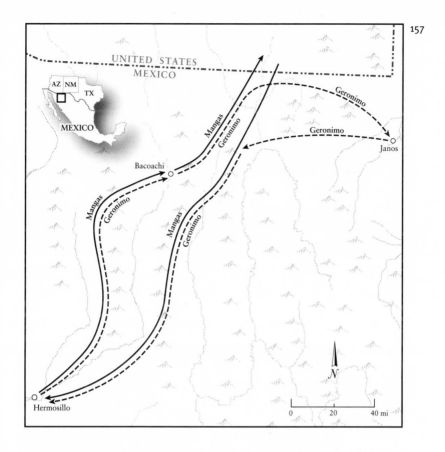

Map 14. Mangas's raid, 1850

Juh, who had been raiding elsewhere in Sonora and rode to the sound of the fight.

At one lull in the battle Geronimo and three companions, armed with only knives, faced two Mexicans with guns in the no-man's-land between the two sides. The Apaches turned to flee to the safety of their comrades, but the Mexicans shot down two and wounded another with a saber. Geronimo reached the mass of Chiricahua warriors, seized a spear from one, and ran back. The Mexican pursuing him reloaded and fired, but missed, so Geronimo impaled him upon the spear. As the second Mexican soldier ran up, Geronimo dodged his saber blow, grappled him to the ground, and killed him with a knife. Geronimo retrieved the saber and brandished it for all the other Apaches to see. As he later remembered, "many [Mexicans] fell by my hand and constantly I led the advance."[3]

After several hours of deadly skirmishing in the fading light of the winter afternoon, darkness fell, ending the battle. Mangas Coloradas and the Chiricahuas continued their trek northward, having killed twenty-six Mexicans and wounded another forty-six, including the commander. One warrior, Tapilá, stopped long enough to take the commander's fancy saddle, and the horse to which it was affixed. The combined force under Mangas, now upward of 350, rode over the mountains to another Mexican town, Bacoachi, where they killed six men, including the mayor, and took five captives. A parley with the Mexicans resulted in the ransoming of two captives but three, including two small boys, remained with the Chiricahuas. After two more days of hard riding the warriors split up, with Irigóllen, Juh, and Geronimo returning to their families at Janos and Mangas Coloradas continuing northward into New Mexico. Mangas, having gathered together most of the leaders and their warriors and given them the confidence, "bordering on arrogance," to defeat the Sonorans soundly, was at the height of his power that winter day as he crossed back over the invisible line of the border, the existence of which would give rise to so many dilemmas for Chiricahuas.[4]

As the winter passed, Mangas learned that the Sonorans were

gathering to take revenge. Since they had penetrated his mountain stronghold before, Mangas moved his people to camp near Janos. Accompanied by several leaders and warriors, including Tapilá, Mangas entered the town, which he knew as Kaskiyeh, to meet with the Mexican peace commissioner. Nothing came of this meeting and Mangas returned to his encampment, but Tapilá remained to barter the fancy saddle he had taken several months earlier. He then stayed for a few days at Irigóllen's ranchería several miles west of Janos and likely drew rations at the presidio. Two days later, in the early morning, Sonorans attacked the Apaches near Janos, as recounted at the opening of chapter 1 in the story of the Kaskiyeh killings. Tapilá and others escaped upriver to join Mangas Coloradas, but Irigóllen was cut down with three men and four women as he attempted to parley. Geronimo and a number of Chiricahuas were in Janos at the time, trading and possibly drinking and gambling, but he along with many more escaped to rendezvous with Mangas that night. In council Mangas Coloradas, realizing how many warriors had been killed or captured, "gave the order to start at once in perfect silence for our homes in Arizona, leaving the dead upon the field."[5]

Not long after Mangas and the Chiricahuas returned to the highlands a party of Americans and Mexicans came to camp at El Cobre. Mangas recognized the Americans as a group he had often seen in Sonora and, accompanied by twelve to fifteen members of his family, paid a visit. He told the American leader, John Russell Bartlett, that he was "a friend of the Americans" and "desired to be at peace with them." And he learned that this party of Americans consisted of neither fur trappers nor soldiers but was there to "mark the line" separating Mexico and the United States. This American told Mangas that all Apaches on the American side of the border would be under the protection of the United States, as long as they did not commit any "thefts or murders" of Americans or Mexicans. If they did so, they would be pursued and punished. Mangas did not comprehend this. The Americans had conquered the Mexicans; why should they protect the Mexicans? And what business was it of the Americans if Chiricahuas raided Mexicans, taking their women for wives and their children as captives, as they had always done? The American response was to insist they were bound to provide this protection, and if Apaches raided Mexicans, the Americans would not "shield them from the consequences."[6]

The dilemma of the border soon became even clearer when two Mexican captive boys, one taken at Bacoachi just months prior, escaped to the American camp. Mangas Coloradas and Delgadito, who were visiting the camp, proposed that the Americans buy them. The American leader refused, advising the Chiricahuas that Americans did not purchase captives, but he also refused to return them. Mangas left the Americans "much offended" and returned several days later, accompanied by Delgadito, Ponce, Baishan, Coletto Amarillo, and some two hundred warriors. This time Mangas addressed the American leader directly: "Why did you take our captives from us?" The explanation that the boys had asked for protection and, by the agreement between Mexico and the United States, they had to be given it, did not satisfy Mangas. He exploded, drawing himself up and projecting all the power and authority a half century of leadership had given him. He had treated the Americans as friends, he exclaimed. He did not threaten their lives or take their animals. He allowed his women and children to visit the Americans. Chiricahuas believed Americans were their friends, so why, he demanded, did they take the captives? Next, Ponce tried to reason with the American, to his utter frustration and anger. Delgadito was finally able to bring the matter to an unsatisfactory conclusion, as the Americans allowed a Mexican to pay for the boys.[7]

The final dilemma became apparent when a Mexican, in the employ of the Americans, killed a Chiricahua of Ponce's group in an argument over the purchase of a whip. When the alarm went up, Mangas Coloradas, Delgadito, and Coletto Amarillo, who were in the American camp at the time, seized their weapons, mounted their horses, and retreated to a nearby hilltop, fearing treachery. Mangas soon learned that the Americans had seized the Mexican and were treating the wounded Chiricahua. Satisfied that Americans were not involved, Mangas let events take their course. After a month in the Americans' care the Chiricahua man died of his wounds. Ponce, backed by Mangas, then asked the American leader for the Mexican, to punish him at El Cobre in sight of the murdered man's kin. The Americans now refused another Chiricahua request, insisting that the murder had been committed on American land and their "great chief" in Santa Fe would punish the killer according to American laws. When Ponce protested this the American leader offered to keep the murderer in chains, working to support the dead Apache's family. Ponce and Mangas left the decision up to the dead man's widow, who chose revenge. After two hours of negotiation the Apache leaders agreed to accept thirty dollars for the dead man. However, for Mangas and the Chiricahuas, no revenge meant no justice.[8]

Thus Mangas grew tired of the Americans at El Cobre. They threatened him if he raided Mexicans. They took away captives. And they refused to allow Chiricahua revenge. So he and the other leaders decided to drive the Americans out by allowing their warriors to raid the unwelcome guests. Several days after the Americans refused to allow revenge, Apaches sneaked three mules out of the Americans' camp. Ten days later warriors drove off twenty-five horses and mules by riding stealthily through low pines and scrub oak into the herd, before startling the animals off with a whoop. Six days after that a larger band of Chiricahuas descended upon the Americans' herd and chased off fifty mules. Finally, two parties drove off more horses and mules, with Delgadito leading one and ensuring the Americans saw him. After this, the Americans decided to move on westward.[9]

As some Chiricahuas raided the Americans at El Cobre, others under Cochise, Miguel Narbona, and Tapilá, now a leader of his own *gò'tàh*, continued attacks into Sonora, killing fifty-nine Mexicans. In retaliation three hundred Sonorans in two columns campaigned, with one column capturing five members of Tapilá's ranchería. Mangas learned that Tapilá had gone to negotiate with the Sonorans for his people's release, and the Mexicans invited him and his party to a feast, got them drunk, and then beat their heads in with clubs. Mangas led a war party of over two hundred Apaches into Sonora in retaliation, attacking three communities and killing at least thirty people. The next spring the Sonorans struck back. Guided by a number of Janeros and two Apaches, Gervacio and Josécito, to an encampment of eighty lodges on the Lago de Guzman northeast of Janos, the Sonorans killed twenty-eight Chiricahuas, including Delgadito. Under assault by the Sonorans, who had killed two experienced Chiricahua leaders in a few months, Mangas Coloradas decided to risk the dilemmas of the border and seek a peace with the Americans.[10]

In the spring after his encounter with the Americans at El Cobre, Mangas Coloradas rode north to camp near the mesa-top Pueblo Indian village of Acoma. There he met with Navajo leaders, agreeing upon a separation of their lands, and he sealed the deal by trading a Mexican captive boy taken at Bacoachi two years earlier for a horse. Alerted that Mangas wished to talk of peace, the Americans soon arrived at the pueblo and set up camp on the mesa. Mangas climbed the stone steps to the top and entered the American leader's tent announcing, "You are the chief of the white men. I am the chief of the red men." Mangas admitted the Chiricahuas wanted peace on the American side of the border and listened to the Americans reading each article of the treaty, agreeing to each one in turn. He accepted for the Chiricahuas the jurisdiction of the United States, agreed to maintain friendly relations, and allowed the Americans to establish posts and agencies in Apache lands.[11]

However, when he heard the articles requiring the return of captives and the end of raids into Mexico, his "eyes widened and [his] expression challenged" the Americans. Mangas insisted that he was there not to make peace with Mexicans but with Americans. With Tapilá's death fresh in his memory, he asked how Chiricahuas could be expected "to be the victims of such treachery and not be revenged?" While the Americans continued to insist on no raiding into Mexico, Mangas believed he had made his point and would later admit he had the tacit approval of the American leader, Colonel Edwin Sumner, to continue his attacks.[12] Mangas clearly felt he had solved the dilemma of the border as he was now safe to continue raiding into Mexico, but safe from attacks by the Americans, and so Chiricahuas began to drift back southward.

"Auxiliaries assisting the citizenry"

In mid-April 1853 Padilla received orders from the political chief of the district, José María Zuloaga. Zuloaga instructed Padilla to take a "party of volunteers from Casas Grandes, Barranco, and that place (Janos)" along with soldiers from the troop on a campaign. Padilla was to reconnoiter the Sierra de Alamo Hueco, the Sierra de la Boca Grande, and the Sierra Florida, all north of Janos and the last on the border between Mexico and the United States. He would attack any Indians he found, and the horses and livestock seized would be distributed among the soldiers and the volunteers. As the volunteers were civilians who served without pay and only for munitions and loot, Zuloaga instructed Padilla to pay "particular attention" to their "good treatment."[13]

Zuloaga's caution was pertinent. While Padilla led out twenty soldiers on April 18, including eighteen-year-old trumpeter Santiago Brito, forty-nine volunteers made up most of his force. For eight days the campaign rode from sunup to sundown, with two Chiricahua scouts an hour ahead of the main body. On April 26 one of the scouts, Gervacio, son of Juan José Compá, spotted signs of an Apache camp and the telltale plumes of smoke from mescal harvesting in the Sierra Florida. Splitting his force into two columns to surround the ranchería, Padilla attacked, killing one man and capturing a young woman. Most of the Indians were dispersed gathering mescal and fled north to the United States, so Padilla occupied the camp, burned all the *jacales* (huts or wickiups), and rounded up twenty-five horses. He then rode back to Corralitos to file his report and turn over his prisoner to Zuloaga.[14]

The inability and suspected unwillingness of the Americans to stop Chiricahua raids as agreed to in Article 11 of the Treaty of

Guadalupe Hidalgo that ended the war between the two nations placed Padilla in a dilemma of his own. Apache aggression necessitated campaigns in response. However, most of the forces at Padilla's disposal were not soldiers but civilians, who were not under military discipline and served only when they wished. Yet these armed civilians were critical to Janos. In June 1853 six soldiers with fourteen civilians pursued Apache raiders, but two months later no soldiers were available to join another group of fourteen Janos residents who set off to track down Indian cattle raiders. When a party of civilian volunteers led by Don Francisco Vázquez recovered a large number of livestock and horses on the Río de Santa María in November, Zuloaga ordered Padilla to march to Don Francisco's support with all available soldiers.[15]

Further, since he now took his orders from Zuloaga, the civilian authority in the district, Padilla distributed most of his few soldiers in small parties to assist the armed civilians of other settlements in their defense, especially Zuloaga's home and mines at Corralitos. In the summer of 1853 Sergeant Prudencio Galindo commanded a detachment to Corralitos that attacked Apaches in the nearby sierra on the sixth and ninth of August. In the first attack Galindo took a local civilian with him and, guided by Gervacio, killed one Indian, took a women named Leonarda captive, and recovered thirteen horses and mules. Three days later Galindo led two soldiers of Janos and Gervacio back into the sierra and killed two Indians and took three horses. Indeed so valuable had Gervacio become to Janos and Padilla that he enrolled the grandson of El Compá in the company. After initially crossing out the preprinted "Soldier" on the contract and writing in "Auxiliary," Padilla settled on listing Gervacio as a "Scout." Identifying him as a "natural de los Apaches," Padilla gave Janos as Gervacio's residence, but listed as his home Corralitos, where he had lived previously, initially as a prisoner; Padilla wrote "Apache" as his religion.[16]

In October 1853 Gervacio joined Padilla and Galindo on a chase of Indians who "robbed" Barranco, recovering what they had taken. Such pursuits became Padilla's main work into the next year.

When Indians raided Corralitos, Padilla chased them into the Sierra de Enmedio, recovering seven animals and capturing one Indian woman. On another occasion a pursuit turned up just three head of livestock. In August 1854 Padilla, again guided by Gervacio, chased and caught a raiding party, killing three and taking twenty-eight steers.

Padilla was rewarded for his tenacity by being promoted to captain of Janos in November after twenty-six years of service, almost half of them in the community. Yet Janeros were increasingly fighting Chiricahuas on their own. An expedition of armed civilians returned to Janos on March 4 and sought to keep the animals they had recovered as a reward to "the people" who had taken them. A campaign of nine soldiers and thirty armed citizens departed the same day. Another party of men from Janos and Casas Grandes rode out at first light on a June morning in 1854 "mounted on good horses."[17]

In May 1855 Padilla, now sole commander of Janos, learned that a party of Indians had crossed the border and was raiding near Janos. Assembling a force of soldiers and armed citizens, likely more of the latter than the former, Padilla cut the trail of twenty Apaches south to the now abandoned Hacienda de Ramos. The next morning Gervacio led scouts following the tracks into the sierras south of the hacienda. After several hours the Janeros overtook two straggling warriors, killing one and capturing the other. This man, Nalze, had ample reason to surrender. A nephew of the leader Itán of Mangas Coloradas's band, Nalze told Padilla that many headmen, including Mangas, wished to make peace with Chihuahua. Padilla in turn had reason to believe him, for some 289 Chiricahuas had recently agreed to a peace and settled near El Carmen. However, Padilla's long experience undoubtedly suggested another motive: that Chiricahuas wished to cross the border to gather mescal near Janos, and the talk of peace was simply to prevent any attacks against their vulnerable camps. The failure of Chiricahuas to return and make peace after a parley in the hills east of Janos made this view more likely, as did the collapse of the

El Carmen treaty with fourteen miners at Corralitos dying in a raid by the previously peaceful Apaches. Despite talks of peace, attacks on Janos continued. Rafael Garza "sustained the honor" of Janos when he, along with eight soldiers and three customs guards, held off seventy-six Chiricahuas in the upper pasture on June 1, 1855.[18]

From October to December 1855 Padilla was preoccupied with another mission. Leading twenty men—nearly all the soldiers he had available—under the command of Commandant General Don Angel Trías, Padilla escorted the U.S-Mexican "Commission of Limits" that surveyed the new boundary between the two nations. Unable to prevent Indian raids across the border, unwilling to pay the costs of doing so, and desiring a southern railroad route, the Americans had proposed to buy a parcel of land south of the Río Gila, in return for abrogation of the original treaty article. The cash-strapped Mexicans agreed to the new treaty in 1853, and surveyors worked throughout all of 1855 to survey, mark, and fix the new boundary. As Padilla saw the new "monuments, mounds, lines and points," he must have grown increasingly dismayed. The border was now even closer to Janos, and many of the sierras often occupied by Chiricahuas and previously within his range, such as the Sierra Florida, were now on the American side of the border, only intensifying his dilemma.[19]

The new year found Padilla's diminishing command spread across the district and the state. Of his fifty-one men eight were in Chihuahua, ten in Corralitos, and seven in El Carmen. Rafael Garza would soon desert the El Carmen detachment while carrying the mail to Chihuahua City, taking his weapon, munitions, and uniform. Among the remaining twenty-six, five were guarding the community and one was in jail, leaving just twenty men for campaigns, pursuits, and sallies. Thus when Padilla learned in May of a raid on Casas Grandes led by Monteras that killed a man and drove off much livestock, he assembled what troops he had, outnumbered and reinforced as was now usual by the *vecinos* of Janos, Barranco, and Corralitos. For three days Padilla followed the raiders' trail northward, again led by Gervacio, and located where they forded the Río Casas Grandes. On the northern bank the raiders split up; most headed for Sonora, but a few continued to drive the livestock toward the new border. Padilla stayed on the trail of the livestock, caught up with the raiders, four in all—surprising them, for they did not expect a pursuit so close to the boundary. Padilla's force of soldiers and armed civilians killed three of the warriors, including the leader Negrito, who had taken over Ponce's group in Mangas's band, and took their scalps for the bounty. The Janeros recovered the livestock and took one Pajarito prisoner, who told Padilla that the raiders had left their families on Mimbres River on the American side of the border, where they were receiving rations.[20]

Padilla did see some success for all his efforts. Itán, Láceres, and Monteras requested a truce on July 30, 1856, offering to exchange Prudencio Arelos of Janos, taken three months earlier, for Nalze, who was Itán's nephew and Monteras's son. Zuloaga agreed to the deal and while no treaty came out of the parley, the captive exchange at Janos convinced other Chiricahuas they could get a better deal on the Mexican side of the line. By mid-August thirty-six Chiricahua resided outside Corralitos, waiting to send a party with Zuloaga to Chihuahua City to meet with the governor. Esquiriba, brother to Láceres, arrived at Janos by the end of the month with some thirteen of his people, having dispatched a delegation led by the influential woman Jusepa to accompany Zuloaga. After narrowly averting Sonoran retaliation on Esquiriba's people, Padilla's hopes for peace quickly foundered.[21]

At midday on September 2, 1856, Mangas Coloradas and thirty to forty leading warriors of Chiricahua swept down on Janos and drove off more than a hundred head of horses. Awakened from his siesta, Padilla watched from the presidial walls, recognizing not only Mangas Coloradas but also Cascos, El Cautívo, Barboncito, Galindo, Perea, and Duransillo. While Cochise was not identified by Padilla as one of these "broncos," he was likely there. Padilla realized the assault was in part revenge for the killing of Negrito, one of Mangas's headmen. Yet it was also an attempt to break up any peace at Janos. Padilla felt betrayed, as Barboncito was one of the Chiricahuas who had visited earlier, talking of peace. He immediately placed Esquiriba and his people under guard, deciding with Zuloaga to use the hostages to force Mangas to return the horse herd and lure other Chiricahuas away from the Americans.[22]

Indeed there was little else Padilla could hope to do. To attack the Chiricahuas in their mountain sanctuaries required forces the state of Chihuahua simply did not have, never mind the fact that Chiricahuas now resided on the American side of the border. Padilla's available forces were still spread out in small detachments at Corralitos, Carmen, and Galeana, made even smaller by the continuing desertions; in August alone there were four, including *Cabo* Guadalupe Madrid, in charge of the detachment at El Carmen. It was quite true, as the commandant general noted in October, that the soldiers of Janos were now serving as "auxiliaries assisting the citizenry" of Janos, Corralitos, and Barranco.[23]

So Padilla sent ten of his remaining soldiers as an escort for Carlota, an Apache woman of Esquiriba's group, whom he dispatched as an emissary to Láceres on the Mimbres River. Carefully crossing the border and avoiding American detection, the soldiers stayed only a short while before taking Carlota and Baquerón back to Janos. Carlota delivered a letter from Féliz Palacios, a Chiricahua leader well known to Padilla, and Baquerón relayed that Láceres was willing to return all the stolen horses for the hostages. After six days Baquerón returned to the rancherias on the Mimbres, carrying Padilla's reply to Palacios. Padilla told "Senor Don Féliz Palacios" that Esquiriba's people would be detained until Láceres, Itán, and Delgadito, along with any others who wanted peace, came to Janos to ratify the peace they had requested with Zuloaga. They would all receive rations, something Padilla knew the Americans were having a hard time providing. There was nothing more he desired, Padilla said, than "a good, big peace." And to ensure that this would happen, Padilla suggested Láceres bring in not only Janos's horses but also Mangas's head.[24]

Palacios showed Padilla's letter to the American agent, Michael Steck. The American wrote to Padilla insisting that Láceres and his band, who were Steck's responsibility, did not carry out the September raid; that had been Mangas Coloradas. Esquiriba was an innocent victim of Mangas's raid, Steck held. While Láceres had tried to recover the horses taken, he had failed, so Steck asked Padilla to influence Zuloaga to free the captives. Padilla, in his response, demurred. All Chiricahuas had been raiding across the border line, including those allied with Láceres. Padilla carefully recounted his capture of Pajarito to show the culpability of Láceres's band. He and his soldiers, he noted, were quite familiar with individual Apache warriors due to long experience and had recognized many during their raids. Once it became clear to Láceres that the Americans could not get his people released from Janos, he gave in, dispatching a warrior called Bartolo to Janos to ask for peace. Deciding to overlook the loss of the Janos horse herd to Mangas Coloradas, Zuloaga agreed. Although neither knew it, it would be the last peace between Chiricahuas and the Presidio of Janos.[25]

On January 2, 1857, Láceres, Poncito, Felipe, and Pascolo, accompanied by nine warriors and fourteen women, came to Janos to ask for peace. Zuloaga escorted Láceres to Corralitos and then to Chihuahua City to ratify the treaty. Láceres returned several weeks later and settled his *gò'tàh* of 149 people a few miles downriver from Janos where they, along with Poncito's thirty-three people, began receiving rations. Over the next two months Delgadito with fifty Apaches and Felipe with ninety-seven joined Láceres in peace at Janos. This concentration of Chiricahuas soon attracted the attention of armed civilians. Some 150 "volunteer men" mustered at Casas Grandes in April. When Padilla learned of them he ordered them to remain in Casas Grandes and refrain from attacking the Apaches living in peace at Janos and Corralitos. The volunteers ignored Padilla's orders and advanced to Janos, where he was forced to detain a hundred of them for insulting the "honor" of the garrison. Yet the commandant general chastised Padilla at the end of the month, stating that such "auxiliary forces" should be the ones to "garrison that frontier." Padilla likely had to agree with his commander for he only had thirty-six men, including twenty-three soldiers, on his muster roll.[26]

The treaty to which the Chiricahuas agreed was a simple one: they would release their captives in exchange for rations. However Padilla received instructions to keep Esquibara's group as hostages to ensure that the Chiricahuas were serious about peace. Further, Padilla was to give rations only in small amounts to show Apaches that Mexicans were not trying to buy their friendship. Only once Apaches proved themselves would the hostages be released, and the commandant general would grant other favors.[27] Padilla undoubtedly knew this hard line without the force to back it up would quickly alienate those Chiricahuas at peace and would not entice any more to come and settle. However, in June, he received a surprise.

North of the border the Americans launched their own campaign into Apachería. To avoid this another 258 Chiricahuas in five rancherías descended into Janos in early summer, including Riñón, Veinte Reales, El Sargento, Victorio, and, much to Padilla's and Zuloaga's shock, Mangas Coloradas. By late summer, however, an epidemic broke out among the more than six hundred Apaches gathered at Janos. Five camps shifted to Corralitos to avoid the sickness, but a number of Chiricahuas returned to the American side of the line. There Chiricahua suspicion fell on the Mexicans, as had often happened in the past, the Apaches claiming they had been poisoned. The Americans, eager to have all Chiricahuas return to the United States, readily accepted this possibility, suggesting Janeros had put arsenic in the rations. His suspicions of Mexicans heightened by the illness among the people, and the American campaign having terminated, Mangas Coloradas abandoned the peace, accompanied by several other groups. By January 1858 only the rancherías of Láceres and Veinte Reales remained at Janos. The local groups of Cigarrito, Dos Reales, Felipe, Poncito, Riñón, and Victorio were still at Corralitos. However when Janeros complained to Padilla in March about the increase in assaults in the district, Padilla was in no position to do anything about it, for as Chiricahuas abandoned the peace, the garrison abandoned the presidio.[28]

On April 1, 1858, Captain Baltasar Padilla mustered the garrison of Janos presidio for the last time. On the muster roll Padilla listed by rank and name all four officers, the armorer, three sergeants, the bugler, three corporals, and nineteen soldiers. But in the last column, "Destinos," the post or assignment of each man, Padilla tallied all thirty-two members of the garrison as "losses," having left military service. The explanation he gave for this mass exodus was an order from the Chihuahua military commander of March 6, 1858, instructing the company to leave its current assignment in support of the Plan of Tacubaya. The Presidio of Janos abandoned its post in support of two coups d'état in Mexico City. The first occurred on December 17, 1857, when General Félix Zuloaga, the commander of the Mexico City garrison and youngest brother of José María Zuloaga, proclaimed his support for the Plan de Tacubaya, nullifying the liberal Constitution of 1857. Barely a month later, on January 11, 1858, General Zuloaga pronounced against President Ignacio Comonfort and, with the support of the Church and the army became president, launching Mexico into the War of the Reform or the Three Years' War.[29] The company of Janos thus abandoned the fight against their traditional Chiricahua foes after nearly 175 years.

"Cut through the tent"

As Janos descended into the maelstrom of war, so did Chiricahuas on the other side of the border. After leaving Janos in the fall Mangas Coloradas returned to his haunts along the Gila River. While the Americans did ration his group, they did so irregularly and provided only corn. Thus, partly to provide for his people and partly to avenge recent deaths in Mexico, Mangas joined with his son-in-law Cochise and raided across the line in late spring. Several months later Mangas and Cochise assembled their warriors and raided across the border again.

Upon his return Mangas faced ever more Americans entering his range, especially miners at El Cobre, who were increasingly joined by more rushing to a new strike to the north at Pinos Altos. The

sight of several hundred prospectors crossing their land and taking up residence in its heart was too much for Chiricahuas. They
determined to harass the miners to force them to leave, as they
had done with the Mexicans and the Americans before, and soon
thefts and killings began. The situation quickly escalated to Mangas leading a large war party to El Cobre. Yet Mangas clearly felt
the raids were preliminary to negotiations, and he did enter the
miners' camp on several occasions to talk, hoping to convince the
miners to leave. The miners handled him roughly on at least one
occasion, later giving rise to the legend that they had seized Mangas and whipped him. Then "suddenly and with no reason" miners attacked the ranchería of Elias and Chabnocito, previously led
by Baishan. As Mangas found himself at war with the Americans,
he received a call for help from Cochise.[30]

Cochise had a problem with the Americans over captives, something that likely did not surprise Mangas. A party of American
soldiers had camped near Cochise and asked to meet. Cochise
went to the American camp, accompanied by his brother Coyuntura, several of his nephews, his second wife, and two children.
After eating, the American leader invited Cochise and Coyuntura
into a tent, where he demanded they turn over a captive boy tak-
en several days earlier. Cochise did not have the boy but offered
to help find him. The American leader agreed to accept Cochise's
help but ordered Coyuntura to look for the boy while Cochise remained a prisoner. Upon hearing this, Cochise instinctively "cut
through the tent" and escaped, but this left his family prisoners of
the Americans. Joined by Mangas and his warriors, Cochise laid
siege to the Americans, who retreated to a stagecoach station. He
asked for his family to be released but the Americans refused, still
demanding the captive boy.[31]

Cochise therefore decided to take some captives to exchange.
He attacked a passing wagon train and seized nine Mexicans and
three Americans. Having no use for the Mexicans, Cochise had
them tortured to death, sparing the Americans to trade for his relatives. Cochise also tried unsuccessfully to ambush the eastbound

stagecoach. At this point Cochise gave up hope, and the Chiricahuas "killed our prisoners, disbanded, and went into hiding in the mountains." Several days later, with their families safe in the sierra, Chiricahuas returned in force to attack the Americans. Cochise sent one party to attack the soldiers as they returned from watering their livestock, and these men succeeded in driving off over fifty mules. At the same time Cochise led another party to attack the station in a failed attempt to free his family. For several days the Americans waited for another attack but were merely under observation by Chiricahua scouts. When the Americans emerged they discovered the mutilated bodies of the dead American captives under some oak trees. Watched by the scouts in increasing horror, the Americans hanged their Chiricahua captives on these same trees, sparing only the women and children.[32]

Cochise set out to take his revenge on the Americans. For sixty days no American was safe. Cochise attacked travelers, settlers, ranchers, soldiers, and miners, killing some 150. Then, as if in response, the Americans abandoned their stagecoach stations, deserted their forts, quit their ranches and small towns, and forsook their mines, leaving Chiricahua lands. As Cochise saw it, his war had been successful in driving out the Americans, save for those at Pinos Altos. So Cochise joined forces with Mangas Coloradas in midsummer and the two placed their warriors near Dziltanatal (Mountain Holds Its Head Up Proudly) Peak on the road to the mines. Throughout the rest of the summer their combined force of several hundred warriors ambushed a number of pack trains and travelers, killing many Americans and Mexicans, taking much stock, and gaining new guns and ammunition.

Buoyed by their success and new armaments, the Chiricahuas attacked Pinos Altos itself at the end of the summer. Surprising the town in the early morning the warriors isolated the miners in their cabins and at their digs. By midday they forced the miners back to the storehouses at the middle of the settlement, but they abandoned the attack when the miners fired a small cannon at them. However, many miners began to abandon the site, a small success. Cochise and

Mangas, as far as they could tell, had driven most of the Americans out of their lands, but the cost had been high. The well-armed Americans killed many irreplaceable warriors, and the leaders Chabnocito, Delgadito, and Esquinaline gave their lives at the head of their men.[33]

The two did not know it at the time, but the Americans had gone to war with each other and withdrew their troops to fight among themselves. Cochise and Mangas Coloradas would learn of this war when, in the summer after the attack on Pinos Altos, scouts warned them of a large body of American soldiers approaching from the west. Cochise made preparations to receive them, joined by Mangas and other leaders—Victorio, Nana, Juh—and their warriors. Cochise and Juh occupied the hills above the only spring on the Americans' route in Apache Pass on the north side of the Chiricahua Mountains, building breastworks of rocks. A half mile away to the west Mangas, Victorio, and Nana took up positions behind rocks and boulders on the steep hillsides above the abandoned stage station. When the Americans straggled into the pass and stopped at the station, the Chiricahuas surrounded them. Mangas initiated the ambush by firing at the rearmost soldiers, while Cochise's force held their fire until the soldiers approached the spring. One group of Americans almost reached water but were driven back by Chiricahua rifle fire and subjected to Chiricahua taunts and scorn. The Americans counterattacked by storming the highest hill above the spring and emplacing two cannon upon it. The soldiers fired the cannon at Cochise's men "causing them to flee into the rocks while shells burst over their heads."[34]

As Cochise engaged the thirst-crazed Americans in the pass, Mangas Coloradas spotted six horsemen break from the western entrance, racing to find their compatriots. He immediately set out in pursuit with forty warriors. One American lagged behind the rest, and Mangas led fifteen warriors after him, firing as they went. A bullet struck the soldier's horse, but the American took cover behind his mount's corpse and commenced firing with a breech-loading gun. Unable to rush the American due to his "lively fusillade," Mangas and his men circled around him, keeping

up a desultory fire for an hour. Then suddenly one of the American's shots hit Mangas in the breast, laying him low. In the growing darkness his warriors gathered their chief into their arms and
retreated. The next day the Americans shot their way through the
pass with cannons clearing the way for the infantry, scattering Cochise's men, but Mangas and his people were not there. So severe
was their leader's wound that they took him to a Mexican doctor
in Janos, risking treachery, although they warned the doctor that
if he killed Mangas, they would kill all the Mexicans.[35]

To the relief of all involved, the doctor managed to extract the
carbine ball and Mangas survived his wounds. But Mexico remained
dangerous with troops in the field seeking Chiricahuas, so Mangas made his way back north of the border. He was tired and wanted peace. More than seventy years old and widely respected, Mangas had no more need to raid and wished to settle down near Pinos
Altos. After consulting with his fellow leaders, including Victorio, who attempted to dissuade him, Mangas entered Pinos Altos
to talk. The Americans seized him as a prisoner and took him to a
nearby fort, where Mangas learned that the Americans were in no
mood for peace, camped as they were in a fort burned down by his
warriors near Dziltanatal Peak, where he and Cochise had attacked
many travelers. Mangas's position that he had simply been defending himself against the miners, whom he saw as a separate band of
whites only loosely allied with the soldiers, carried no weight; Mangas remained a prisoner. That cold winter night the soldiers guarding
Mangas tortured him by heating their bayonet blades and placing
them on his exposed limbs. When he rose on an elbow to admonish
them in Spanish that he was no child to be played with, the guards
shot him. After a perilous lifetime of living in a community of violence, Mangas Coloradas died at the hands of the Americans.[36]

"Against the barbarians"

Mangas Coloradas's return to Janos for medical attention in 1863
was not a surprise to the community. The end of the garrison had
not meant the end of relations with Chiricahuas, either cooperative

or violent. The last document to survive from the presidial archive decried a raid in the Valle de San Buenaventura on July 1, 1858, the same locale as the first recorded Apache raid back in 1682. Janos and its sister communities in the region were not helpless in the face of raids, as a class of civilian chiefs grew out of the steadily increasing role armed civilians had played in campaigns over the preceding decades. Juan Mata Ortiz of Galeana was one such chief, active in campaigns against Apaches from an early age, mobilizing and organizing his fellow *vecinos*, and securing weapons, mounts, and supplies. Mata Ortiz received support in his endeavors from José María Zuloaga, who returned to the district sometime in 1859 or 1860. While Zuloaga led the conservative faction in Chihuahua during the War of the Reform and briefly served as governor in 1859, from which the liberal triumph unseated him, his relation by marriage to the rising liberal Terrazas clan secured him in his position as the political chief of northwestern Chihuahua.[37]

Back in his base at Corralitos, Zuloaga entered into negotiations for peace with a number of Chiricahuas in the summer of 1860, including some from Cochise's band. Given that Apaches could raid into Mexico while leaving their families in security on the American side of the border, Zuloaga believed the only way to control them was to settle them near Mexican communities, where close scrutiny could be maintained. Zuloaga's plan ran into the basic dilemma of the border for Janos: without troops or "full-time specialists in violence" to control the boundary or monitor the peace establishments, the community was on its own. The Chiricahuas soon returned to their lands north of the border, from where they continued to raid. One attack took a pack mule train just east of Casas Grandes and armed civilians set out in pursuit. They surprised the Apaches at their breakfast, firing a volley into the twelve warriors, dropping one and causing the others to scatter. As the Mexicans pursued the fleeing warriors the "dead" Apache regained consciousness and ran for cover, hurried on by rifle fire. Unbeknownst to the Mexicans, Geronimo had just made another of his escapes.[38]

Yet when they were not organized for a campaign or pursuit,

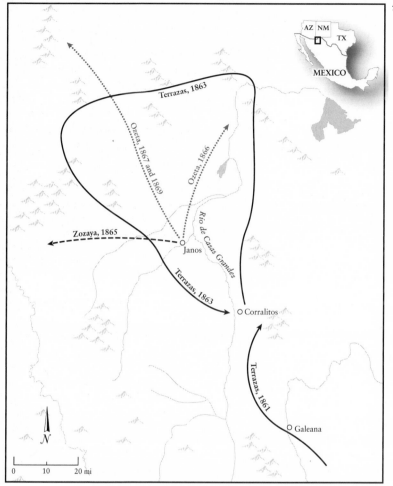

Map 15. Mexican campaigns, 1860s

Janeros would willingly trade with Chiricahuas. In the summer of 1861 Cochise and Mangas Coloradas exchanged their plunder from American travelers for ammunition and alcohol at Janos. The community would also participate in campaigns under Mata Ortiz "against the barbarians" when given the opportunity. One such opportunity arose when Joaquín Terrazas, cousin of Chihuahuan governor Luis Terrazas, led a campaign in August and September 1861 that killed eleven Apaches in the Sierra de Corral de Piedras near Corralitos. While this campaign disrupted the Chiricahua trade at Janos and Corralitos, by the spring of 1862 it had resumed. A party of warriors from Cochise's band drove more than a hundred horses to trade at Janos and Corralitos. Americans trailed the stock to Corralitos, where they took nine Chiricahua—one man, three women, and five children—from Zuloaga's house and executed the man and women. That summer Janeros joined a group of volunteers from the district of Guerrero to the south in attacking a ranchería near Janos and taking eleven prisoners.[39]

Terrazas returned to the Janos region again in July 1863, marching with a small force of cavalry to Corralitos, where he "formed a campaign with the *vecinos*" of the district, undoubtedly under the command of Mata Ortiz. Terrazas, Mata Ortiz, and the Janeros in the force struck out northward to the U.S.-Mexican border, traced it westward, and then returned south to Janos and Corralitos, where the *vecinos* retired to their towns. It was after the departure of this campaign that Mangas Coloradas's warriors held Janos hostage for the medical treatment of their leader. Unorganized and likely outnumbered, the Janeros had little option but to cooperate. This lack of organization would continue for several more years as Terrazas ceased to campaign in the northwest part of the state and instead focused on "preparing forces for the national defense against the French invasion."[40]

As Terrazas held the forces of the state in the capital an American campaign under Lieutenant Colonel Nelson Davis crossed the border into northwestern Chihuahua to search out Apaches who had fled American attacks north of the Gila in July 1864. After

searching the mountains north of Janos, Davis continued to Corralitos where he confronted Zuloaga with the charge that he was
"selling power and lead to the Indians." Zuloaga vehemently denied this, pointing out that he had "almost absolute authority and
jurisdiction over this part of the State," and not only did he not sell
ammunition to Apaches but he also prohibited anyone else from doing so, as far as he was able. Zuloaga was "anxious to have the hostile Apaches subdued or exterminated," as his losses to their raids
were quite high, as was the expense of keeping armed men to protect his mines, trains, and stock. While Davis left convinced that
the complaints made against Zuloaga were "without foundation
in fact," the charges were likely quite true. What Zuloaga failed to
mention was that he did not trade when he was strong enough to
attack but was quite willing to do so, as was Janos, when he was
unready or unable to do violence against Chiricahuas.[41]

Janos continued this basic pattern. When three Sonoran survivors of a Chiricahua ambush in Higueros Canyon fifty miles
west of Janos, likely led by Cochise and Juh, stumbled into Janos
on April 5, 1865, Juan José Zozaya, the past peace commissioner,
led twenty-three Janeros out in relief. Cautiously scouting the site,
Zozaya determined that three previous parties had been attacked
and wiped out by a force numbering between 150 and 200 warriors well armed with rifles and revolvers. Yet in the next year Sonorans would complain that Chiricahuas showed up every Saturday
at Casas Grandes or Janos to trade plunder and gold for ammunition. One Sonoran, Francisco Martínez, saw Cochise "with his entire band and a great deal of stock" at Janos in August 1866. The
authorities, likely including Zozaya, treated Cochise "very well"
and seemed "very happy to see him." Martínez's friend tried to
buy back his own horses taken in Sonora, but the Apaches refused
to trade for anything other than gunpowder or bullet lead. However when Cayetano Ozeta led a group of state-supported volunteers from Guerrero to Janos in December, Janeros joined him in
attacking Cochise's camp northeast of the community, killing five
men and one woman and taking four captives.[42]

Ozeta remained in the region and launched a campaign in the spring of the next year that followed an Apache trail across the border into the southern Chiricahua Mountains. There he surprised a local group led by Tuscas, who clearly felt safe on the American side of the border. Ozeta succeeded in taking the entire ranchería, killing eight warriors and four women and capturing twenty-six more, along with recovering a Mexican captive. That fall, however, with Apache hostilities in Sonora as bad as they had ever been, Sonoran authorities launched an investigation of Janos, blaming the community for encouraging Chiricahua attacks. The commission found that Janos had a local peace with Apaches, particularly Cochise. Chiricahuas traded stolen livestock for guns and ammunition with the Janeros, who then sold it to the Americans. The Sonorans even claimed Janeros warned Chiricahuas of Mexican campaigns. The accusations of trade were quite true, but the Chihuahuan government realized that without adequate security, Janos had little option but to trade with the Apaches. The government therefore authorized Ozeta to recruit a unit of armed civilians to serve at Janos early in 1868, the first garrison at the ex-presidio for nearly ten years.[43]

But even Ozeta realized the usefulness of treating with Chiricahuas whenever possible. When Cochise, pressured on both sides of the border, sent six Chiricahuas to negotiate a treaty at Janos, Ozeta was willing to talk. That was until he learned of an attack on Casas Grandes that wounded one Mexican and stampeded fifty head of livestock, at which point he seized the Chiricahuas as prisoners. Cochise's latest ploy came about the time Zuloaga died on June 31, 1868. Having entered service in 1816 and retiring as a captain in 1839, Zuloaga was the last of the men who remembered the general peace of the colonial and early national periods based on campaigns, captive exchanges, and rations. The men who followed—Terrazas, Mata Ortiz, Ozeta—knew less of long-term peace with Chiricahuas and more of regular violence.[44]

Hence when Chiricahuas tried again to negotiate a peace at Janos in October to buy breathing space and time, Ozeta was initially willing to talk. But when a force of Sonorans attacked the Apache encampments he readily abandoned any hope for peace and seized the twelve Chiricahua negotiators. Ozeta then organized an attack on a ranchería north of Janos, taking in triumph to Chihuahua City ten prisoners and twelve scalps, including that of José Mangas, brother to Mangas Coloradas. In August of 1869 Ozeta led a campaign that once again crossed into American territory, this time to Guadalupe Canyon, where his men surprised two Chiricahuas, a man and a boy, wounding the man before capturing both. The man told Ozeta an encampment of over a hundred Apaches was four miles to the north, led by men "very well known in Janos by their savage raids." Ozeta hurried to the camp but found it abandoned. After remaining overnight Ozeta retreated into Mexico to the Sierra de Enmedio, hoping the Chiricahuas would follow so that he could attack. This ploy failed and Ozeta returned to Janos on September 17.[45]

"Americans are everywhere"

Before Ozeta's seizure of the peace delegation in the fall of 1868 Cochise had had enough of Mexico and returned to the American side of the border. He realized he would have to make a peace with the Americans. In the winter he accosted an American patrol or "scout," telling the American officer that he had lost one hundred people over the last year, most to sickness but many to the Americans. Where ten years earlier he had led a thousand Apaches, barely a hundred remained. "The Americans," he declared, "are everywhere and we must live in bad places to shun them." The logic of a community of violence required that Cochise first do violence before asking for any peace, so raids on the American side of the line increased, making the next two years the "bloodiest" the Americans had seen.[46]

In the fall of that first year Cochise ambushed a mail stagecoach, killing all six Americans, and drove off a herd of over two hundred cattle the next day. The Americans set out in dogged pursuit, all day and through the night. At dawn on the second day the Americans caught Cochise and after a sharp fight recovered all the cattle and most of the mail. But the Americans kept coming after Cochise, more and more joining the chase. Cochise was barely able to fight them to a stalemate and make his escape. Coming of age after the period of general war with the Spanish, Cochise had never experienced this kind of persistence. He retreated northward away from the border mountains.[47]

Cochise waited out the winter above the Gila River, safe from Americans and Mexicans, but returned southward to near the border in the spring and resumed his raids on both sides. After another bloody spring and summer Cochise was ready to talk of peace and sent his wife Dos-teh-seh to the Americans. She stated Cochise "wanted to make peace with the whites and was tired of war." Cochise clearly felt he had done enough violence to get a peace. He considered joining Lozo, Mangas Coloradas's son Salvadora, and Victorio in their reservation at Cañada Alamosa across the mountains in New Mexico, and met in council with the Americans there. Cochise made it clear that Chiricahuas did not want "to be put in a corral," to which the American replied "tell me . . . where you want your rations issued." Cochise would remember this offer.[48]

Cochise did not yet settle, staying the winter instead along the border in Arizona, from where he and his warriors carried out raids in the spring and summer, something Cochise euphemistically called "making a living" when he spoke with the Americans. By the summer he was avoiding raiding Americans to avoid any pursuits but continued crossing into Mexico. With the coming of fall and the looming winter Cochise decided to settle at Cañada Alamosa, first running off fifty-four horses and seven mules from an army herd to help make the trip. He arrived with thirty warriors and two hundred women and children, only to learn that the Americans now wanted to move the reservation north to Tularosa. As his people were safe and rationed, even if poorly, Cochise bided his time at Cañada Alamosa over the winter. In the spring Chiricahua and American leaders met in council, where Cochise refused to go to Tularosa. When the Americans announced the reservation would move anyway, Cochise abandoned this attempt at peace and returned to the mountains along the border from where his warriors continued to "make a living."[49]

With Terrazas off fighting yet another civil war, Cochise again approached Janos in the summer to ask for peace. The authorities at Janos insisted he had to go to Galeana to talk, likely with Mata Ortiz, but bad memories of Galeana prevented Cochise from going. He and his people remained near Janos for over a month trading what they had taken from the Americans. By the fall Cochise returned across the border to the Dragoon Mountains, where he made a peace with the Americans, but on his terms. Cochise agreed to peace in return for a reservation centered on his strongholds and hideouts in the mountains of southeastern Arizona along the border. The Americans agreed, although some realized the temptation to raid into Mexico would be great.[50]

American concerns held true, for Cochise stated he had made peace with the Americans, not the Mexicans. While raiding against Americans ceased, crossings into Mexico continued. These incursions only increased when more Chiricahuas moved to Cochise's reservation from Chihuahua and the abandoned reservation at Tularosa. Part of the problem was the inability of the Americans to supply the promised rations, meaning Chiricahuas had a continuing need to raid into Mexico. But revenge was the heart of the matter. When an army officer confronted Cochise over the raids, he replied that the raids were carried out by "many young people whose parents and relatives have been killed by Mexicans." The forays continued with Apaches displaying silver-mounted saddles and bridles taken in Mexico and Mexican lace on children's clothing. One warrior traded a silver-plated revolver he took off a Mexican officer he had killed. And still the Americans recovered captives from Chiricahuas whenever possible. When Geronimo brought a captive Mexican boy to the reservation the Americans took him away.[51]

After a year of this existence and with mounting complaints from Mexico, Cochise realized he had to act or else American soldiers would take over the reservation. He helped Americans

recover livestock taken from Mexico and, as his health deteriorat-
ed, held a council with all the Chiricahua leaders and their warriors, telling them they had to cease raiding or leave the security
of the reservation. A number of local groups did leave, giving Cochise's reservation some respite and stability. But Cochise died on
the morning of June 8, 1874, leaving leadership of his band to his
son Taza.[52] While Cochise lived in a community of violence, he
used violence to be able to die in peace. But he never overcame the
dilemma of the border.

The creation of the border between the United States and Mexico created a security dilemma for both Chiricahua and Janos as
actions the communities took to provide security for themselves
ultimately threatened their survival. If Chiricahuas stayed on the
Mexican side of the border they faced treachery and attacks. But if
they crossed to the American side seeking security for their families, they could not live the way they wanted. As Mangas Coloradas
and Cochise both discovered, Americans would not let them take
or keep captives. Captives were critical for the community as they
increased Chiricahua numbers and were channels for negotiations
and exchanges between communities.[53] Nor would the Americans
allow them to raid across the line into Mexico. This threatened the
community since raids, via the novice complex, were the means by
which boys became men and by which men became leaders among
their people. Raiding also provided the resources for men to care
for their families and the all-important puberty or Maiden's ceremony by which girls became valuable, marriage-eligible women.
The inability of the Americans to provide enough rations to a family group for daily survival, let alone a four-day ceremony, meant
Chiricahuas would continue raiding to make a living, as Cochise
put it, especially into Mexico.[54]

   They did so as Chiricahuas never had any interest in a permanent peace with Mexico. Immediate memories of decades' worth
of Mexican scalp hunting, treacherous towns, and unprovoked attacks firmly placed Mexicans in Chiricahua minds as their natural

enemy. But decades of raiding also caused Chiricahuas to see Mexicans as their "vassals," whose purpose was to raise livestock for raiders to take. Decreasing Mexican military power caused an increasing lack of respect for Mexicans and a growing sense of Chiricahua superiority. Chiricahuas had a low regard for Mexicans and saw killing one as an honorable achievement, especially since killings were often for revenge. But Americans would not allow Chiricahuas to take revenge upon Mexicans, as Mangas Coloradas discovered when a Mexican killed a Chiricahua and the Americans refused to turn him over so that his people could satisfy their need for revenge. Cochise clearly understood that he would be unable to stop many raiders from going into Mexico for they went to seek revenge. And Chiricahuas learned that Americans would enforce their prohibitions with military force, threatening the security they sought.[55]

For Janos the dilemma was different but no less threatening to the community's survival in the long term. The creation of the border and subsequent political turmoil in Mexico only continued the steady decrease of the garrison of Janos and led to its eventual dissolution. This made Janeros solely responsible for their own security, a development that would ultimately threaten the Mexican state. While the national government had tried to provide a defense of the border with the creation of military colonies in 1848, the minister of war and navy in 1853 ended this experiment. The minister authorized the reorganization of presidial companies because presidial troopers were "natives of those frontiers," knew the country, and had spent the major part of their lives at war with the "barbarian Indians." The reorganization did not include any more material or fiscal support, meaning numbers remained low at Janos, barely fifty in total in April 1856. To increase the size and usefulness of the remaining companies, Janos was amalgamated with the presidial company of Old San Elizario, now at El Paso, although the men of the garrison remained at Janos; but the companies were split again a year later. On his final parade in 1858 Padilla mustered only thirty-two men, one-third of his authorized strength.[56]

While Emperor Maximilian authorized presidial companies during the 1860s, his conservative government was never in any position to organize them. This tainted presidial companies in the eyes of the victorious liberals, so Janos was again designated a military colony in 1868, but over a decade and a half later nothing had happened. The result of this inability to garrison Janos and the entire northern border was an increasing militarization of society. Anyone who could organize and group citizens into a force, provide them with weapons, mounts, and supplies, and take the force out on campaign was considered a *militar* (military man or soldier) in the slang of the day.[57] This meant that Janos came to see violence as the means to relate not only to Chiricahua but ultimately with the Mexican state on both the local and national level. Needless to say this threatened the state, and its response would threaten the security and survival of Janos. But in 1875 that day had not yet arrived, and Janos still had to ensure its own security from the "persecutions" of the "barbarians."

| Chapter 7

Communities' End
Persecution and Imprisonment, 1875–1910

In the last decades of the nineteenth century Chiricahua and Janos gradually ceased to interact with each other and ceased to be communities of violence. The state government of Chihuahua sought to defend itself from Apache raids, culminating in the battle at Tres Castillos, fought solely by armed civilian volunteers, including many from Janos, with no help from the national government. The Chiricahua survivors of Tres Castillos were soon joined by others who left reservations in the United States and would ultimately come under the influence of Geronimo. For several years Geronimo and Chiricahuas with him survived both American and Mexican attacks. Fearing treachery in Mexico they finally surrendered and accepted imprisonment away from the borderlands. The beginning of the end for Janos came with the end of the Apache wars. The Mexican national state now had the security to survey and sell "excess" lands, including those of Janos, threatening the survival of the community. Janos thus provided the "ideal recruits" to start the Mexican Revolution of 1910–20. They ultimately lost the revolution as the resulting Mexican state was finally able to make violence an unattractive strategy for survival, ending Janos as a community of violence. Chiricahua ended as a community of violence due to exile and imprisonment away from the borderlands.

"Persecute the barbarians"

Cochise never solved the dilemma of the border for Chiricahua, and Terrazas continued to face it with Janos. Although promoted to "Sub-Inspector of the Military Colonies of the State of Chihuahua" in 1873, Terrazas still did not have enough forces at hand to prevent Apache violations of the border and continued to rely upon armed civilian volunteers. In the spring of 1873, per the governor's orders, Terrazas placed a detachment in Janos before setting off on a campaign to "persecute the barbarians" through the cantons of Guerrero, Degollado, and Galeana, where Apaches continued to surprise "towns, ranches, and haciendas." Every few months during this campaign Terrazas halted his troops near towns "where Apaches had killed or robbed, whose *vecinos* entered the service of the campaign."[1]

In July of the next year Terrazas received an order from the minister of war in Mexico City ordering him to recruit a force, first to cover the town of Gallego and then to defend Janos. These troops were to continue to recruit and organize *vecinos* of the towns, haciendas, and ranches attacked by Apaches, paying them for their time on campaign with federal funds. By October Terrazas had a force of fifty men, mounted, with saddles and equipment. Their weapons and munitions, however, were of various classes and calibers. But these men were not in the field when Juh showed up at Janos in December 1874, having left Cochise's reservation, and once again sounding out the possibility of peace in Mexico. The killing of one of Juh's peace envoys by Sonorans ended this attempt. In February 1875 Terrazas received enough saddles and bridles, Remington rifles with twenty thousand cartridges, and uniforms to organize a hundred-man "Chihuahua Colony Squadron." Terrazas based his new squadron in Carrizal in March and assigned detachments of likely no more than ten or fifteen men to four towns, including Janos. The rest of the squadron, augmented by armed civilians, "persecuted barbarians."[2]

The detachment at Janos was authorized to call upon *vecinos* to augment the force for "prompt persecution" whenever Indians appeared in the area, either entering or leaving with their loot. For the rest of the year, "with the *vecinos* of the town and those in the area," the Janos detachment frequently scouted the area for Apaches, who typically avoided them by crossing the border into the United States. But in June a party of armed civilians from Carrizal encountered Chiricahuas in the Sierra de Pilares and in the ensuring chase captured an Indian woman. In June 1876 Terrazas reunited his squadron to fight the rebellion of Porfirio Díaz. The Janos detachment did not join him until mid-July as it had been serving on a campaign. Mata Ortiz, now *jefe político* of Janos, accompanied the detachment, leading a party of armed civilians from the towns of his district.[3]

Terrazas and Mata Ortiz defeated the rebels at Avalos outside Chihuahua City in August, but the rebellion proved successful everywhere else in Mexico. When Díaz dispatched forces to take control of Chihuahua in 1877 the Terrazas cousins, Luis and Joaquín, retired to "the private life" and released their troops. Mata Ortiz "retired" back to Galeana and once again faced having to secure his district with only the armed civilians of the towns. Yet he and Joaquín Terrazas would soon serve together again. The new governor quickly alienated many of the political elite in Chihuahua by imposing an extraordinary tax to finance the war against the Apaches. They rebelled and soon defeated the governor. By November 1879 Luis Terrazas was governor once again. A large federal force under General Gerónimo Treviño arrived in December to put down the rebellion, but Treviño accepted Luis Terrazas as governor, and soon his cousin would be back in the saddle persecuting barbarians.[4]

The cause of Joaquin Terrazas's return to the campaign trail was the departure of Victorio from his American reservation. By this time Chiricahuas had divided into two factions. One, led by Cochise's son Taza, agreed to keep the peace with the Americans on the reservation. The other faction had no single leader, although Juh was the best known; it included most of the younger warriors and their families and saw the reservation as a refuge from which to raid into Mexico. Actions by this second faction, and a continuing inability to supply the Chiricahua reservation, caused the Americans to decide the Chiricahuas had to leave their reservation and move to San Carlos, away from their mountains and away from Mexico. Taza agreed to go and led his faction there, while other leaders, including Juh, fled across the border, where they were safe as the Mexicans were focused on their own internal battles. San Carlos proved a miserable place, and when warriors from Mexico visited and told of raids and good lives, many at San Carlos decided to leave. Victorio led a large group away from the reservation but soon surrendered to the pursuing Americans. However, when he learned that he was to be tried in American courts for horse stealing and murder, he left for the last time in August 1879 with 75 warriors and 375 women and children, and headed for the border.[5]

Victorio crossed into Mexico and encamped at a *tinaja* (water hole), which would soon be named for him, in the Sierra de la Candelaria. From there raiders dispersed seeking horses and mules to aid in their flight. Victorio also dispatched scouts to watch the nearby Mexican town of Carrizal. When they reported "much coming of men and talking in the plaza" Victorio feared treachery. Sánchez, one of his warriors, volunteered to go to the town, since he had been a captive in Chihuahua for many years and could pass as a Mexican. Donning the clothes of a *vaquero* he had earlier killed, and mounted on a horse bearing the Terrazas brand, Sánchez rode into Carrizal, drank at the cantina, talked with men in the plaza, and rode out of town. Sánchez reported to Victorio that Carrizal planned to invite the Chiricahuas to a feast, get them drunk, and kill them. A day or so later a Tarahumara Indian came to the camp and invited Victorio to Carrizal. Since the Tarahumara saw only a small number of men with Victorio as the raiders were still away, he was allowed to leave unharmed. When the raiders returned Victorio moved his camp deeper into the sierra and laid an ambush with his men on the north side and the rest under Nana to the south. Soon eighteen Mexicans rode into the trap in single file, following the trail. Victorio's warriors opened fire first, forcing the

Mexicans into the rocks on their southern flank, where Nana's men killed them all. The mayor of Carrizal dispatched another party, this time thirty-five men. Victorio allowed them to begin to bury the dead before attacking, killing another fifteen and driving off the remainder "horseless." Collecting horses, weapons, and precious ammunition, Victorio moved his band to the lagoons near the border.[6]

Terrazas learned of the "double massacre" in the Candelarias in November 1879. As General Treviño had accepted Luis Terrazas's return to the governorship, federal troops were available to campaign against the Apaches for the first time. Colonel Ponciano Cisneros, with a hundred cavalry, thirty infantry, and a mountain artillery piece, rendezvoused with Terrazas at El Carmen in mid-December. Terrazas gave Cisneros command of the campaign, which then headed for Galeana. Upon their arrival the two commanders learned that Juan Mata Ortiz, once again *jefe político* of the district, had gone to Corralitos to recruit *vecinos* for the campaign. Cisneros and Terrazas then marched for Corralitos and discovered they had once again missed the hard-riding Mata Ortiz, now on his way to aid men from Ascención who were surrounded by Indians near the Lago de Guzman. Cisneros thus led his force northward and at Ascención met Mata Ortiz, who reported that the *vecinos* were saved, but Indians had destroyed a party of smugglers and retired to the northwest with "a great, stolen, herd of horses and mules."[7]

Mata Ortiz was undoubtedly glad to see the soldiers as he simply did not have enough men to remain ready to fight the Apaches. When Juh visited Casas Grandes that summer with eighty warriors, "there was no means to fight them." With the men of the place dispersed to their plows and herds and succor from other towns hours away, the town was in no position to offer resistance. So he and his armed civilians gladly joined Cisneros's campaign as it moved along the border. Scouts discovered an abandoned Chiricahua camp with a trail leading back into the United States, and Cisneros headed back south and east to Carrizal. Here Mata Ortiz and his *vecinos*, fatigued by their earlier exertions and the campaign, retired to their towns at year's end.[8]

During the summer of 1880 Victorio crossed back across the border into Mexico, pursued by American troops. Mata Ortiz received orders from the governor to take to the field with his "volunteer auxiliaries" at the end of June. His operations in the northwestern part of the state were to complement those of Colonel Aldofo Valle's federal troops in the northeast. Valle ended his campaign in early August after a bitter fight with Victorio in the Sierra de los Pinos above the Rio Grande. While Victorio crossed the river, he was unable to stay on the American side since soldiers occupied the water holes, so he fell back into Mexico. Mata Ortiz thus received another set of orders from the governor within a few weeks directing him to recruit as many "armed civilians" as possible for a campaign under the command of Terrazas. The state government would pay four *reales* a day for those who served on foot and six a day for those who brought their own horse. The standard premium for an Indian warrior's scalp or for captured women and children would be paid, per the law. In addition two thousand pesos would be paid for Victorio, dead or alive.

Mata Ortiz immediately dispatched scouts to watch the trails and water holes near the lagoons along the border and sent word to all the towns in his district, including Janos, to gather at Corralitos. By the time Terrazas joined him nearly a month later, with barely fifty men, Mata Ortiz had 119 armed men ready to march. These men, including many Janeros, were not surprised when Terrazas told them that Colonel Valle's federal troops, some garrisoned at nearby El Carmen and Carrizal, would not be joining the campaign. Once again, as had been the case for over two decades, Janos and her sister towns would fight Chiricahuas alone. Despite the thirty Public Security troops and twenty cavalrymen who joined Terrazas and Mata Ortiz as they rode out of Corralitos heading east, the last great campaign of the Apache wars in Chihuahua would be mainly fought by civilians.[9]

Mata Ortiz's scouts caught up with the campaign at a water hole

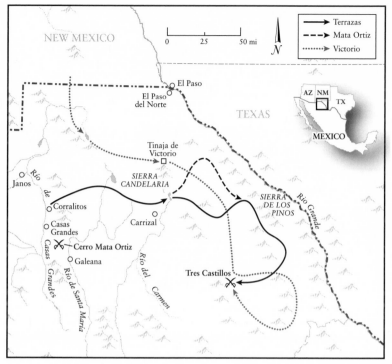

Map 16. Mata Ortiz, Terrazas, and Victorio, 1880

north of Carrizal, reporting they had seen no Indians but did spy tracks heading east. By this time another hundred civilians from Guerrero, Carrizal, and the towns around El Paso del Norte had joined Terrazas. Concerned that this force would soon run out of supplies the colonel ordered more rations from El Paso and divided his force into two columns. Terrazas took one column eastward while Mata Ortiz, now second in command of the campaign, rode north and east to meet the expected supply train from El Norte. Four days later he guided the train to rendezvous with Terrazas in the sierras above the Rio Grande. There he learned that his commander had lost the trail, so for two days the force rested, resupplied, and scouted the surrounding mountains. Mata Ortiz and Terrazas determined the Chiricahuas must be to the south and headed that direction, preceded by scouts. The campaign again struck the Apaches' trail, which seemed fresh. Terrazas cut ninety men from his force "who seemed worthless" and again divided into two columns. Mata Ortiz took a column south and found nothing after an all-night search, but upon rejoining Terrazas's column, which had gone west, he learned that more tracks had been found, pointing to a set of three rocky peaks rising one hundred feet above the desert floor and known as Tres Castillos.[10]

Terrazas and his small escort rode ahead of the main force. Looking through his field glasses Terrazas spotted a small dust cloud to the south heading to Tres Castillos. He watched for an hour and spotted two more dust clouds raised by Apaches heading for Tres Castillos. Victorio had directed his people gather at the landmark to rest and prepare to cross Chihuahua, headed for the Sierra Madre to the west and Sonora beyond. Terrazas and Mata Ortiz had gotten to his rally point first. It was late in the day when Terrazas met the main force led by Mata Ortiz. Terrazas placed his column on the left of the line of march and Mata Ortiz's to the right, each with a front of ten men, in an attempt to disguise the true size of the force. As the mid-October sun set Terrazas and Mata Ortiz neared the hills. Two groups of Chiricahuas had already reached the southern hill and spotted the Mexicans when they were about a thousand yards away. Thirty warriors headed toward the column. When they came within rifle range two Tarahumara Indians with Terrazas dashed forward and fired, killing one warrior. The rest of the Apaches fell back to the hills.[11]

In the waning light Terrazas led his column around the southern peak to the left as Mata Ortiz led his to the right, firing as they went. Apaches abandoned their horses and mules, saddled and packed, to flee into the rocks along the slopes. As the darkness fell the Mexicans surrounded the Chiricahua, and in the light of a new morning the fighting resumed. The Mexicans drove the Apaches back from their rock parapets by rifle fire and then went among the boulders, fighting hand to hand. Terrazas cited Mata Ortiz and Mauricio Corredor, leader of the Tarahumara Indians, for gallantry during this fighting. Eventually only two warriors held out in a cave for over two hours, well armed and supplied with ammunition, ignoring all calls to surrender, even those by captured Chiricahuas, until they too were killed. The near-destruction of Victorio's band cost Terrazas only three men killed and ten wounded. Mexicans killed sixty-two warriors and sixteen women and children and scalped them for the bounty. Terrazas also took 68 prisoners, 120 horses, 38 mules, and 12 burros and rescued two captive Mexican boys. Not until one of the rescued boys pointed out the body did Terrazas realize that "one of those killed was Victorio."[12]

The campaign returned to Chihuahua City, feted as the heroes of Tres Castillos. Terrazas and Mata Ortiz, "looking worn and travel stained," followed a brass band and an "immense throng of people . . . mad with excitement" into the city. The Chiricahua prisoners, mounted on ponies and mules, came next. The pack trains and men followed, the men four abreast and "bloody and dirty in the extreme," bearing the seventy-eight scalps. Corredor received credit for shooting Victorio and carried his scalp, "tinged visibly with grey." The procession halted at a prison and all the prisoners "dismounted and were passed in." The next day all the smaller children and girls up to thirteen were given away, "taken into the best and wealthiest families in the city." The governor took two, a boy and a girl, while another "gentlemen" took three. Corredor was presented with a crimson jacket, a vest and pants of black doeskin trimmed with silver, and a white hat "covered with spangles." After their fiesta in the city, Mata Ortiz and his men, including the Janeros, returned home with their share of the scalp bounties, knowing they had once again defended themselves against the Apaches with no help from the national state.[13]

The Dead People

There were Chiricahua survivors from Tres Castillos. They regrouped under Nana and set off for the Sierra Madre on the western horizon, taking revenge as they could. Gathering the thirty or so warriors who had survived, Nana attacked a party of Mexicans on the road south of Carrizal. Chiricahuas killed nine Mexicans, including one who was riding in Victorio's saddle. His body they carefully mutilated, slashing it into pieces. Terrazas too was attacked and barely managed to escape, with only one of his ten-man escort. Reaching refuge in the mountains Nana led his people back across the border into the Mogollon Mountains for the winter. There he married his recently widowed niece, Guyan, to his *segundo* (second), Kaytennae. Returning to Mexico with the coming of spring, Nana and Kaytennae secreted their families in the mountains and set off on a raid for revenge. Pursued by Mata Ortiz, Nana crossed the border back to the American side and rampaged through the territory of New Mexico for two months. He and his warriors covered three thousand miles, fought the Americans seven different times, and attacked twelve ranches and towns. They killed five soldiers and thirty civilians, wounded at least twenty-five more, and ran off hundreds of head of horses and cattle. As he crossed back into Mexico Nana likely reflected that despite the amazing success of his raiding, he and his people were still *indeh*, the dead people.[14]

Juh's and Geronimo's groups soon joined Nana's in the Sierra Madre. Juh and Geronimo had lived at the San Carlos reservation for several years but grew "dissatisfied" with the Americans

over the quantity of rations and not being allowed to harvest mescal. While Nana raided New Mexico, an Apache named Noch-ay-
del-kline gained great influence on the reservation by teaching a
dance to commune with the spirits of the dead and return the dead
leaders to life. The Americans grew alarmed and moved to arrest
Noch-ay-del-kline on Cibicue Creek. Fighting broke out, killing
many soldiers and Apaches. Fearful of a general uprising the Americans rushed troops to San Carlos. This alarmed Juh and Geronimo, who headed for Mexico, where they were met with "rifle fire
from the *vecinos* of Janos."[15]

The Chiricahuas had many skirmishes with Mexicans through
the fall and into the winter, even as they traded at Janos and Casas
Grandes. The mountains were no longer a safe refuge as Mexican
troops gathered in strength, so many that the Chiricahuas "could
not hope to fight them successfully." By the spring Geronimo realized the Chiricahuas needed reinforcements. He knew Loco had
four hundred people in his *gò'tàh* at San Carlos, including seventy-five warriors. So Geronimo called a council with Nana and Juh,
where he expressed his fear that many of Loco's people would die
from the heat, suffer for food, and perish from bad water. All agreed
it would be better if Loco's group came to Mexico, although they
realized they would have to force Loco to go. While Juh negotiated with Terrazas near Janos, Geronimo led a small party of warriors to San Carlos, where they fell on Loco's camp, killing two
Apache scouts who came to investigate, and forced Loco's people
to abandon the reservation.[16]

Geronimo led the Chiricahuas southward, threatening to kill
anyone who refused to come. He struck into the mountains and
continued to move, wary of pursuing American soldiers. Yet Geronimo stopped for several days to allow a family to celebrate the all-
important Maiden or puberty ceremony. After two fights, including one on the Mexican side of the border where Geronimo did
not expect the Americans to follow, the Chiricahuas shook their
pursuers. A day or so later the Chiricahuas continued southward
along an arroyo west of Janos. As the main body of women and

children walked past the advance guard of warriors, who were taking a smoke break, Mexicans boiled out of the ravines along the arroyo "shooting down women and children right and left." As the families fled from the Mexican attack Geronimo rallied thirty warriors, dug rifle pits, and fired upon the Mexicans. After several abortive attacks the Mexicans withdrew at midday, but this proved to be a ruse, as Geronimo suspected, and attacks resumed. Geronimo was finally able to lead his warriors and a few women who had assisted them to rejoin their families after night fell, crawling through a grass fire set by the Mexicans. But the Mexican attack had killed seventy-eight and captured another twenty or thirty, mainly women and children, costing the Chiricahuas Geronimo led from San Carlos half of their families.[17]

Geronimo guided the survivors into Juh's stronghold in the mountains southwest of Casas Grandes. Loco's people joined Juh's and Nana's groups in a band under Juh and Geronimo, consisting not only of Chiricahuas but also Mescalero and Western Apaches, Navajos, and Mexican and American captives grown to manhood. Having lost in the Mexican attack much of what they had taken from San Carlos, Juh and Geronimo decided to trade at Casas Grandes. They led a third of the band to camp an hour east of the town and sought peace in the traditional manner by sending a woman. She arranged for a meeting outside the town between the Mexicans and Juh and Geronimo. The Mexicans agreed to allow the Indians to come into the town to trade, or gamble, or drink.[18]

In the past the two Chiricahua leaders had often sought peace at Casas Grandes in order to trade. The previous autumn they had met with Terrazas before going to the San Carlos reservation. So for two days Chiricahuas freely entered Casas Grandes, traded, drank at the cantina, and moved their camp to just outside the town walls. But Terrazas's orders were now to "capture or kill Juh and Geronimo." He led one column up the left side of the Río Casas Grandes, and Mata Ortiz led a column along the right bank to attack the Chiricahuas. Mata Ortiz's men fell upon the camp outside Casas Grandes early in the morning, killing or capturing

forty-three Chiricahuas, mainly women and children and including one of Geronimo's wives, and seizing all their horses. Inside the
town Mexicans barricaded the cantina door, trapping the Chiricahuas inside, and killed them, it was later claimed, with the fumes
from a bomb made of dried chile peppers. Juh and Geronimo were
in the town but realized their danger and managed to escape. As
Geronimo fled he taunted Terrazas, calling him "treacherous," and
Mata Ortiz, whom he called the "Fat Captain," saying he would kill
him not with bullets, or knives, or a lance, or arrows but with fire.[19]

With Terrazas searching the mountains of Chihuahua for them,
Juh and Geronimo chose to move away, splitting the band, with
each man leading one part. For the rest of the summer and into the
fall the Chiricahuas raided Sonora and the Americans before re-
uniting at the edge of the great canyon in the Sierra Madre. There
Juh and Geronimo decided to take their revenge on Mata Ortiz.
They moved the band near to Mata Ortiz's base at Galeana and
held a war dance. They then concealed most of the warriors in a
ravine along the road north of the town and sent a small party of
warriors to Mata Ortiz's *rancho* outside the town. Just after dawn
these men assaulted one of Mata Ortiz's *vaqueros* and ran off a
number of his cattle and horses. Mata Ortiz immediately set out in
pursuit with twenty-five *vecinos*. As he rode along the road Chiricahua warriors swarmed out of the ravine and attacked. Realizing he was outnumbered and outgunned, Mata Ortiz led his men
to the top of a low, conical hill where they dismounted and built
a low barricade of rocks. Chiricahuas quickly surrounded Mata
Ortiz. The older warriors under Juh, Geronimo, and Nana fired
upon Mata Ortiz's fighters as the younger warriors moved around
the other side of the hill and crept in among the Mexicans. Only
three Mexicans escaped the ensuing hand to hand fighting, which
killed twenty-one *vecinos* and Mata Ortiz. Later accounts insisted
Geronimo was good to his word and burned Mata Ortiz to death.[20]

Having taken their revenge Juh and Geronimo crossed back
over the Sierra Madre to avoid Chihuahuan retribution as Terrazas scoured the mountains. Their band again split, each leading

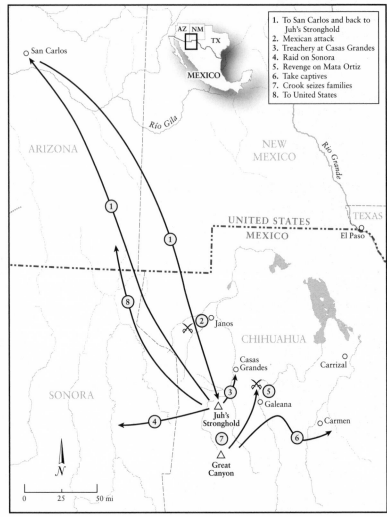

1. To San Carlos and back to
   Juh's Stronghold
2. Mexican attack
3. Treachery at Casas Grandes
4. Raid on Sonora
5. Revenge on Mata Ortiz
6. Take captives
7. Crook seizes families
8. To United States

San Carlos

Río Gila

ARIZONA

NEW
MEXICO

Río Grande

UNITED STATES
MEXICO

TEXAS

El Paso

Janos

CHIHUAHUA

Casas
Grandes

Carrizal

Galeana

SONORA

Juh's
Stronghold

Carmen

Great
Canyon

N

0   25   50 mi

Map 17. Geronimo, 1880–83

his own *gò'tàh*. Geronimo's group enjoyed success in raiding Sonora and the United States and also fought off Mexican troops who attacked their camp by rolling rocks down on top of them. Mexicans from Temosachic, however, attacked Juh's ranchería, killing two warriors, killing and capturing a number of women and children including Juh's wife, and wounding his favorite daughter Jacali. Juh tracked the raiders down and attacked them, killing six Mexicans, but losing another four irreplaceable warriors. Dissatisfied with Juh's leadership, most of the families opted to join Geronimo. Old, tired, and seeking quiet, Juh retreated further into the mountains.[21]

Geronimo now led around forty families and upwards of eighty warriors, not counting boys undergoing their apprenticeships. Many of these new families had members held captive in Chihuahua. To cement his hold on leadership Geronimo held a council with the family leaders. They decided to raid Chihuahua to take prisoners who could then be exchanged for Chiricahuas in a peace negotiation at Casas Grandes. Geronimo hid his people in several camps in the mountains and led about half of the warriors and apprentices into Chihuahua. They crossed the main road south of Galeana by walking on their heels to leave small holes in the dirt that did not look like human tracks. Geronimo then led them into the hills southeast of San Buenaventura, where they found evidence of old Apache camps. So contracted had their range become that these Chiricahuas did not recognize the signs of their ancestors' lives but thought they were from Lipan Apaches, who lived far to the east along the Rio Grande. They waited along the road south of El Carmen and captured six women, wives of soldiers at Casas Grandes. Geronimo released one old woman to tell the Mexicans he had captives he wished to trade. Then Geronimo suddenly learned that all the families left in the mountains were now held by American troops. He led the warriors and their captives back to the camps as quickly as he could.[22]

When Geronimo arrived at his base camp he discovered that American soldiers, guided by Apache scouts, including Chiricahuas, had crossed the border into Mexico. After several weeks of searching they had discovered Geronimo's camps and seized the families. Geronimo thus met in conference with the American leader, General Crook, who took Geronimo's captives away and returned them to the Mexicans. Yet so dangerous had Mexico become that after several meetings, Geronimo and the rest of the leaders agreed to return to San Carlos. While Loco and Nana and their rancherias accompanied Crook, Juh did not, refusing to go. Geronimo asked for more time to gather together his scattered people and allow the women to finish roasting mescal. Then he would meet the Americans at the border. For nearly a year Geronimo delayed, raiding the Mexicans for cattle and horses and making two final unsuccessful attempts to enter into peace at Casas Grandes in exchange for the return of the imprisoned Chiricahuas. He then crossed the border back into the United States driving his herd. Upon Geronimo's reaching San Carlos, General Crook took the herd away, despite Geronimo's protestations that the cattle and horses were not American but had been taken in war against Mexicans. Juh was not with him, having died from a heart attack while in the mountains of Mexico, now another of the *indeh*.[23]

Geronimo returned to the reservation, settled among the pines along Turkey Creek, and tried to live his life. This proved difficult for not only did the Americans take away Chiricahua captives and cattle; they also now interfered with Chiricahua families. Specifically they forbade the women making *tizwin* (corn beer) and the men drinking it. The Americans also sought to prevent men from punishing their wives for misbehavior and adultery by beating or mutilation: nose cutting. A year after Geronimo's return the American agent arrested a man for disciplining his wife, breaking her arm in two places. He then arrested another man for holding a *tizwin* drinking party. Chiricahua leaders, including Geronimo, held a council and decided to confront the American, after an all-night *tizwin* drink. They met the American armed and complained that they had kept the peace as they had promised General Crook. But never in their talks with the general had he ever told them they would not be able to live the way they wanted with their families. Old Nana limped out of the meeting after telling the American that he could not advise Nana how to treat women as the American was just a boy and Nana had been killing men when he was born. Chihuahua, another leader, was still intoxicated when he taunted the American, asking if he was going to put all the Chiricahuas in jail as they had been drinking *tizwin*. The American told the Chiricahua leaders he would ask General Crook for directions. For days the Chiricahuas waited for a reply as suspicions grew and rumors flew that soldiers were coming to arrest the leaders and would kill them if they resisted. Geronimo decided he had had enough. He abandoned the reservation for what would be his last time and headed for Mexico.[24]

Geronimo was not alone as he fled across the border for he had persuaded Naiche, Cochise's son, and Chihuahua that they too were in danger, and they accompanied him with their people, some four hundred in all. The Americans pursued in several parties, guided by Chiricahua scouts. The scouts attacked the refugees' camps on several occasions, ultimately taking some one hundred women and children as prisoners back to the reservation. For the rest of that summer and into the fall Chiricahua raiding parties struck across the border into the United States, often trying to recover their families. Chiricahua scouts guarded these families and led soldiers in pursuit of the raiders, who fell back into the Sierra Madre as winter approached.[25]

Mauricio Corredor heard of the Chiricahua return to his mountains and joined a party of volunteers led by Santana Pérez in late 1885. After two weeks of traversing broken tracks on foot the Mexicans spotted Apaches among the ridges and canyons. After sunset the volunteers marched through the frigid night so that at sunrise they were in a position to open fire on the Indians. After an hour of exchanging fire and insults with the Apaches the Mexicans realized these were not "wild or hostile Indians" but American scouts led by two officers, one of whom fell at the first volley. But during the hour-long firefight Corredor received "a bullet in the breast, the same traversing his body diagonally from right to left." So Corredor ended his time as a member of a community of violence, felled by an Apache bullet, as he probably always expected he would die, albeit one fired by a scout in American service.[26]

Many parties of Mexicans and Americans scoured the Sierra Madre in search of Geronimo that spring. So when he learned that General Crook had crossed the border and wanted to talk, Geronimo went to meet him. Geronimo reiterated that he had fled the reservation because Crook had ordered his arrest and imprisonment and that he was to be killed if he resisted. While Crook denied it, Geronimo later confided, "I firmly believe that he did issue orders for me to be put in prison, or to be killed in case I offered resistance." The general presented his ultimatum. If Geronimo did not surrender, Crook would give him a three-day start and then send all the soldiers and scouts after him and all his people. If Geronimo did surrender, their lives would be spared, though the men would have to be imprisoned for two years in the east before returning to their families. Chihuahua and most of the several hundred Chiricahuas preferred imprisonment to further warfare and agreed to accompany Crook back to San Carlos.[27]

Geronimo did not. Again fearing "treachery," he led Naiche, twenty warriors, fourteen women, and two boys back into the mountains of Mexico. American troops with Chiricahua scouts and Mexican soldiers and volunteers pursued Geronimo's little group. To avoid the daily skirmishes the group split up even further. Geronimo took six men and four women back across the border to wait for the troops to leave. Upon his group's return to Mexico "we attacked every Mexican we found, even if for no other reason than to kill." Geronimo and Naiche reunited the group, but the troops had not left and continued to trail and skirmish with the Chiricahuas. A small party of soldiers and scouts spotted Geronimo in the later summer of 1886. Two Chiricahua scouts approached Geronimo with a message from the new American general, Nelson Miles. If Geronimo and his men surrendered, they would be reunited with their families. At first Geronimo wanted to reject

the proposal, but his three half-brothers decided they would surrender to be with their families. Realizing he had lost the support
of his warriors, Geronimo surrendered to General Miles several
weeks later, accepting imprisonment far away from the Southwestern Borderlands, signaling the end of the Chiricahuas' existence as
a community of violence.[28]

The End for Janos

Janos's ending took longer, even though the Presidio of Janos had
ended its existence on April 1, 1858. Present for that last muster
was *Cabo* Santiago Brito, who would continue to live as a member of a community of violence. Brito had joined the company in
1849 as a *clarín* (trumpeter) at the age of fourteen. While family
legend would later have him a Yaqui Indian, his enlistment papers
showed Brito as a native and resident of Janos. As the trumpeter
he did not serve on active service until he was eighteen years old,
when he took part in an attack on rebellious Apaches in the Sierra
de Florida on May 2, 1853, capturing an Indian woman and twenty-seven horses. In November 1854, the same year he was admitted to the rank of soldier, he married Georgia Abalos, also a native of the presidio, and he enrolled his younger brother Tomás in
the presidial school in December. Padilla soon promoted Brito to
corporal, on January 1, 1855, and took *Cabo* Brito in pursuits of
Apache raiders in both 1855 and 1856, the last killing three warriors, rescuing a captive, and recovering five steers. Given his loyalty and competence, Brito likely rode with Padilla and Zuloaga
during the War of the Reform.[29]

His actions after the conservative defeat in 1859 are unclear, but
sometime during the next two decades Brito made his way to Pinos
Altos in New Mexico Territory, where he worked as a miner, mu-
leteer, and freighter. He posed for a picture in the 1870s, still with
his trumpet and carrying a pistol. Brito also remarried, this time to
a Mexican woman named Selma, and had two sons, Frank C. Brito born 1877 and Joe a year later. In April 1898 Frank was working as a dollar-a-day cowboy on the Circle Bar "way out beyond"

Silver City, New Mexico, when he received a message from his father to come back home at once. Frank rode the ten hours back to Pinos Altos, got there at midnight, and found the house all lit up. Santiago Brito came out and said he had news from Fort Bayard that "we were going to war with Spain." He said there was a call for cowboy volunteers and told Frank and his brother Joe to ride to Silver City and sign up. On May 6, 1898, Frank and Joe became privates in the New Mexican contingent of the 1st U.S. Volunteer Cavalry Regiment, which the papers were already calling the "Rough Riders." Frank and Joe were assigned to Captain George Curry's Troop H in Santa Fe and departed for the regimental training depot in San Antonio on May 8.

Much to the brothers' mortification, Troop H was one of the four left behind in Tampa, Florida, due to a lack of shipping, and they missed the battles and diseases of Cuba. Joe reenlisted in a volunteer regiment for service in the Philippines, where he was killed. Frank returned to southwestern New Mexico, where he served at a fireman, jailer, and deputy sheriff of Doña Ana County. He returned to active service in 1916 with a company of the New Mexico National Guard. Two of Frank's sons served in World War II, one of whom, named Santiago for his grandfather, fought in the D-Day invasion of Normandy, and four grandsons served in Vietnam. Frank Brito, son of Santiago Brito, died on April 22, 1973, the penultimate Rough Rider.[30]

The Britos' Mexican cousins did not fare as well. The end of conflict with the Apaches meant land in the borderlands was now valuable. The Mexican state surveyed and sold off "excess" or "unclaimed" land to oligarchs and foreigners. Janos lost rights to about three-fourths of its communal land. With the loss of land—territory depended upon for survival—communities felt they were now threatened and turned to violence as the basis of relations with the Mexican state, much as they had with Indians. Tomochic, a small mountain village, rose in rebellion in the early 1890s. Much like in the campaigns from the final days of the Apache wars, an expedition of federal troops supported by local armed *vecino* volunteers, led by Santana Pérez, set out to attack the town. Pérez and his men refused to fire on the *vecinos* of Tomochic, who had served with them on Indian campaigns.[31] Further attacks destroyed the community, but the resistance of Tomochic put communities like Janos into a conundrum.

Janos had previously defended "civilization" from "barbarians," but now it in turn was cast as "barbarian," inhibiting the march of "civilization." By the first decade of the twentieth century Janos found itself under direct assault by a 1905 land law. In protest Janos argued for its rights to municipal lands as a community "who suffered from the invasions of the barbarians, who our fathers fought."[32] While the people of Janos lost this legal battle, their experience and existence as a community of violence made Janeros "the ideal recruits to start" the Mexican Revolution of 1910–20.[33] However Janos as a community of violence, like all the *serrano* (mountain) communities of northwestern Chihuahua, ultimately lost the revolution.[34] The revolution resulted in a Mexican state able to generate enough power to make violence an unattractive strategy for communal survival in the borderlands and heralding the end for Janos.[35]

Chiricahua Exile

While Janos's end resulted from a convoluted set of connections and confrontations with the rising Mexican state, the Chiricahuas' end was much simpler and more brutal: separation from Janos via exile away from the borderlands. Geronimo's and Naiche's *gò'tàh* was aboard a train heading east almost immediately after their surrender. The day prior to Geronimo's departure Americans surrounded those Chiricahuas on the reservation, disarmed them, loaded them onto wagons, and drove them ninety miles to a railroad. They were then sent east to Fort Marion, Florida. Numbering just over four hundred, they included the scouts whose depredations while on the hunt for Geronimo—killing cattle, murdering and robbing Mexicans, burning sugar cane fields—gave the Americans little faith that Chiricahuas would not return to raiding into Mexico, living as a community of violence, if given the chance. Geronimo's group did not join those at Fort Marion. The Americans stopped his train in San Antonio, Texas. The territorial governments of both Arizona and New Mexico wished to bring charges against him, charges that would certainly result in a death sentence. General Miles had thus gotten Geronimo out of the territories with some haste. For over a month Geronimo anxiously awaited his fate. The Americans finally decided he and his warriors would got to Fort Pickens, Florida, while their women and children would go on to Fort Marion on the other side of the state.[36]

This separation was bitter for Geronimo as it broke the conventions of his surrender. After six months the Americans relented and allowed the families of those men at Fort Pickens to join them. A year after that Geronimo rejoined the Chiricahuas, now at Mount Vernon Barracks, Alabama. For seven years Chiricahuas did their best to live in the low, hot, and muggy climate of the American Southeast, suffering badly from tuberculosis. They were then relocated once again, this time to Fort Sill, Oklahoma, numbering barely 350 persons. Finally in 1912, twenty-six years after their surrender and exile, the Chiricahuas were allowed to return to the Southwestern Borderlands to the Mescalero Reservation in southeastern New Mexico. Seventy-eight families elected to stay at Fort Sill, and 183 chose to go and live with their Mescalero cousins. Geronimo was not among them, having died in 1909.[37]

Geronimo settled into Fort Sill, farming and raising cattle, which he especially enjoyed. But some Chiricahuas held him responsible for their plight, saying "we would not be in our present trouble if not for men like him." It was true, but it was also unfair. Geronimo was simply a member of a community that related to Mexicans via violence. He carried reminders of this existence in the form of a suite of wounds: a bullet in the right thigh, a saber scar below the left knee, a scar on the head from a musket butt, a scar just below the left eye, a bullet wound in the left side, and one in the back. He had killed many Mexicans, by his own account. Decades later he still had "no love for the Mexicans," considering them "always treacherous and malicious." If he were young, Geronimo claimed, and followed the warpath, it would lead once again to Mexico.[38]

A few years prior to his death Geronimo attended the World's Fair in Saint Louis, Missouri. At first he did not want to go, but the chance to make needed money for his family from selling photos and giving autographs changed his mind. With his "keeper" and guards Geronimo wandered the midway, seeing sword fighters, an escape artist, a magic show, and a dancing bear. He rode the ferris wheel, went into a fun house, and watched glass blowers. He also noticed "little brown people" who, like him, had been taken prisoner by the U.S. Army. Geronimo enjoyed his time at the fair, but his final remembrance of it showed him as a member of a community of violence to the end. "During all the time I was at the Fair no one tried to harm me in any way. Had this been among the Mexicans I am sure I should have been compelled to defend myself often."[39]

| Conclusion

Borderland Communities of Violence

This work posits the centrality of violence in relations within and between borderland communities. Violence was how these communities established, maintained, or changed their relationships. Violence often drove the communities to peaceful dealings — negotiations, trade, treaties — that had the possibility of future violence looming over them, as these contacts between them could lead to acts of violence, which in turn might carry the potential of future peace. The assessment is focused on two communities, Chiricahua Apaches and the Janos presidio, with communities being broadly defined as sets of relationships among families and individuals to ensure cooperation for survival. Chiricahua and Janos were in a borderland where no one polity had an enduring monopoly on the legitimate use of violence.

Violence was therefore at the center of those relationships by which both Janos and Chiricahua made their communities, via the incorporation of the original Indians of region as wives or into the caste system and then via captives from each other, to the extent that the two communities were likely genetically related. Violence created families by turning boys into men through participation in campaigns and raids, which led ultimately to marriage. Violence loomed over the provisioning and security of these families, creating and maintaining the necessary status. When rationing ended, both communities sought to secure themselves via violent acts of revenge and retaliation, even as trades and exchanges continued sporadically. This placed both Chiricahua and Janos into a security dilemma in which actions they took to secure themselves only caused greater insecurity, finally leading to the end of both as communities of violence.

Borderlands and Communities of Violence

As noted at the start of this work, the study of borderlands is no stranger to violence. What place does the concept of communities of violence have in our understanding of borderlands as both local places and global processes? As a place, the Southwestern Borderlands have traditionally been represented by the concept of the Spanish Borderlands: those parts of the United States from California to Florida that were once claimed by Spain. This conceptualization placed the borderlands into United States history, however.[1]

Questioning this characterization, scholars have increasingly viewed the Southwestern Borderlands as a transnational space. Ramón Gutiérrez and Elliot Young have recently called for the "writing of transnational history" in the borderlands that would focus on "transnations" and explore the tensions that overflow the boundaries of the nation-state. Ultimately a transnational Southwestern Borderlands history "would pay attention to both relations between nation-states and more multi-polar relations among cultural groups."[2] Cultural groups are in many ways communities as defined in this work: sets of increasingly extended kinship ties or affinities with shared ethnic identities, familiar languages, and common moral and material practices. Culture is expressed in those hundreds of visual, olfactory, sensory, and auditory cues by which members of communities determine with whom they are expected to cooperate and reciprocate and with whom they are not. Recent research notes that the interaction of multiple cultural or ethnic groups in the short and near terms lowers the willingness to trust, ability to cooperate, and capability to reciprocate between the groups, causing friction among them.[3]

Under certain conditions, such as those found in borderlands where no group has a legitimate monopoly of power, this friction can lead to violence. Young, writing with Samuel Truett, noted that "when groups met in the borderlands, the encounter was sometimes peaceful, often violent, always contested."[4] Thus transnational scholars of the Southwestern Borderlands need to take into account the reality that relations between cultural groups, or communities, may well be configured by violence or the potentiality of violence, hence the search for a sense of security. Borderlands as transnational places create spaces for communities of violence. So violence will remain a critical part of the study of the borderlands as a place.

Borderlands have also been seen as process, with global implications. Jeremy Adelman and Stephen Aron attempted to describe a borderland process for North America, positing a shift from frontier to borderland to border. By frontier Adelman and Aron meant "a meeting place of peoples in which geographic and cultural borders were not clearly defined." Rising European imperial rivalry created borderlands, "the contested borders between colonial domains," conflicts over which "shaped the peculiar and contingent character of frontier relations." Borders came to be when states claimed "exclusive dominions over all territories" within an international boundary.[5]

Commentators on Adelman and Aron's article were quick to point out that the transitions from frontier to borderland to border were more often than not accompanied by violence. Evan Haefeli noted that borderlands "were actually *more* destructive and less accommodating" than the frontiers that preceded them.[6] John R. Wunder and Pekka Hämäläinen found Adelman and Aron depicted borderlands as "eerie lethal places."[7] Adelman and Aron's response to their commentators acknowledged the role of violence and "that Indians did not triumph in their struggle against Europeans."[8] Violence thus plays a key role in borderlands as a global process of ever increasing domination of native peoples by imperial and then national states. Relations between and among settler and indigenous individuals, families, and communities, shaped by violence, lie at the heart of borderlands as a global process.

Fittingly it is James Brooks—who opened the path so many borderlands works have followed, including this one—who has once again led the way. Brooks has begun to explore "the predicament of hybridity" in the identities of individuals, families, and communities in nineteenth-century pastoral borderlands at the edges of settler imperialism and nationalism across the globe. His individuals include Shamil Basayev, leader of Chechen resistance to Russian expansion in the Caucasus from 1834 to 1859, and Andrés Martínez, a New Mexican captured by Apaches and traded to Kiowas but fully accepted by them and named Andele. The family Brooks explored was that of James Connolly, who would be the governor of Vancouver and elevated to the nobility, and his wife Amelia Douglas, who came from the mixed community of Home Guard Cree, allies and auxiliaries of the Hudson Bay Company in western Canada. Brooks also explored the Griqua of South Africa, a mixed community that formed north of the Orange River, herding and raiding cattle, taking captives, and selling slaves.[9] Brooks later added various South American indigenous peoples—Pehuenche, Mapuche, Tehuelche, Araucanian—who also sought to form their own mixed communities on the pastoral borderlands of the Pampas in the first half of the nineteenth century.[10] From a community of violence perspective, the predicament faced by all these hybrid identities—individual, family, community—is that they "came to be under conditions of intercultural conflict or warfare."[11] Violence, in other words, dominated the relations among and between these communities. Even when viewed as a global process, borderlands still have a place for communities of violence.

Borderland Communities of Violence

In his studies Brooks proceeds "on the assumption that our long century just ended has become, for the 21st century, an analytical obstacle."[12] This insight may explain some of our present-day concerns and uncertainties, for communities of violence remain in the Southwestern Borderlands, and while their forms are quite different, their functions are eerily, historically, familiar. These communities of violence may be called drug trafficking organizations, transnational criminal organizations, mafias, *narcotraficantes*, or cartels, but they are still based upon groups of families, sets of relationships, a defined if indeterminate territory, and a need for cooperation. Today's communities of violence go by the names the Arellano Felix Organization, the Sinaloa Cartel, Beltran Leyva Organization, Los Zetas, the Gulf Cartel, La Familia Michoacana, and the Carrillo Fuentes Organization. These communities spread across the international border and include drug growers, drug producers, traffickers, smugglers, distributors, gang members, and consumers, in addition to financial officers, *sicarios* (hitmen), chiefs of the all-important *plazas* (smuggling corridors), and cartel leaders. The communities further extend to corrupted officials, co-opted law enforcement, intimidated media, and fearful citizens on both sides of the border.[13]

The region around the border between the United States and Mexico is still a borderland where neither nation state has a legitimate monopoly on the use of violence across the entire region. International law and the imperatives of sovereignty limit what either state can do across the border and thus in the borderland. In addition, at the geopolitical level, the complete security of the border is not an imperative for either the United States or Mexico. The United States needs the Southwest to ensure access to the Pacific Ocean and provide a buffer for the bread basket and transportation hub of the Greater Mississippi Valley. For Mexico, the northern border too serves as a buffer zone for its central core around Mexico City, but the more power the Mexican state must project beyond the core, the less cost-effective control of the northern border becomes.[14] Violence in the Southwestern Borderlands thus remains useable and useful.

Violence keeps the drug supply chain moving from production areas along transportation routes to the smuggling corridors and the distribution nodes beyond. Violence and the threat of violence intimidate and co-opt local authorities and civilian populations along the supply chain, keeping it moving. Violence and the threat of violence provide the "lubricant" that makes the supply chain function. The illicit transfer of the product means the contractual basis of property rights is not available. Deals, agreements, and understandings between money men, producers, transporters, smugglers, and distributers are enforced not by lawyers but by gunmen. When violence is used by the cartels it is spectacularly brutal, and the results are made public to send the message that agreements must be kept or consequences will be suffered. Violence is also the means by which cartels increase their market share, since the illicit nature of the product's movement from producer to user removes the usual ways of reducing price or increasing quality of product, and no lawsuits can be filed over unfair practices. So violence is used to take over competitors' supply chains, especially the lucrative smuggling corridors. Again, violence used in this pursuit is spectacularly brutal to send the message of a true hostile takeover.[15] Violence is thus the means whereby today's communities of violence establish, maintain, advance and change relations within communities and between themselves, the state, and civil society.

What, then, does an understanding of historical communities of violence tell us about potential solutions to today's communities of violence? The critical recognition is that today's communities of violence are as tightly bound in a cycle of revenge and retaliation as were our historical comparisons. The spiraling violence from killings and counterkillings forced the Mexican state's hand in 2005 and led to the deployment of federal military and, increasingly, federal police forces to border cities. This placed the cartels into their version of the security dilemma. If they continued to operate, they would be vulnerable to federal forces. But if they scaled back their operations, they would be vulnerable to takeovers by other cartels. Hence the cartels increased their violence, to ensure that their competitors could not take advantage of the federal presence, to try to take advantage of it themselves to take over more territory, and to establish a relationship with the federal forces via their preferred means: violence. Over the five years from 2005 through 2009 the deaths caused by drug-related violence in Mexico rose from 1,537 killed in 2005 to 2,221 killed in 2006, 2,673 killed in 2007, 5,630 killed in 2008, and 9,635 killed in 2009. Most of those killed were members of the cartels, and many were killed in the northern border states.[16] At the time of this writing in mid-2010 it appears that the cartels have effectively used violence to establish a relationship with the local, state, and federal governments that gives the cartels the initiative in the borderlands, if not outright control.[17]

What a historical understanding of communities of violence suggests is that the cycle of violence has to be disrupted by making violence less useful, less attractive, and by ensuring that potential punishments outweigh possible rewards. Mexico and the United States must strive to maintain a monopoly on the legitimate use of violence in the borderlands, since, as Steven Pinker has noted, "adjudication by an armed authority" is the best general violence-reduction technique known.[18] But it is legitimacy that will be key. Mexico is attempting to rebuild and reintroduce police forces and reform its legal institutions, even as it learns to be a multiparty democracy.[19] The United States needs to address the growing perception among its own citizens that it is unwilling to secure the border, even as it must work to reform older border and enforcement policies.[20] It is critical that the United States and Mexico work as partners in the borderlands, for no use of force, enforcement, or policy changes can be legitimate as long as both sides of the border can blame each other for the problem.[21]

In the end violence will remain instrumental in the streams of human existence, especially in places where no one has a legitimate monopoly on its use, such as borderlands. Borderlands too will remain. As twentieth-century structures of governance come under the pressures of globalization, new borderlands, sometimes called ungoverned or undergoverned spaces, are appearing as cracks on the geopolitical surface of the globe. In the seams of poorly defined and poor states, at the junctions of vague borders, in blighted urban areas or suburban slums—all borderlands around and between state sovereignties and traditional tenets—new communities of violence come into existence, whether we call them smugglers, mafias, militants, militias, paramilitaries, terrorists, or "violent non-state actors."[22] We will find communities of violence in borderlands yesterday, today, and tomorrow.

| Acknowledgments

This book has had a long gestation period and I have many people to thank; my sincerest apologies if I have forgotten any. I can trace the germ of the idea back to an initial unsuccessful thesis proposal for Dan Tyler at Colorado State University. He was able to see that I did not know enough to pursue the idea. My pursuit of this knowledge landed me eventually at Northern Arizona University, where one raw spring day I walked into Susan Deeds's office as a potential graduate student and walked out as her student. Anyone who knows her knows the magnitude of that shift.

In Flagstaff I enjoyed the challenge and companionship of a wide-ranging graduate cohort: Cynthia Bruner, Laura Camp, Mike Egan, Toby Green, Tracy Goode, Kristin Mann, Dave Nesheim, Gabe Rhodes, Victoria Spenser, and John Westerlund. My committee at NAU—Susan Deeds, Karen Vieira Powers, Sanjay Joshi, Eric Meeks, and Irene Matthews—oversaw the dissertation that provided the foundation for much of this book.

Upon completion of my PhD the state of the job market for historians, combined with my strong desire to remain in the Rocky Mountain West, led me to take a job with the federal government as a historian. I have to thank Tom Trask, Gene Haase, Tom Fuller, and Patrick Murray, who as my supervisors were accepting of my academic pursuits. I also have to thank my colleagues Patricia Goude, Scott Johnson, John Lacomia, and John Baker.

Since I am employed outside the academy no august foundation provided monetary assistance for research, no learned society ensured a place to write, and no kind chair or dean allowed me time off from other duties to complete the manuscript. This has been a work of personal persistence.

That is not to say that I did not have help. James Brooks, David Weber, and Ross Frank all gave encouragement and inspiration at critical moments when I was ready to give it all up. Cynthia Radding arranged for me to have a position at the Latin American and Iberian Institute that afforded me the access necessary to complete the final research for the book. Sam Truett listened to my ideas, selflessly shared his own, provided crucial insights, and bought beers, all contributing to the completion of this work. Brian DeLay and his family were always welcoming and always supportive. Karl Jacoby was kindly interested in my concepts and unselfishly shared his own.

A chance meeting with Pekka Hämäläinen on a cold, snowy morning in Denver led to the book in its current form. Pekka was unstinting in his critiques, unwavering in his honesty, and unquestionable in his support. He directed me to Matthew Bokovoy at the University of Nebraska Press, who saw far better than I could the potential of the manuscript and was willing to take a risk for it to be the inaugural volume in a new series. I also have to thank the press's two readers for the insight their fresh eyes provided. Sally Antrobus and Sabrina Stellrecht worked to get the manuscript in shape, for which I am grateful.

As I was in the process of completing the manuscript I relocated to Colorado's Front Range. Here I discovered a community that runs from the cañon to the open space to the brewery, featuring hikes, dogs, skis, bikes, and craft beer. I am humbled by how I have been welcomed into this community, whose inhabitants remind me every day that making a community is hard work.

I also need to thank my family. My wife, Gretchen Merten,

regularly got me outside into the Arizona, New Mexico, and Colorado high country to hike, run, backpack, bike, snowshoe, ski, or snowboard. Whatever sanity I have left I owe to her love and insistence. And I remain adamant that she is the smart one. I have to thank my sister Ann Doyle, her husband Tom, and their children Bryan and Caitlyn for always welcoming me into their home and putting up with their wayward and slightly weird brother-in-law/uncle. My father, Gary Blyth, not only taught me how to ride and shoot but also read every word of the manuscript.

Sadly my mother, Carolyn Blyth, died as the manuscript was entering the initial editorial process. She fought a brave and dignified battle with Parkinson's for nearly a decade. It was she who really made me a historian. Words cannot express my loss, but I have provided some seventy-five thousand of them in memoriam.

Lance R. Blyth
Cheyenne Cañon
Colorado

| Notes

Preface

   1. Nirenberg, *Communities of Violence*, 127, 9.

1. Communities of Violence

   1. Griffen, *Apaches at War and Peace*, 237–39; Sweeney, *Mangas Coloradas*, 218–25.

   2. Geronimo, *His Own Story*, 75–83; Debo, *Geronimo*, 13, 34–40; Sweeney, "'I Had Lost All.'"

   3. Hoja de Servicio, Teniente don Baltasar Padilla, Janos, December 31, 1851, Janos Collection, 39 reels of microfilm, Cline Library, Northern Arizona University, reel 33, 1851 (hereafter cited as JC reel:year).

   4. As noted, for my concept of communities of violence I am indebted to Nirenberg, *Communities of Violence*.

   5. Langfur, "Moved by Terror," 258. White's *Middle Ground*, esp. 75–82, is the now classic description of these processes in North America, but see Herman's "Romance on the Middle Ground," noting that the middle ground "is a brutal place, a place of constant warfare, violence, and disease" (280).

   6. Brooks, *Captives and Cousins*, 35.

   7. Gearhard, *North Frontier*, 229–33. To avoid anachronistic national descriptors and in despair of any better term, "Hispanic" is used in this work to describe those people in the Americas who descended from people of the Spanish and Basque-speaking areas of the Iberian Peninsula.

8. Opler, "Chiricahua Apache," 401. Since the membership in these bands was very fluid, and in the interest of clarity, in this work I define members of all three bands as Chiricahua unless band identification plays a role.

9. Berreby, *Us and Them.*

10. Bowles, "Group Competition," 1569–72, and see the comment by Robert Boyd, "The Puzzle of Human Sociality," 1555–56; Ridley, *Origins of Virtue*, 149–71.

11. See Wade, *Before the Dawn*, 8–9, 84–86, 148–58; Keeley, *War Before Civilization*; LeBlanc, with Register, *Constant Battles*; and, for the century just past, Ferguson, *War of the World.*

12. Parker, "Toward an Understanding." For another understanding of borderland processes see Adelman and Aaron, "From Borderlands to Borders," and the responses in *American Historical Review* 104 (1999): 1222–39.

13. Opler, *An Apache Life-Way.*

14. Lane, "Economic Consequences of Organized Violence," 404. Baretta and Markoff, "Civilization and Barbarism," 589–93 relied upon Lane's insight, and Donna J. Guy and Thomas E. Sheridan, "On Frontiers: The Northern and Southern Edges of the Spanish Empire in the Americas," in Guy and Sheridan, eds., *Contested Ground*, 10–12, relied upon Baretta and Markoff's. The concept ultimately descends from Weber, *Theory of Social and Economic Organization*, 154.

15. Pinker, *The Blank Slate*, 318–29.

16. I have drawn on the essays on violence by Göran Aijmer, Jon Abbink, Anton Blok, and Nigel Rapport in Aijmer and Abbink, eds., *Meanings of Violence*, quotes on 23, 24, 8. Eisner, "Uses of Violence," notes that "violence is *an instrument* that serves to achieve specific goals" (44, emphasis in original).

17. Griffen, *Apaches at War and Peace.*

18. Brooks, *Captives and Cousins.*

19. Barr, *Peace Came in the Form of a Woman.*

20. Hämäläinen, *Comanche Empire.*

21. Blackhawk, *Violence Over the Land.*

22. DeLay, *War of a Thousand Deserts.*

23. Jacoby, *Shadows at Dawn.*

24. Farmer, "Borderlands of Brutality," notes that much of the work has focused on Native American violence.

25. Part of the Janos archive is described at http://www.lib.utexas.edu/benson/Mex_ Archives/Janos.html.

26. For the use of oral traditions as an archive see Echo-Hawk, "Ancient History in the New World," and Colwell-Chanthaphonh, "Western Apache

Oral Histories." For cautionary notes see Mason, "Archaeology and Native North American Oral Traditions," and Schaafsma, "Truth Dwells in the Deeps."

27. Pérez de Villagrá, *A History of New Mexico*, 149, reports "Moorish and Christian games," understood as a performance of *Moros y cristianos* by Simmons, *The Last Conquistador*, 117–18, among others. This presentation follows the script in Lucero-White Lea, *Literary Folklore*, 107–12, and draws the quotes from Espinoza de Luján, *Los Moros y Cristianos*, 16–24.

28. Bishko, "The Spanish and Portuguese Reconquest," 396–455. For a recent synopsis of the Reconquista see Tyerman, *God's War*, 650–73.

29. Espinoza de Luján, *Los Moros y Cristianos*, 1–3; Lucero-White Lea, *Literary Folklore*, 21–25; Harris, *Aztecs, Moors, and Christians*, 61; Martin, *Governance and Society in Colonial Mexico*, 40, 100, 104, 108, 118.

30. Lamadrid, *Hermanitos Comanchitos*, 21–26.

31. For an engaging narration of the conquest of New Mexico and its rebellious result see Roberts, *The Pueblo Revolt*.

32. Simmons, *The Last Conquistador*, 134–41.

33. Pérez de Villagrá, *Historia de la Nueva México, 1610*, 266.

34. Simmons, *The Last Conquistador*, 142–44.

35. Simmons, *The Last Conquistador*, 144–46. Kessell, *Pueblos, Spaniards*, 41–43, suggests that Oñate may not have carried out the mutilations as ordered, but instead showed clemency, possibly at the last minute in a bit of "conquest theater," and pardoned the Indians in the hope of reconciliation, a vain hope as it turned out.

36. Vazquez de Coronado's Letter to the King, October 20, 1541, in Flint and Flint, eds., *Documents of the Coronado Expedition*, 319–20; in the same volume, see The Relación de la Jornada de Cíbola, Pedro de Castañeda de Nájera's Narrative, 1560s, 408; and The Relación del Suceso, 1540s, 501.

37. "Origin of the Apache Indians," in Geronimo, *His Own Story*, 49–50. For other tellings of this tale see "The Moccasin Game for Day or Night" in Opler, *Myths and Tales of the Chiricahua*, 23–27, and "The Gambling Game for Night and Day," in Hoijer and Opler, *Chiricahua and Mescalero Apache Texts*, 14–16.

38. For an overview of the debates around the migration route for and time of arrival of Apaches in the Southwest, see the papers in Wilcox and Masse, eds., *The Protohistoric Period in the North American Southwest*, especially David Wilcox, "The Entry of Athapaskans into the American Southwest: The Problem Today," 213–56; David A. Gregory, "Western Apache Archeology: Problems and Approaches," 257–74; David M. Brugge, "Comments

on Athabaskans and Sumas," 282–90; and Curtis F. Schaafsma, "Early Apacheans in the Southwest: A Review," 291–320. Perry, *Western Apache Heritage*, 101–75, and Towner, *Defending the Dinétah*, 193–216, provide recent interpretations.

39. Nancy P. Hickerson, "The War for the Southern Plains, 1500–1700," in Flint and Flint, eds., *Coronado Expedition*, 187, emphasis in original; Donald J. Blakeslee et al., "Bison Hunters of the Llano in 1541: A Panel Discussion," in Flint and Flint, eds., *Coronado Expedition*, 178.

40. Spielmann, "Interaction among Nonhierarchical Societies," 11.

41. "The Child of the Water," in Hoijer and Opler, *Chiricahua and Mescalero Apache Texts*, 8–9.

42. "The Birth of Child of the Water and the Slaying of the Monsters," in Opler, *Myths and Tales of the Chiricahua*, 10.

43. For Child of the Water see "The Birth of Child of the Water and the Slaying of the Monsters," in Opler, *Myths and Tales of the Chiricahua*, 2–14; and "The Child of the Water," "The Killing of the Giant," "The Killing of the Bull," "The Killing of the Eagles," and "The Killing of the Prairie Dogs," in Hoijer and Opler, *Chiricahua and Mescalero Apache Texts*, 5–13. For the variations among these see Opler, "Three Types of Variations."

44. Anderson, *Indian Southwest*, discusses "Apacheanization," while Spicer, *Cycles of Conquest*, 281–333, considers the "Spanish Program."

45. Reedy-Maschner and Maschner, "Marauding Middlemen," 707–9.

46. Maschner and Reedy-Maschner, "Raid, Retreat, Defend," 22–23.

47. Daly and Wilson, *Homicide*, 221–51, explores this phenomenon.

48. McMurtry, *Oh What a Slaughter* 6; Barash, "Targets of Aggression."

49. Boehm, *Blood Revenge*, 54.

50. Chirot and McCauley, *Why Not Kill Them All?*, 31–33.

51. Gat, "Human Motivational Complex, Part II," 78–80, provides a good short discussion of the security dilemma.

52. Vandervort, *Indian Wars*.

2. Refugees and Migrants

1. Forbes, *Apache, Navaho, and Spaniard*, 178–81.

2. Gutiérrez, *When Jesus Came*, 101–8.

3. Order of governor and captain-general of El Parral, Parral, September 24, 1680, in Hackett, *Revolt of the Pueblo Indians*, 1:185–66, cvi–cix.

4. Naylor and Polzer, eds., *Presidio and Militia*, 528, n. 1; Griffen, *Indian Assimilation*, 88.

5. Antonio de Otermín to Francisco Ramírez, alcalde mayor of Casas Grandes, El Paso, October 9, 1681, in Hackett, *Revolt of the Pueblo Indians*, 2:154–55.

6. Forbes, *Apache, Navaho, and Spaniard*, 200–3; Francisco Ramírez de Salazar to the Marqués de la Laguna, viceroy of New Spain, Casas Grandes, April 14, 1685, in Naylor and Polzer, *Presidio and Militia*, 528–29.

7. Ramírez to the viceroy, Casas Grandes, April 14, 1685, and Roque Madrid to the governor, Casas Grandes, October 3, 1684, in Naylor and Polzer, *Presidio and Militia*, 529–30 and 507–8, respectively.

8. Ramírez to the viceroy, Casas Grandes, April 14, 1685; Madrid to the governor, Casas Grandes, October 3, 1684; and Declaration of Roque Madrid, El Paso, April 12, 1685, in Naylor and Polzer, *Presidio and Militia*, 530–31, 508, and 542, respectively.

9. Ramírez to the viceroy, Casas Grandes, April 14, 1685, in Naylor and Polzer, *Presidio and Militia*, 531–32.

10. Griffen, *Indian Assimilation*, 19–20; Thomas H. Naylor, "Athapaskans They Weren't: The Suma Rebels Executed at Casas Grandes in 1685," in Wilcox and Masse, *Protohistoric Period*, 276.

11. Naylor and Polzer, *Presidio and Militia*, 548–49.

12. Ramírez to the viceroy, Casas Grandes, April 14, 1685, in Naylor and Polzer, *Presidio and Militia*, 530–31.

13. Don Juan de Oñate, San Juan Bautista, February 23, 1599, in Hammond and Rey, eds., *Don Juan de Oñate*, 398–400.

14. Schaafsma, *Apaches de Navajo*, 231; Perry, *Western Apache Heritage*, 164–65, 174; "Killer-of-Enemies at Picuris" and "Killer-of Enemies at Taos and His Departure," in Opler, *Myths and Tales of the Jicarilla*, 100–109.

15. Kessell, *Kiva, Cross, and Crown*, 136–37. Memorial of Fray Francisco de Velasco, April 9, 1609; Order of Viceroy Velasco; Governor Peralta's Instructions, all in Hammond and Rey, *Don Juan de Oñate*, 1094–95, 1059, and 1089, respectively.

16. "Killer-of-Enemies, with Coyote's Assistance, Gets the Cattle Away from the Crows," in Opler, *Myths and Tales of the Chiricahua*, 15–18.

17. Kessell, *Kiva, Cross, and Crown*, 137–38; Brooks, *Captives and Cousins*, 48–51; Benavides, *Memorial of Fray Alonso*, 56–57.

18. "The Foolish People and the White Men" and "The Foolish People Run Away," in Hoijer and Opler, *Chiricahua and Mescalero Apache Texts*, 36–37.

19. Benavides, *Memorial of Fray Alonso*, 42–43; Forbes, *Apache, Navaho, and Spaniard*, 117–18, 134.

20. Worcester, "Spread of Horses," 226–27; Forbes, "Appearance of the

Mounted Indian," 200–1; "The Foolish People and the Horse," in Hoijer and Opler, *Chiricahua and Mescalero Apache Texts*, 37. See Clark, *They Sang For Horses*, for the complete incorporation of the horse into Apache culture.

21. Forbes, *Apache, Navaho, and Spaniard*, 162–63, 166–67, 181.

22. "White-Painted Woman Instructs the Chiricahua in the Puberty Rite," in Opler, *Myths and Tales of the Chiricahua*, 15; Report and Relation of the New Conversions by Eusebio Francisco Kino, 1710, in Bolton, ed., *Spanish Explorations*, 451. To avoid a multitude of names, I use "Chiricahua" throughout to refer to those Apaches living in the areas associated with the three historic Chiricahua bands, the Eastern, Central, and Southern. See Opler, "Chiricahua Apache," 401–2.

23. Fray Nicolás to Francisco Xavier, El Paso, January 30, 1682, in Hackett, *Revolt of the Pueblo Indians*, 2:367; Forbes, *Apache, Navaho, and Spaniard*, 190–91.

24. Forbes, *Apache, Navaho, and Spaniard*, 209.

25. Juan Fernández de la Fuente to Diego de Vargas, Janos, 16 April 1691, in Kessell and Hendricks, eds., *By Force of Arms*, 65–66.

26. "The Adventures of the Foolish People on a Raid," in Opler, *Myths and Tales of the Chiricahua*, 86.

27. Opler, *An Apache Life-Way*, 332–33.

28. Letter of Antonio de Otermín, March 29, 1682, quoted in Forbes, *Apache, Navaho, and Spaniard*, 191.

29. Fernández to Vargas, Janos, 16 April 1691; Vargas to the Conde de Galve, El Paso, 14 August 1691; and Vargas to Fernández, n.p., 9 September 1691, all in Kessell and Hendricks, *By Force of Arms*, 66–67, 77, and 84–85, respectively.

30. Vargas to the Conde de Galve, El Paso, 4 October 1691, in Kessell and Hendricks, *By Force of Arms*, 91–92.

31. Letter of Juan Fernández de la Fuente, December 12, 1691, quoted in Forbes, *Apache, Navaho, and Spaniard*, 230–31; "The Gahe Who Fought the Mexican Soldiers," in Opler, *Myths and Tales of the Chiricahua*, 78.

32. Reports of Juan Fernández de la Fuente, July 26 and 31, 1692, cited in Forbes, *Apache, Navaho, and Spaniard*, 234.

33. Report of Juan Fernández de la Fuente, August 14, 1692, cited in Forbes, *Apache, Navaho, and Spaniard*, 235; Residents of Sonora to the viceroy, San Juan Bautista, February 6, 1693, in Hackett, ed., *Historical Documents* 2:294–95.

34. Fernández to Don Pedro de Almazán, Janos, September 18, 1693, in Hackett, *Historical Documents*, 2:372–73; Moorhead, *The Presidio*, 22–23.

35. Diego García de Valdes to Maestre de Campo don Joseph Francisco Marín, Parral, September 26, 1693, Raphael de Ibarguen to Joseph Francisco Marín, Parral, September 20, 1693; and Marín to Conde de Galve, Parral, September 30, 1693, all in Hackett, *Historical Documents*, 2:378–79, 382–83, and 399–401, respectively.

36. Marín to Conde de Galve, Parral, September 30, 1693, in Hackett, *Historical Documents*, 2:394–95; "White-Painted Woman Instructs the Chiricahua in the Puberty Rite," in Opler, *Myths and Tales of the Chiricahua*, 15.

37. This draws upon the campaign report of Captain Fernández translated as "A Campaign against the Pimas, 1695," in Naylor and Polzer, *Presidio and Militia*, 589–96, 641–48. For the Chiricahua division of time see Opler, *An Apache Life-Way*, 354–55.

38. Anderson, *Indian Southwest*, 105–6; Madrid to the governor, Casas Grandes, October 3, 1684, in Naylor and Polzer, *Presidio and Militia*, 507; Forbes, *Apache, Navaho, and Spaniard*, 191. For the original inhabitants see Schaafsma, "Ethnohistoric Groups."

39. Lorenz and Smith, "Distribution of Four Founding mtDNA Haplogroups," 320; Mahli et al., "Native American mtDNA Prehistory," 120–21. See Reséndez and Kemp, "Genetics and the History of Latin America," for the use of historical genetic evidence.

40. "A Campaign against the Pimas, 1695," in Naylor and Polzer, *Presidio and Militia*, 643; Opler, *An Apache Life-Way*, 354–86.

41. Opler, *An Apache Life-Way*, 163–81.

42. "Coyote Has Intercourse with His Mother-in-law," in Opler, *Myths and Tales of the Chiricahua*, 40–41.

43. Opler, *An Apache Life-Way*, 250.

44. "A Campaign against the Pimas, 1695," in Naylor and Polzer, *Presidio and Militia*, 589–96, 641–44.

45. "A Campaign against the Pimas, 1695," 644–47.

46. "A Campaign against the Pimas, 1695," 647–55.

47. Forbes, *Apache, Navaho, and Spaniard*, 278–79.

48. Griffen, *Indian Assimilation*, 90–93.

49. Jackson, *Race, Caste, and Status*; Cope, *Limits of Racial Domination*; Griffen, *Indian Assimilation*, 92. For a full discussion of the *sistema de castas* at Janos presidio see Blyth, "The Presidio of Janos," chap. 1.

50. Mission 2000 Searchable Spanish Mission Records, Tumacácori National Historical Park, http://home.nps.gov/applications/tuma/search.cfm (hereafter cited as Mission 2000), Baptism, Janos, April 18, 1729; Baptism, Janos, September 30, 1733; Baptism, Janos, January 13, 1750. Griffen, *Indian Assimilation*, 92; Lafora, *Frontiers of New Spain*, 100.

51. Mission 2000, Baptism, Janos, April 24, 1741; Baptism, Janos, April 2, 1743; Burial, Janos, July 17, 1748.

52. Libro de capellán, Janos, October 1724, JC 8:1768; Mission 2000, Burial, Janos, November 3, 1724, November 16, 1724, November 20, 1724.

53. Griffen, *Indian Assimilation*, 91–93, tables 7 and 8. For the experience of such detribalized Indians to the north of Janos in New Mexico, the *genízaros*, see Ebright and Hendricks, *Witches of Abiquiu*, 27–47.

54. Mission 2000, Baptism, Janos, April 18, 1729; Burial, Janos, October 12, 1730; Baptism, Janos, September 16, 1724; Gómez Robledo, Francisco Ignacio (ID: 5344).

55. Opler, *An Apache Life-Way*, 350.

56. Opler, *An Apache Life-Way*, 351; Mission 2000, Burial, Janos, June 3, 1753.

57. "Coyote Makes Woman Valuable by Breaking the Teeth in Her Vagina," in Opler, *Myths and Tales of the Chiricahua*, 70.

58. Opler, *An Apache Life-Way*, 351; Mission 2000, Burial, Janos, June 30, 1749.

59. *Reglamento para todos los presidios de las Provincias internas de esta Governación . . . Año de 1729* (hereafter Reglamento de 1729), in Naylor and Polzer, eds., *Pedro de Rivera*, 279.

60. "The Creation," in Hoijer and Opler, *Chiricahua and Mescalero Apache Texts*, 13–14.

3. Fierce Dancing and the Muster Roll

1. Hoja de servicio, Sargento Marcelino Antonio de Herrero, Janos, January 16, 1766, Archivo General de la Nación, Mexico City, Ramo Provincias Internas (hereafter AGN, PI), vol. 95, fol. 210.

2. This narration and the following paragraphs draw on Diario de novedades . . . , Janos, January 1757–November 1758, JC 7:1700s (Griffen, *Apaches at War and Peace*, 24–27, summarizes this document).

3. Griffen, *Apaches at War and Peace*, 24; Barr, *Peace Came in the Form of a Woman*, 2; Reglamento de 1729, in Naylor and Polzer, *Pedro de Rivera*, 279.

4. Mission 2000, Burial, Janos, September 16, 1757.

5. Hoja de servicio, Teniente de Capitan Don Joseph Camilio Chacon, Janos, January 15, 1766, AGN, PI, vol. 95, exp. 6, fol. 211.

6. Santiago Ruiz de Ael, Janos, January 4, 1759, January 6, 1759, April 4, 1759, JC 7:1759; Mission 2000, Burial, Janos, May 25, 1759; Marriage, Janos, February 4, 1753.

7. Hoja de servicio, Sargento Marcelino Antonio de Herrero, Janos, January 16, 1766, AGN, PI, vol. 95, fol. 210.

8. Opler, "Outline of Chiricahua Apache Social Organization," 179–84.

9. Lafora, *Frontiers of New Spain*, 79; Juan Antonio de Mendoza to Francisco José de Leyzaola, San Felipe, October 30, 1760, JC 7:1760; Mendoza to Leyzaola, San Felipe, December 14, 1760, JC 7:1760; Griffen, *Apaches at War and Peace*, 28–29.

10. José Carlos de Agüero to Leyzaola, Durango, August 4, 1761, JC 7:1760; Lafora, *Frontiers of New Spain*, 78–79.

11. Lafora, *Frontiers of New Spain*, 79–80.

12. Hugo O'Conor's Report to Teodoro de Croix, July 22, 1777, in Cutter, ed., *Defenses of Northern New Spain*, 42; Navarro García, *Don José de Gálvez*, 189–90.

13. Lista de revista, Janos, January 1, 1774, JC 8:1774; Bolton, "French Intrusions"; Christiansen, "The Presidio and the Borderlands," 33; Hoja de servicio, Capitán don Juan Bautista Perú, Janos, December 31, 1786, Records of the Presidio de San Felipe y Santiago de Janos, 1706–1858, Benson Latin American Collection, General Libraries, University of Texas at Austin, Folder 4A, Section 3 (hereafter cited as Janos Records, JR folder-section).

14. The Report of Hugo O'Conor, January 30, 1776, in Moore and Beene, eds., "The Interior Provinces," 275; Christiansen, "The Presidio and the Borderlands," 35–36.

15. *Reglamento e instrucción para los presidios que se han de formar en la línea de frontera de Nueva España. Resuelto por el Rey Nuestro Señor en cédula de 10 de Septiembre de 1772* (hereafter Reglamento de 1772), in Brinckerhoff and Faulk, *Lancers for the King*, 14–17; Listas de revistas, Janos, November 1, 1774, and January 1, 1775, JC 8:1774.

16. O'Conor's Report to Croix, July 22, 1777, in Cutter, *Defenses of Northern New Spain*, 88; Reglamento de 1772, in Brinckerhoff and Faulk, *Lancers for the King*, 26–27, 40–41. For more on recruitment patterns see Blyth, "The Presidio of Janos," 181–83.

17. Hoja de servicio, Cadete don Joaquín Perú, Janos, August 30, 1777, JC 8:1778; Navarro García, *Don José de Gálvez*, 238–41; Libro de capellán, Janos, June 2, 1775, JC 8:1768.

18. Filiación, José Tapia, Chihuahua, April 27, 1772, JC 9:1784; Carta de suplicación, Janos, June 9, 1776, and Diligencia de matrimonio, Janos, June 11, 1776, JR 1–3.

19. Extracto de principales . . . , Durango, October 11, 1777, in Brinckerhoff and Faulk, *Lancers for the King*, 109–10; Hoja de servicio, Cadete don Joaquín Perú, Janos, August 30, 1777, and Lista de revista, Janos, May 1, 1778, JC 8:1778; Perú to comandante inspector, Janos, November

8, 1777, JR 1-6; Carrasco to the viceroy, San Buenaventura, May 30, 1786, AGN, PI, vol. 41, fols. 406–9.

20. Griffen, *Apaches at War and Peace*, 39–41; Listas de revistas, Janos, February 1, 1778, March 1, 1778, May 1, 1778, JC 8:1778.

21. Moorhead, *The Presidio*, 82–83; Reglamento de 1772, in Brinckerhoff and Faulk, *Lancers for the King*, 20–21; Estado . . . , Chihuahua, February 14, 1774, AGN, PI, vol. 88, fol. 245. Also see Blyth, "The Presidio of Janos," 75–87.

22. Reglamento de 1772, in Brinckerhoff and Faulk, *Lancers for the King*, 22–23; Cargos contra Juan Perú, Janos, October 17–19, 1778, JR 3-19; Diego de Borica to Perú, El Paso, February 28, 1782, JC 9:1782. Hagle, "Military Life on New Spain's Northern Frontier," 66–67, stated that more documents in the Janos archive deal with the selling, buying, and care of horses than with any other subject. Also see Blyth, "The Presidio of Janos," 204–16.

23. Reglamento de 1772, in Brinckerhoff and Faulk, *Lancers for the King*, 32–33; Borica to Comandante de Janos, Chihuahua, August 1, 1781, JR 4-2, and February 4, 1784, JR 4A-2; Comandante General to Comandante de Janos, Chihuahua, January 19, 1789, JC 9:1789.

24. Listas de revistas, Janos, July 1, 1778, and November 1, 1778; Estado de la furerza, Janos, November 1, 1778; JC 8:1778.

25. Filiación, Antonio Cornelio Delgado, Chihuahua, March 1, 1776, JC 9:1789; Libro de capellán, Janos, August 21, 1779, JC 7:1768.

26. Moorhead, *The Presidio*, 206–11; Reglamento de 1772, in Brinckerhoff and Faulk, *Lancers for the King*, 44–49; Listas de revistas, Janos, March 1, 1779, April 1, 1779, JC 8:1778.

27. Listas de revistas, Janos, October 1, 1779, August 1, 1780, December 1, 1780, JC 8:1778.

28. Nuevo pie en que debern ponerse las Compañías Presidiales . . . , Arispe, April 18, 1782, JC 9:1782; Extractos de las revistas, Janos, 1783, JR 4-4; Hoja de servicio, Capitán don Juan Bautista Perú, Janos, December 31, 1786, JR 4A-3; Filiación, Bernardo Sepúlveda, 4a Compañía Volante, August 1, 1778, JC 19:1814; Filiación, Fernando Grijalba, Janos, March 23, 1783, JC 10:1795; Libro de capellán, Janos, 1783, JC 7:1768.

29. Filiación, Vicente Mariano Santillon, Querétaro, May 16, 1784, JC 9:1788.

30. Listas de revistas, Janos, 1785, JR 4A-2; Hoja de servicio, Capitán don Juan Bautista Perú, Janos, December 31, 1786, JR 4A-3; Extracto de la revista, Janos, January 1, 1786, JR 4A-3.

31. Opler, *An Apache Life-Way*, 356–58.

32. Griffen, *Apaches at War and Peace*, 29; Opler, "Outline of Chiricahua Apache Social Organization," 180–83, 232–34.

33. Opler, *An Apache Life-Way*, 336–37.

34. Juan Perú to Comandante Inspector, Janos, November 8, 1777, JR 1-6.

35. Narciso de Tapia to Narcisco Muñiz, Janos, December 14, 1777, JR 3-1; Muñiz to Tapia, Carrizal, December 15, 1777, JC 8:1778; Tapia to Muñiz, Janos, December 23, 1777, JR 3-1.

36. "Old Apache Customs," in Hoijer and Opler, *Chiricahua and Mescalero Apache Texts*, 45–47; Opler, *An Apache Life-Way*, 332–34.

37. Opler and Hoijer, "The Raid and War-Path Language," 618–24, 629, 634.

38. Tapia to Muñiz, Janos, January 17, 1778, JR 3-1.

39. Opler, *An Apache Life-Way*, 463; Opler, "Outline of Chiricahua Apache Social Organization," 177; Lafora, *Frontiers of New Spain*, 79; O'Conor to Croix, July 22, 1777, in Cutter, *Defenses of Northern New Spain*, 70. These three bands correspond to the historical Chihene, Chokonen, and Nednhi, or Central, Eastern, and Southern bands.

40. Griffen, *Apaches at War and Peace*, 40–41; Tapia, Janos, February 11, 1778, JR 3-1.

41. Tapia to Muñiz, Janos, February 28, 1778, JR 3-1.

42. Teodoro de Croix to Perú, Chihuahua, June 20, 1778, JR 3-1.

43. Comandante de Janos to Diego Borica, Janos, September 5, 1778, JR 3-1.

44. Lista de revista, Janos, November 1, 1778, JC 8:1778; Borica to Perú, San Buenaventura, November 2, 1778; Croix to Comandante de Janos, Chihuahua, February 22, 1779, JR 3-3.

45. Griffen, *Apaches at War and Peace*, 43–44.

46. Griffen, *Apaches at War and Peace*, 44–46; Weber, *Bárbaros*, 156–59.

47. Croix to Peru, Arizpe, January 2, 1783, JR 4-4; Croix to Peru, Arizpe, April 14, 1783, JR 4-4; Griffen, *Apaches at War and Peace*, 46.

48. Griffen, *Apaches at War and Peace*, 47–48; Perú to Diego de Borica, Janos, February 1, 1785, JR 4A-2.

49. Opler, *An Apache Life-Way*, 352–54, 144.

50. "Coyote Makes Woman Valuable by Breaking the Teeth in Her Vagina," in Opler, *Myths and Tales of the Chiricahua*, 70; Griffen, *Apaches at War and Peace*, 48.

51. "Rengel's Instruction for Campaign against the Gila, November 8, 1785," in Thomas, ed., *Forgotten Frontiers*, 275–79.

52. "Diary of Captain Cordero against the Gilas in Southern New Mexico and Arizona, November–December 1785," and "Diary of Captain Martinez

against the Gilas in Southern New Mexico, November–December 1785," in Thomas, *Forgotten Frontiers*, 286–87 and 281–82, respectively.

53. "Diary of Captain Cordero," 288.

54. Diary of Captain Cordero," 288; "Cordero to Rengel, December 14, 1785," in Thomas, *Forgotten Frontiers*, 291.

55. Weber, *The Spanish Frontier*, 204–35.

56. Swann, *Tierra Adentro*, 128; Fenn, *Pox Americana*, 135–66.

57. Blyth, "The Presidio of Janos," 123–29; Opler, *An Apache Life-Way*, 416–18; Opler, "Outline of Chiricahua Apache Social Organization," 204–5.

58. Opler, "Outline of Chiricahua Apache Social Organization," 200–4; Opler, *An Apache Life-Way*, 154–63.

59. Blyth, "The Presidio of Janos," 121–23.

4. A Vigilant Peace

1. Hoja de servicio, Capitán don Antonio Cordero, Janos, December 31, 1786, JR 4A-3.

2. Hoja de servicio, Capitán don Juan Bautista Perú, Janos, December 31, 1786, JR 4A-3.

3. Moorhead, *The Apache Frontier*, 123. For the larger context see Weber, *Bárbaros*, 138–77, esp. 156–59. Gálvez served on a campaign from Janos in June and July 1769. See McCarty, "Bernardo de Galvez."

4. Gálvez, *Instructions*, 34–38, 50; Moorhead, *The Apache Frontier*, 124–32, summarizes the document.

5. Gálvez, *Instructions*, 40–43.

6. Hoja de servicio, Capitán don Antonio Cordero, Janos, December 31, 1787, JR 5-1.

7. Matson and Schroeder, eds., "Cordero's Description of the Apache," 339, 341, 349, 350.

8. Diario de novedades, Janos, November 4, 1786, JC 39:1787; Comandante de Janos to Comandante General, Janos, April 1, 1787, JC 39:1787; Jacobo Ugarte to Cordero, Arispe, April 8, 1787, JC 39:1787; Moorhead, *The Apache Frontier*, 186; Hoja de servicio, Capitán don Antonio Cordero, Janos, December 31, 1787, JR 5-1.

9. Joseph Antonio Rengel to Cordero, El Paso, May 24, 1787, JR 5-1; Moorhead, *The Apache Frontier*, 188.

10. Gálvez, *Instructions*, 80–85; Moorhead, *The Apache Frontier*, 189–90; Griffen, *Apaches at War and Peace*, 59; Hoja de servicio, Capitán don Antonio Cordero, Janos, December 31, 1787, JR 5-1.

11. Hoja de servicio, Capitán don Antonio Cordero, Janos, December 31,

1788, JR 5-2; Diario de los operaciones, Chihuahua, April 28, 1788, AGN, PI, vol. 128, exp. 3; Griffen, *Apaches at War and Peace*, 61–62.

12. Lista de revista, Janos, September 1, 1788, JR 5-2; Jacobo Ugarte y Loyola to Manuel Antonio Flores, San Bartolomé, September 22, 1788 AGN, PI, vol. 127, fol. 299.

13. Josef Vato to Comandante de Janos, August 22, 1788, AGN, PI, vol. 127, fol. 300; Cordero to Comandante General, Janos, August 24, 1788, AGN, PI, vol. 127, fol. 301; Ugarte to Flores, Hacienda de la Zarca, November 1, 1788, AGN, PI, vol. 127, fol. 305; Comandante de Janos, August 24, 1788, JC 38:24; Hoja de servicio, Sargento Fermín González, Janos, December 31, 1810, JC 1:1810.

14. Griffen, *Apaches at War and Peace*, 63; Comandante de Janos to Comandante General, Janos, December 18, 1789, JC 9:1789.

15. Ugarte to Cordero, San Buenaventura, September 18, 1788, JR 5-2. Griffen, "The Compás," tells the full tale of the Compás.

16. Ugarte to Juan Bautista de Anza, San Bartolome, December 12, 1788, AGN, PI, vol. 128, exp. 4. Moorhead, "Spanish Deportation of Hostile Apaches," and Archer, "Deportation of Barbarian Indians," are the standard works on Apache deportation, recently joined by Santiago, *Jar of Severed Hands*. Conrad, "Military Service," perceptively noted that "military commanders used the *threat* of deportation to leverage Apache headmen."

17. Diego de Borica to Cordero, Chihuahua, March 25 and March 29, 1790, JR 6A-2; Griffen, *Apaches at War and Peace*, 71; Archer, "Deportation of Barbarian Indians," 378–79; Moorhead, *The Apache Frontier*, 198–99.

18. Cano to Antonio Muñoz, El Carmen, November 8, 1790, JR 6A-1; José de Tovar to Muñoz, Janos, August 29, 1790, JR 6A-1; Griffen, "The Compás," 26.

19. Cordero to Comandante de Janos, Chihuahua, August 22, 1790, JR 6A-1; Pedro de Nava to Ramón de Casanova, Chihuahua, June 7, 1791, JR 7-1.

20. Cordero to Casanova, Janos, December 4, 1790, JR 6A-1.

21. Griffen, *Apaches at War and Peace*, 72–73, 75–76; Cordero to Ugarte, Janos, July 1, 1791, JR 7-1.

22. Griffen, "The Compás," 28; Pedro de Nava, Instrucción . . . , Chihuahua, October 14, 1791, JC 13:1788, translated in Hendricks and Timmons, *San Elizario*, 102–9. Also see Griffen, *Apaches at War and Peace*, 101–2, for the rations and goods given to Apaches.

23. Griffen, "The Compás," 27, 29. See Griffen, "Chiricahua Apache Population," for a population analysis.

24. Griffen, "The Compás," 29–30.

25. Opler, *An Apache Life-Way*, 354–65; Griffen, "The Compás," 30, 44–45; Matson and Schroeder, "Cordero's Description of the Apache," 340.

26. Opler, *An Apache Life-Way*, 365–71.

27. Opler, *An Apache Life-Way*, 375–85; Matson and Schroeder, "Cordero's Description of the Apache," 339.

28. Opler, "Cause and Effect in Apachean Agriculture," 1143–45; Opler, *An Apache Life-Way*, 82–134.

29. Matson and Schroeder, "Cordero's Description of the Apache," 347, 341; Opler, *An Apache Life-Way*, 407.

30. "Coyote's Enemy Sends Him Away on Rising Rock and Steals His Wife," "Coyote Seeks his Family and Kills His Rival," "Coyote Kills His Rival by Making Him Swallow Hot Stones," "The Woman Who Pretended Sickness and Death to Be with Her Lover," "The Unfaithful Wife Found Out by Her Husband," and "The Woman Who Pretended Sickness to Be with Her Lover," in Opler, *Myths and Tales of the Chiricahua*, 28–31, 63–65, 87–89.

31. Opler, "Outline of Chiricahua Apache Social Organization," 223; Opler, *An Apache Life-Way*, 141–42, 408–10; Matson and Schroeder, "Cordero's Description of the Apache," 342.

32. Extractos de la revista, Janos, November 2 and December 2, 1793, JC 10:1793; Libro de capellán, Janos, August 21, 1779, JC 7:1768; Padrón . . . , Janos, January 1, 1793, JR 8-2.

33. Ugarte to Manuel Antonio Flores, Hacienda de la Zarca, November 1, 1788, AGN, PI, vol. 177, fol. 305; Lista de revista, Janos, October 1, 1776, JC 8:1774; Lista de revista, Janos, December 1, 1780, JC 8:1778; Relación . . . , Janos, May 9, 1797, JR 14-2.

34. Pedro de Nava to Manuel de Casanova, Chihuahua, December 7, 1793, JR 9-2.

35. Padrones, Janos, December 31, 1791, JR 6A-2 and 7-2; 1792, JR 8-2; 1796, JR 12-1; 1799, JR 15-2.

36. Blyth, "The Presidio of Janos," 161–63.

37. de la Teja, ed., and Wheat, trans., "Ramón de Murillo's Plan," 521; Blyth, "The Presidio of Janos," 163–64; Ruxton, *Adventures in the Rocky Mountains*, 115; Clarke, *Travels in Mexico*, 61–72. See Meyer, "Health and Medical Practice," for medical practices in the region.

38. Cordero to Comandante de Janos, Chihuahua, May 13, 1794, JR 10-2; Nava to Comandante de Janos, November 17, 1795; Nava, November 7, 1795, JC 10:1795.

39. Griffen, *Apaches at War and Peace*, 91–93, 103–4; Pedro de Nava, Instrucción . . . , Chihuahua, October 14, 1791, JC 13:1788; Cortés, *Views*

from the Apache Frontier, 29–30; John, ed., and Wheat, trans., "Views from a Desk in Chihuahua," 155.

40. Griffen, "The Compás," 30–32; Nava to Comandante de Janos, Chihuahua, February 8, 1797, JR 14-1.

41. Griffen, *Apaches at War and Peace,* 88–89.

42. Nava to Comandante de Janos, Chihuahau, August 24, 1799, JR 15-2; Nava to Joseph de Tovar, Chihuahua, August 5, 1803, JC 15:1803.

43. Nemesio Salcedo to Tovar, Chihuahua, March 7, 1804, JR 17-2; Cumpá to Comandante General, February 1, 1805, JC 15:1809; Apache Census, Janos, December 31, 1810, JC 11:1812; Juan José [?] to Varela, Janos, August 15, 1810, JR 19-4; Griffen, "The Compás," 32–34. For evidence of Apache agricultural practices at this time see Babcock, "Turning Apaches into Spaniards," 112, 125, 218.

44. Griffen, *Apaches at War and Peace,* 78–80; Nava, Instrucción . . . , Chihuahua, October 14, 1791, JC 13:1788.

45. Babcock, "Turning Apaches into Spaniards," 263–69; Griffen, "Chiricahua Apache Population," 160–66.

46. Filiación, Manuel Albino Rodriquez, Janos, October 17, 1792, JC 14:1823; Filiación, Albino Parra, Janos, January 1, 1800, JC 1:1810; Extracto de la revista, Janos, November 1, 1800, JC 14:1800; Extracto de la revista, Janos, February 1, 1801, JR 16-1.

47. Blyth, "The Presidio of Janos," 50–51; Pike, *Expeditions of Zebulon Montgomery Pike,* 2:796.

48. Extracto de la revista, Janos, May 1, 1801, JC 14:1801; Extracto de la revista, Janos, November 1, 1797, JC 14:1700s; Padrón, Janos, December 31, 1803, JR 17-2; Extracto de la revista, Janos, January 1, 1809, JC 15:1809.

49. Hoja de servicio, Capitán don José Ronquillo, Janos, December 31, 1810, JC 1:1810; Census, Janos, December 31, 1810, JC 1:1810.

50. Filiación, José Valentín Ronquillo, San Buenaventura, May 9, 1791, JR 25-1; Promotion List, Janos, September 20, 1812, JR 19-4; Cordero to Comandante de Janos, Chihuahua, May 22, 1792; January 27, 1792; January 10, 1792, JR 8-1.

51. Hoja de servicio, Primer Alférez Don José Ignacio Ronquillo, Janos, December 31, 1817, JC 3:1817.

52. Hoja de servicio, Teniente don José Ignacio Ronquillo, Cerrogordo, December 31, 1821, JR 24A-2.

53. Supply Receipts, Janos, January 10, March 6, May 31, 1811, JR 20-2; May 6 and May 9, 1811, JC 1:1811, October 1, 1812, JC 2:1812; Lista . . . , Janos, 1814, JR 21-1; Filiación, José Marrufo, Janos, January 1, 1814, JR 47-2; José Marrufo to Ronquillo, Janos, February 8, 1814, JC 2:1814.

54. Griffen, "The Compás," 34, 37; Griffen, *Apaches at War and Peace*, 89–90; Griffen, "Chiricahua Apache Population," 167–71.

55. Alberto Maynez to Ayudante Inspector, Janos, January 26, 1818; Lombán to Comandante de Janos, Chihuahua, October 2, 1818, JR 23-1.

56. Radding, *Wandering Peoples*, 292–93; Filiación, José Valentín Ronquillo, San Buenaventura, May 9, 1791, JR 25-1; Hoja de servicio, Teniente don José Ignacio Ronquillo, Cerrogordo, December 31, 1821, JR 24A-2.

57. Noticía de Alta y Baja, Janos, January 1, 1821, JC 13:1821.

58. Hoja de servicio, Teniente don José Ignacio Ronquillo, Cerro Gordo, December 31, 1821, JR 24A-2; Comandante General las Provincias Internas de Occidente a las tropas, Chihuahua, August 26, 1821, JC 13:1821; Comandante de Janos to Comandante General, Janos, July 30, 1821; JC 13:1821; Comandante de Janos to Comandante General, Janos, September 20, 1821, JR 24A-1.

59. Pie de lista y Extracto de la revista, Janos, December 1, 1821, JC 13: 1821; Listas y Extractos de la revista, Janos, January 1, February 1, and December 1, 1823, JR 25-3; Filiación, José Valentín Ronquillo, San Buenaventura, May 9, 1791, JR 25-1; Hoja de servicio, Alférez graduado Teniente don José Ignacio Ronquillo, Janos, December 31, 1823, JR 25-3.

60. Estado de la fuerza, Janos, November 1, 1824, JC 16:1824; Estado de la fuerza, Janos, October 1, 1825, JC 17:1825; Relacion, October 1, 1825, JR 26-2; Noticía de los jefes . . . , Chihuahua, September 30, 1825, JC 17:1825; Estado que manifiesta la fuerza . . . , México, February 3, 1826, JC 17:1826; Estada de la fuerza, Janos, May 1, 1826, JC 17:1826.

61. Griffen, *Apaches at War and Peace*, 125–29.

62. Griffen, "The Compás," 37–38; Simon Elías to Comandante de Janos, Chihuahua, May 29, 1828, JC 21:1828, and January 18, 1829, JC 22:1829.

63. Pattie, *Personal Narrative*, 66–67, 76–77.

64. Griffen, "The Compás," 34–45; Babcock, "Turning Apaches into Spaniards," table 4.2, 333; Comandante de Janos to Comandante General, Janos, January 11, 1830; Petition, Janos, January 11, 1830, JC 20:1828.

65. Babcock, "Rethinking the Establecimientos," similarly argues that Apaches settled primarily for protection and rations.

66. Babcock, "Turning Apaches into Spaniards," 268–82; Blyth, "The Presidio of Janos," 153–59.

67. Blyth, "The Presidio of Janos," 97–99.

68. Blyth, "The Presidio of Janos," 158–59, 162–63.

5. War, Peace, War

1. Libro de defunciones, Janos, 1831, JR 24A-1; Estado de la fuerza, Janos, February 1, 1832, JR 34-2.

2. Griffen, *Utmost Good Faith*, 30; Griffen, *Apaches at War and Peace*, 139–43.

3. Bases principales para conceder la paz a los apaches sublevados en el estado de Chihuahua, José Joaquín Calvo, Encinillas, July 28, 1832, JC 5:1832; Calvo to Comandante de Janos, Chihuahua, September 18, 1832, JC 24:1832; Griffen, *Apaches at War and Peace*, 142.

4. Mariano Ponce de León to Comandante de Janos, San Buenaventura, February 24, 1833, JC 25:1833; Juan José Compá to Mariano Varela, Carcay, April 25, 1833, JC 25:1832.

5. Compá to Varela, Carcay, May 1, 1833; Varela to Compá, May 1, 1833, JC 25:1832; Compá to Varela, [no date], JC 26:1833; Griffen, *Apaches at War and Peace*, 146–47.

6. Rickard, "Chino Enterprise"; Walker, "Copper Genesis."

7. Letter to Commandant General, El Cobre, January 6, 1834, JC 26:1834.

8. Cayetano Justiniana to Secretario Interno, El Paso, October 9, 1834; Ronquillo to Calvo, El Paso, October 15, 1834, JR 36-1; Griffen, *Apaches at War and Peace*, 149–51.

9. Griffen, *Apaches at War and Peace*, 157–60; Comandante del Cobre to Ayudante Inspector, El Cobre, April 12, 1835, JC 28:1838.

10. Compá to Comandante General, El Cobre, April 22, 1835, JC 28:1839; "The Mountain Spirits Help a Fleeing Chiricahua," in Opler, "Mountain Spirits," 129–30.

11. Quoted in Griffen, *Apaches at War and Peace*, 160.

12. Mariano Rodríguez Rey to Comandante General, May 12, 1836, JR 38-2.

13. Rodríguez Rey to Comandante General, June 21, 1836, JR 38-2; Griffen, *Apaches at War and Peace*, 167–68.

14. Griffen, *Apaches at War and Peace*, 172.

15. Strickland, "Birth and Death of a Legend," 272.

16. Strickland, "Birth and Death of a Legend," 273–74, and John Johnson to José Joaquin Calvo, Janos, April 24, 1837, 277–78.

17. Griffen, *Apaches at War and Peace*, 174–75.

18. Hoja de servicio, Sargento Jóse Padilla, San Elizario, October 14, 1840, JC 28:1840; Diario de novedades, Janos, September 1840, JC 28:1840; Comandante de Janos to Comandante General, Janos, October 1 and 20, 1840, JR 41-1.

19. Smith, *Borderlander*, 99–101.

20. Smith, *Borderlander*, 102–3, 109–12.

21. Lista y extracto de la revista, Janos, February 1, 1840, JR 41-1; Comandante de Janos to Comandante General, September 20, 1840, JR 41-1.

22. Blyth, "The Presidio of Janos," 159–60; Comandante General to Comandante de Janos, El Paso, July 28, 1841, JC 29:1841; Subprefecto de Janos to Comandante de Janos, Casas Grandes, April 26, 1842, JC 29:1842.

23. Hoja de servicio, Primer Alférez Don José Padilla, Janos, December 31, 1841, JC 29:1841; Extractos de revista, Janos, January 1 and April 1, 1841, JC 29:1841; Noticia de los individuos de tropa . . . , Janos, January 9, 1841, JC 29:1841; Griffen, *Utmost Good Faith*, 60–61; Hoja de servicio, Primer Teniente Don Baltasar Padilla, Janos, December 31, 1851, JC 33:1851.

24. Filiaciones, Janos, July, August, 1841, JC 29:1841; Filiaciones, Janos, November 24, 1841, JR 41-2; Lista y extracto de la revista, Janos, January 1, 1842, JR 42-2; Fernandez to Comandante de Janos, Chihuahua, October 26, 1841, JC 29:1841.

25. Estado de fuerza, Janos, June 1, 1842, JC 30:1842; Griffen, *Apaches at War and Peace*, 190.

26. Griffen, *Apaches at War and Peace*, 191, 194; Griffen, *Utmost Good Faith*, 192–94.

27. Estado de Fuerza, Janos, September 1, 1842, JC 29:1842; Varela to Comandante de Janos, December 22 and 31, 1842, JR 42-1; Griffen, "Chiricahua Apache Population," 172–75.

28. Griffen, *Apaches at War and Peace*, 196, 206; Comandante de Janos to Comandante General, Janos, February 7, 1843, JR 43-1; José Mariano Monterde to Comandante de Janos, Chihuahua, February 23, 1843, JR 43-1.

29. Comandante de Janos to Comandante General, Janos, April 25, 1843, JR 43-1. Sweeney, *Mangas Coloradas*, 27–28, makes the Fuerte as Mangas Coloradas connection.

30. Comandante de Janos to Comandante General, Janos, May 8, 1843, JR 43-1; Comandante de Janos to Comandante General, Janos, May 28, 1843, JR 43-1.

31. Comandante de Janos to Comandante General, Janos, June 24, 1843, JR 43-1.

32. Hoja de servicio, Primer Teniente Don Baltasar Padilla, Janos, December 31, 1851, JC 33:1851; José María Zuloaga to Comandante General, Janos, July 13, 1843, JR 43-1; Comandante de Janos to Comandante General, Janos, November 1 and 7, 1843, JR 43-1.

33. Listas para la revista, Janos, February 1 and December 1, 1844, JC 31:1844; Griffen, *Utmost Good Faith*, 145; Hoja de servicio, Primer Teniente Don Baltasar Padilla, Janos, December 31, 1851, JC 33:1851; Griffen, *Apaches at War and Peace*, 208.

34. Hoja de servicio, Primer Teniente Don Baltasar Padilla, Janos, December

31, 1851, JC 33:1851; Diario de las operaciones, Janos, June 4, 1845, JC 32:1849; Noticia, Janos, June 10, 1845, JR 45-2; Francisco García Conde to Capítan de Janos, Chihuahua, July 1, 1845, JC 31:1845.

35. Griffen, *Utmost Good Faith*, 292–93, 295; Hoja de servicio, Primer Teniente Don Baltasar Padilla, Janos, December 31, 1851, JC 33:1851; Estado de fuerza, Janos, January 1, 1846, JC 31:1845.

36. Smith, *Borderlander*, 149–55; Griffen, *Apaches at War and Peace*, 215–16; Sweeney, *Mangas Coloradas*, 155.

37. Betzinez, *I Fought with Geronimo*, 3–4, misidentifies Galeana as Ramos; Sweeney, *Mangas Coloradas*, 134; Ruxton, *Adventures in Mexico*, 158–59. Smith, *Borderlander*, 162–67, considers Mexican, Apache, and American accounts of the massacre.

38. Betzinez, *I Fought with Geronimo*, 4; Sweeney, *Mangas Coloradas*, 3–4, 17; U.S. Congress, *Condition of the Indian Tribes: Report of the Joint Special Committee, Appointed under Joint Resolution of March 3, 1867* (39th Cong, 2d sess., 1867), 328.

39. Betzinez, *I Fought with Geronimo*, 4–5.

40. Betzinez, *I Fought with Geronimo*, 5–6; Opler, *An Apache Life-Way*, 386–93.

41. Betzinez, *I Fought with Geronimo*, 6–7.

42. Betzinez, *I Fought with Geronimo*, 7–9; Sweeney, *Mangas Coloradas*, 91.

43. Sweeney, *Mangas Coloradas*, 143–44.

44. Luis Jáuregui, "Chihuahua en la tormenta: Su situación política durante la guerra con las Estados Unidos, Septiembre de 1846–Julio de 1848," in Vázquez, *México al tiempo de su guerra*, 143–47, 153–54; Dawson, *Doniphan's Epic March*, 142–62; Wilcox, *History of the Mexican War*, 541–43.

45. Listas y extractos de la revistas, Janos, February 1 and March 1, 1849, JC 32:1849 and JR 48-2; Padilla to Zuloaga, Janos, February 21, 1849, JC 32:1849.

46. Comandante de Janos to Comandante General, Janos, March 22 and March 29, 1849, JC 32:1849.

47. Clarke, *Travels in Mexico*, 54–55; Padilla to Angel Trías, Janos, May 26, 1849, JC 32:1849; Smith, "Scalp Hunt in Chihuahua," 118.

48. Sweeney, *Mangas Coloradas*, 171; Zuloaga to Padilla, Corralitos, June 11, 1849, JC 32:1849; Padilla to Zuloaga, Janos, June 30, 1849, JC 32:1849.

49. Sweeney, *Mangas Coloradas*, 172; Padilla to Comandante General, Janos, June 30, 1849, JC 32:1849.

50. Harris, *Gila Trail*, 64–66; Griffen, *Apaches at War and Peace*, 228; Sweeney, *Mangas Coloradas*, 173.

51. Padilla to Comandante General, Janos, September 12, 1849, JC 32:1849; Hoja de servicio, Capitán Don Baltasar Padilla, Janos, December 31, 1857, JR 53-1.

52. Padilla to Inspector de las Colonias Militares, Janos, September 15, 1849, JC 32:1849; Filiaciones, Macedonio Ornelas, San Buenaventura, July 21, 1842, and José Almansa, Janos, January 16, 1849, JR 48-2.

53. Diario de novedades, Janos, October 11–12, 1849, JR 48-2.

54. Hoja de servicio, Capitán Don Baltasar Padilla, Janos, December 31, 1857, JR 53-1; Cunningham and Hewitt, "A 'lovely land full of roses and thorns,'" 398; Griffen, *Apaches at War and Peace*, 235.

55. Padilla to Comandante General, Janos, April 30, 1850, JC 33:1850; Sweeney, *Mangas Coloradas*, 202.

56. Padilla to Jefe Político, Janos, May 22, 1850, JC 33:1850; Sweeney, *Mangas Coloradas*, 203–4.

57. Sweeney, *Mangas Coloradas*, 209, 205–6.

58. Griffen, *Utmost Good Faith*, 197–213; Jastrzembski, "Treacherous Towns," 193.

59. Cole, *Chiricahua Apache*, 84–87.

60. Weber, *The Mexican Frontier*, 103. For the internal politics of Mexican Indian policy prior to 1846 see DeLay, *War of a Thousand Deserts*, 141–64 and 194–225.

61. Griffen, *Utmost Good Faith*, 164–65.

62. Blyth, "The Presidio of Janos," 61, 64–65.

63. Faulk, trans. and ed., "Projected Military Colonies." The law and regulation found their way to Janos as a copy in Chihuahua, June 4, 1849, JC 31:1849.

64. Clarke, *Travels in Mexico*, 69–70; Betzinez, *I Fought with Geronimo*, 27–28; Sweeney, *Mangas Coloradas*, 224.

65. Elias to Justiniani, Chihuahua, July 9, 1835, JR 37-1.

6. Border Dilemmas

1. Sweeney, *Mangas Coloradas*, 209–10; Geronimo, *His Own Story*, 80–81.

2. Geronimo, *His Own Story*, 82.

3. Sweeney, *Mangas Coloradas*, 210; Geronimo, *His Own Story*, 82–83.

4. Sweeney, *Mangas Coloradas*, 211–14, 218.

5. Sweeney, *Mangas Coloradas*, 217–19; Geronimo, *His Own Story*, 76–77; Betzinez, *I Fought with Geronimo*, 17.

6. Bartlett, *Personal Narrative*, 1:300–1.

7. Bartlett, *Personal Narrative*, 1:311–17; Cremony, *Life among the Apaches*, 58–66.

8. Bartlett, *Personal Narrative*, 1:331–39.

9. Bartlett, *Personal Narrative*, 1:343, 346–47, 349, 351, 353–54.

10. Sweeney, *Mangas Coloradas*, 241–43, 252–54.

11. *Santa Fe Weekly Gazette*, November 20, 1852, and January 26, 1856, cited in Sweeney, *Mangas Coloradas*, 258–59.

12. Sweeney, *Mangas Coloradas*, 260.

13. Zuloaga to Padilla, Corralitos, April 15, 1853, JC 34:1853.

14. Diario de Campaña, Corralitos, April 30, 1853, JC 34:1853; Contrato del Clarin, Santiago Brito, Janos, October 1, 1849, JC 32:1849.

15. Griswold del Castillo, *Treaty of Guadalupe Hidalgo*, 190–91; Comandante de Janos, June 9, 1853, and August 30, 1853; Zuloaga to Comandante de Janos, Corralitos, November 2, 1853, JC 34:1853.

16. Relacion . . . , Corralitos, October 23, 1853; Contrato del Explorador, Gervacio Dias, Janos, July 9, 1853, JC 34:1853.

17. Hoja de servicio, Capitán Don Baltasar Padilla, Janos, December 31, 1857, JR 53-1; Comandante Militar to Ayudante Inspector, Janos, March 13, 1854; Diario de novedades, Janos, March 13, 1854; Comisario de Janos, Janos, June 3, 1854, JC 35:1854.

18. Comandante de Janos to Comandante General, Janos, May 28, 1855, JC 36:1856; Sweeney, *Mangas Coloradas*, 317–18; Filiación, Rafael Garza, Janos, June 1, 1854, JC 37:1856.

19. Hoja de servicio, Capitán Don Baltasar Padilla, Janos, December 31, 1857, JR 53-1; Griswold del Castillo, *Treaty of Guadalupe Hidalgo*, 58–61; Emory, "Running the Line," 238.

20. Estado de fuerza, Janos, March 1, 1856, JC 36:1856; Filiación, Rafael Garza, Janos, June 1, 1854, JC 37:1856; Padilla to Michael Steck, Janos, November 3, 1856, JC 36:1856.

21. Zuloaga to Comandante de Janos, Corralitos, July 31, 1856, JC 36:1856; Sweeney, *Mangas Coloradas*, 336.

22. Padilla to Steck, Janos, November 3, 1856, Padilla to Zuloaga, September 2 and 3, 1856, JC 36:1856.

23. Lista para la revista, Janos, September 1, 1856, JC 37:1856; José Merino to Captain of San Elisario, Chihuahua, October 22, 1856, JC 36:1855.

24. Diario de novedades, Janos, September, 1856, JC 36:1856; Padilla to Féliz Palacios, Janos, September 29, 1856, quoted in Griffen, *Apaches at War and Peace*, 263.

25. Steck to Padilla, Janos, October 18, 1856; Padilla to Steck, November 3, 1856, JC 36:1856; Diario de novedades, Janos, December, 1856; Zuloaga to Presidente Jefe de Janos, Corralitos, December 23, 1856, JC 37:1857.

26. Comandante de Janos to Comandante General, Janos, January 2, 1857; Merino to Padilla, Chihuahua, March 31, 1857, JR 53-1; Griffen, *Apaches at War and Peace*, 253; Comandante de Janos to Don Esmergildo Quintana, Janos, April 3, 1857, JC 37:1857; Comandante Militar a la Frontera de Janos to Zuloaga, Janos, April 5, 1857, JR 53-1; José Merino to Capitán de Janos, Chihuahua, April 27, 1857, JC 37:1857; Lista y extracto de la revista, Janos, May 1, 1857, JC 37:1857.

27. Merino to Comandante de Janos, Chihuahua, February 4, 1857, JC 37:1857.

28. Sweeney, *Mangas Coloradas*, 352–59; Griffen, *Apaches at War and Peace*, 255, 257; Casares to Padilla, Janos, March 21, 1857, JR 53-1.

29. Lista y extracto de la revista, Janos, April 1, 1858, JC 37:1858; Brian R. Hamnett, "Wars of Reform (Three Years War)," in Werner, ed., *Encyclopedia of Mexico*, 1601–4.

30. Sweeney, *Mangas Coloradas*, 362–66, 370–72, 384, 387–89, 395, 398; Betzinez, *I Fought with Geronimo*, 43.

31. Sweeney, *Cochise*, 150–53; Betzinez, *I Fought with Geronimo*, 40–41.

32. Sweeney, *Cochise*, 155–63; Geronimo, *His Own Story*, 116–17.

33. Sweeney, *Cochise*, 170–78; Sweeney, *Mangas Coloradas*, 412–26.

34. Ball, *Indeh*, 19–20; Sweeney, *Mangas Coloradas*, 431–35; Betzinez, *I Fought with Geronimo*, 42.

35. Cremony, *Life among the Apaches*, 158–60, 176; Ball, *Indeh*, 20.

36. Ball, *In the Days of Victorio*, 47–48; Sweeney, *Mangas Coloradas*, 444, 448–57.

37. Letter to Presidente de la Hacienda de Corralitos, Janos, July 13, 1858, JC 37:1858; Almada, *Diccionario de historia*, 438–39; Wasserman, *Capitalist, Caciques, and Revolution*, 15; Jordán, *Crónica de un País Bárbaro*, 250–60.

38. Sweeney, *Cochise*, 138–39; Geronimo, *His Own Story*, 87–88.

39. Sweeney, *Cochise*, 183, 188, 194, 206–7; Terrazas, *Memorias*, 23–25.

40. Terrazas, *Memorias*, 27–28, 31.

41. Report of Lieut. Col. Nelson H. Davis, Santa Fe, New Mexico, October 17, 1864, in *The War of the Rebellion*, series I, vol. 41, part I, 125–30.

42. Sweeney, *Cochise*, 228–30, 244–45.

43. Sweeney, *Cochise*, 249, 252–53.

44. Sweeney, *Cochise*, 256; Almada, *Diccionario de historia*, 576.

45. Sweeney, *Cochise*, 258, 267.

46. Sweeney, *Cochise*, 263–65.

47. Sweeney, *Cochise*, 268–77.

48. Sweeney, *Cochise*, 278, 282, 287–88, 297–99.

49. Sweeney, *Cochise*, 287–88, 297–99, 304, 207, 316, 323, 325, 338–40.

50. Terrazas, *Memorias*, 50–57; Sweeney, *Cochise*, 344–45, 356, 363–66.

51. Sweeney, *Cochise*, 367, 370–74, 369–70, 372–74, 378–79, 382–84.

52. Sweeney, *Cochise*, 386–87, 395.

53. Brooks, *Captives and Cousins*.

54. Cole, *Chiricahua Apache*, 170–71, 175.

55. Jastrzembski, "An Enemy's Ethnography," 85–115; Thrapp, *Conquest of Apacheria*.

56. Frias to Padilla, Chihuahua, August 2, 1853, JC 34:1853; Listas para la revista, Janos, April 1, 1856, JR 52-2; February 1, 1857, JC 33:1851.

57. Chartrand, *Mexican Adventure*, 23; Bancroft, *History of the North Mexican States*, 613; Orozco Orozco, *Las guerras indias*, 23–28.

7. Communities' End

1. Terrazas, *Memorias*, 57–58.

2. Terrazas, *Memorias*, 59, 61; Sweeney, *Cochise*, 392.

3. Terrazas, *Memorias*, 61–68; Almada, *Diccionario de historia*, 439.

4. Wasserman, *Capitalist, Caciques, and Revolution*, 35–36.

5. Cole, *Chiricahua Apache*, 152–53, 156–58, 161–63; Thrapp, *Victorio*, 75.

6. Ball, *In the Days of Victorio*, 12–15; Thrapp, *Victorio*, 253.

7. Terrazas, *Memorias*, 68–70.

8. Thrapp, *Victorio*, 256, 286–88; Terrazas, *Memorias*, 70.

9. Chamberlain, *Victorio: Apache Warrior and Chief*, 190–92; Crimmins, "Colonel Buell's Expedition"; El Governador Gral. Luis Terrazas, Chihuahua, June 28, 1880, in Chávez, "Extincion de los Apaches Victorio," 337–38; Terrazas, *Memorias*, 71–75.

10. Terrazas, *Memorias*, 75–78; Thrapp, *Victorio*, 301.

11. Terrazas, *Memorias*, 79; Ball, *In the Days of Victorio*, 88–94.

12. Terrazas, *Memorias*, 80–81; Ball, *In the Days of Victorio*, 94–100; Thrapp, *Victorio*, 303–4.

13. Thrapp, *Victorio*, 310–11; Terrazas, *Memorias*, 82.

14. Lekson, *Nana's Raid*, 6–10, 32; Thrapp, *Conquest of Apacheria*, 209; Terrazas, *Memorias*, 83–84.

15. Debo, *Geronimo*, 127–32; Thrapp, *Juh: An Incredible Indian*, 21–28; quote from Terrazas, *Memorias*, 85.

16. Geronimo, *His Own Story*, 107; Ball, *In the Days of Victorio*, 136–39; Thrapp, *Juh: An Incredible Indian*, 29–30; Sweeney, *From Cochise to Geronimo*, 202–6.

17. Betzinez, *I Fought with Geronimo*, 56–75; Geronimo, *His Own Story*, 108–9.

18. Betzinez, *I Fought with Geronimo*, 77–80.

19. Terrazas, *Memorias*, 85–88; Geronimo, *His Own Story*, 106; Ball, *In the Days of Victorio*, 133; Sweeney, *From Cochise to Geronimo*, 234–35.

20. Betzinez, *I Fought with Geronimo*, 81–95; Terrazas, *Memorias*, 90–91; Ball, *In the Days of Victorio*, 134–35; Sweeney, *From Cochise to Geronimo*, 251–54.

21. Terrazas, *Memorias*, 91–92; Betzinez, *I Fought with Geronimo*, 97–112; Ball, *Indeh*, 70–72.

22. Betzinez, *I Fought with Geronimo*, 112–15.

23. Debo, *Geronimo*, 183–88, 197–202; Terrazas, *Memorias*, 92–93; Thrapp, *Juh: An Incredible Indian*, 39.

24. Debo, *Geronimo*, 222–25, 234–36; Betzinez, *I Fought with Geronimo*, 129; Geronimo, *His Own Story*, 129.

25. Debo, *Geronimo*, 243–48.

26. Deposition of Santana Perez, January 13, 1886, in United States Department of State, *Executive Documents*, 601–2; Opler, "A Chiricahua Apache's Account," 373–74.

27. Geronimo, *His Own Story*, 131; Betzinez, *I Fought with Geronimo*, 134–35.

28. Geronimo, *His Own Story*, 132–34; Betzinez, *I Fought with Geronimo*, 138–39.

29. Contrato del Clarin, Santiago Brito, Janos, October 1, 1849, JC 32:1849; Brito to Capitán de la Compañía, Janos, November 1, 1854, JR 51-1; Relación que manifiesta los niños . . . , Janos, December 1, 1854, JC 35:1854; Lista y extracto de la revista, Janos, April 1, 1858, JC 37:1858.

30. Sweeney, *Mangas Coloradas*, 230; Walker, *Boys of '98*, 15–17, 93–94, 143–44, 280–81.

31. Lloyd, *El proceso de modernización*, 74; Vanderwood, *Power of God*, 249–50. Katz, *Life and Times of Pancho Villa*, 16–40, is the most recent synthesis of this process.

32. Nugent, "'Are We Not [Civilized] Men?'"; Jane-Dale Lloyd, "*Rancheros* and Rebellion: The Case of Northwestern Chihuahua, 1905–1909," in Nugent, ed., *Rural Revolt in Mexico*, 107–33; Katz, *Life and Times of Pancho Villa*, 35.

33. Knight, *Mexican Revolution*, 127.

34. Alonso, *Thread of Blood*, and Nugent, *Spent Cartridges of Revolution*, both make this point.

35. See the essays in Joseph and Nugent, eds., *Everyday Forms of State Formation*.

36. Debo, *Geronimo*, 297–308; Cole, *Chiricahua Apache*, 164–65; Jastrzembski, "An Enemy's Ethnography," 106–12. Also see Stockel, *Shame and Endurance.*

37. Geronimo, *His Own Story*, 139–44; Debo, *Geronimo*, 326, 334, 364–65; Cole, *Chiricahua Apache*, 165–68. For the Fort Sill experience see Turcheneske, *The Chiricahua Apache Prisoners.*

38. Opler, "A Chiricahua Apache's Account," 368; Geronimo, *His Own Story*, 110.

39. Geronimo, *His Own Story*, 155–62.

Conclusion

1. The most recent recounting of the Spanish Borderlands is Weber's *The Spanish Frontier in North America*, but also see Weber, "The Spanish Borderlands, Historiography Redux."

2. Gutiérrez and Young, "Transnationalizing Borderlands History," 53.

3. Putnam, "*E Pluribus Unum.*"

4. Truett and Young, "Making Transnational History," 1–32, quote p. 23.

5. Adelman and Aron, "From Borderlands to Borders," 815–16.

6. Haefeli, "Use of North American Borderlands," 1223, emphasis in original.

7. Wunder and Hämäläinen, "Of Lethal Places," 1229.

8. Adelman and Aron, "Of Lively Exchanges," 1239.

9. Brooks, "Life Proceeds from the Name."

10. Brooks, "Seductions and Betrayals."

11. Brooks, "Seductions and Betrayals," 260.

12. Brooks, "Life Proceeds from the Name," 183.

13. Cook, "Mexico's Drug Cartels"; Stratfor, "Mexican Drug Cartels."

14. Stratfor, "Geopolitics of Mexico."

15. Freeman, "State of Siege."

16. Sanchez, "Aumenta Nivel de Violencia del Narco."

17. Stratfor, "Mexico and the Failed State Revisited."

18. Pinker, *The Blank Slate*, 330.

19. Hanson, "Mexico's Drug War."

20. Meyers, "U.S. Border Enforcement." DeLay, "19th-Century Lessons," draws the connections between the borderland policies past and present.

21. For suggestions of how this could be done see Bonner and Rozental, "Managing the United States–Mexico Border."

22. For a discussion of ungoverned spaces see Patrick, "Are 'Ungoverned Spaces' a Threat?" Williams, "Violent Non-State Actors," provides a typology of violent nonstate actors.

| Glossary

aguaje: Water hole
alcalde mayor: Magistrate
alférez: Ensign
caballada: Horse herd
cabo: Corporal
cadete: Cadet
calabozo: Jail
calidad: Status
campaña: A campaign or patrol
capitán: Captain
capitancillos: Literally little captains; referred to Apache leaders
carabinero: Carabineer, a senior soldier
castas: Descendants of mixed ethnicities in the caste system
Chihene: The "red paint people" or Eastern Band of Chiricahua, known to the Spanish as Chiricaguis
Chokonen: The Central Band of Chiricahua, known to the Spanish as Gileños
compañía volante: Mobile company, one not assigned a permanent garrison
comandante inspector: Chief inspector
comandante general: Commandant general

correduría, correría: A chase or pursuit

coyote: Descendant of a mestizo and an Indian woman in the caste system

criado: An Indian child reared as a Hispanic

cuera: Leather body armor

dikohe: A novice on the raid

esclavo: Slave

escopeta: A short musket

Españoles: Descendants of Spaniards or Europeans in the caste system

exploradores: Scouts

filiación: Enlistment paper

función de guerra, funciones: Skirmish, skirmishes

gahe: Mountain spirits of the Chiricahua Apaches

gandule: An Indian warrior in the Southwestern Borderlands; from the Arabic *gandur*, meaning rogue, rascal, or vagabond

gò'tàh: An extended family encampment; also a local group of family encampments

guardia de caballada: Horse herd guards

habilitado: Quartermaster

hacienda: A large farm

indios: Descendants of Indians in the caste system

inválido: Retiree

jasquie: Valiant

mestizo: Descendant of an *Español* and an Indian woman in the caste system

moros y cristianos: Moors and Christians

mulato: Descendant of an *Español* and a negro woman in the caste system

negros: Descendants of Africans in the caste system

Nednhi: The "enemy people" or Southern Band of Chiricahua, known to the Spaniards as Mimbreños

padrino/padrina: Godfather/godmother

partidas: Detachments of soldiers

piezas: Literally pieces, used to refer to Indians killed or captured; eventually used to refer to scalps taken

piloncillo: A molded cone of sugar

pinole: Parched corn

plazas: Positions on a muster roll

presidio: A garrison community

Provincias Internas: Internal Provinces, referred to New Spain's northern provinces

Querechos: Ancestral Apaches, Apacheans

ranchería: Indian settlement

rancho: Ranch

Reconquista: Literally reconquest; figuratively the centuries-long recovery of the Iberian peninsula from its Muslim conquerors

sarapes: Cloaks

sistema de castas: Caste system

soldado: Soldier

tambor: Musician

teniente: Lieutenant

tizwin: "Grey water," a weak maize beer.

tropa de cuera: Leather jacket troop

tropa ligera: Light troop

vaquero: Cowboy

vecino: Neighbor or citizen

Bibliography

Archival Sources

Archivo General de la Nación. Mexico City. Ramo Provincias Internas.
Cited as AGN, PI.

Janos Collection. 39 reels of microfilm. Cline Library, Northern Arizona
University. Cited as JC reel:year.

Janos Records. Records of the Presidio de San Felipe y Santiago de Janos,
1706–1858. Benson Latin American Collection, General Libraries,
University of Texas at Austin. Cited as JR folder-section.

Mission 2000 Searchable Spanish Mission Records. Tumacácori National Historical Park. http://home.nps.gov/applications/tuma/search.cfm.
Cited as Mission 2000.

Published Sources

Adelman, Jeremy, and Stephen Aaron. "From Borderlands to Borders: Empires, Nation-States, and the Peoples In-Between in North American
History." *American Historical Review* 104 (1999): 814–41.

———. "Of Lively Exchanges and Larger Perspectives." *American Historical Review* 104 (1999): 1235–39.

Aijmer, Göran, and Jon Abbink, eds. *Meanings of Violence: A Cross Cultural Perspective.* New York: Berg, 2000.

Almada, Francisco R. *Diccionario de historia, geografía, y biografía chi-
huahuenses.* Chihuahua: Talleres Gráficos, 1927.

Alonso, Ana María. *Thread of Blood: Colonialism, Revolution, and*

Gender on Mexico's Northern Frontier. Tucson: University of Arizona Press, 1995.

Anderson, Gary Clayton. *The Indian Southwest, 1580–1830: Ethnogenesis and Reinvention.* Norman: University of Oklahoma Press, 1999.

Archer, Christon I. "The Deportation of Barbarian Indians from the Internal Provinces of New Spain, 1789–1810." *Americas* 29 (1973): 376–85.

Arnal, Luis. "El sistema presidial en el septentrión novohispano: Evolución y estrategia de poblamientolamiento." *Revista Electrónica de Geografía y Ciencias Sociales,* vol. 10, núm. 218 (26), 1 de agosto de 2006.

Babcock, Matthew. "Rethinking the Establecimientos: Why Apaches Settled on Spanish-Run Reservations, 1786–1793." *New Mexico Historical Review* 84 (2009): 363–97.

———. "Turning Apaches into Spaniards: North America's Forgotten Indian Reservations." PhD diss., Southern Methodist University, 2008.

Ball, Eve. *In the Days of Victorio: Recollections of a Warm Springs Apache.* Tucson: University of Arizona Press, 1970.

———. *Indeh: An Apache Odyssey.* Norman: University of Oklahoma Press, 1988.

Bancroft, Hubert Howe. *History of the North Mexican States and Texas,* Vol. 2: *1801–1889.* San Francisco: History Company Publishers, 1889.

Barash, David P. "The Targets of Aggression." *Chronicle Review,* October 5, 2007.

Baretta, Silvio R. Duncan, and John Markoff. "Civilization and Barbarism: Cattle Frontiers in Latin America." *Comparative Studies in Society and History* 20 (1978): 587–620.

Barr, Juliana. *Peace Came in the Form of a Woman: Indians and Spaniards in the Texas Borderlands.* Chapel Hill: University of North Carolina Press, 2007.

Bartlett, John Russell. *Personal Narrative of Explorations and Incidents in Texas, New Mexico, California, Sonora, and Chihuahua, Connected with the United States and Mexican Boundary, during the Years 1850, '51, '52, and '53.* 2 vols. New York: D. Appleton and Company, 1854.

Benavides, Alonso de. *The Memorial of Fray Alonso de Benavides, 1630.* Trans. Mrs. Edward E. Ayer, ed. Frederick Webb Hodge and Charles Fletcher Lummis. Chicago, 1916; Albuquerque: Horn and Wallace, 1965.

Berreby, David. *Us and Them: Understanding Your Tribal Mind*. New York: Little, Brown and Company, 2005.

Betzinez, Jason. *I Fought with Geronimo*. Lincoln: University of Nebraska Press, 1987.

Bishko, Charles Julian. "The Spanish and Portuguese Reconquest, 1095–1492." In *A History of the Crusades*, Vol. 3: *The Fourteenth and Fifteenth Centuries*, ed. by Harry W. Hazard, 396–455. Madison: University of Wisconsin Press, 1975.

Blackhawk, Ned. *Violence Over the Land: Indians and Empires in the Early American West*. Cambridge: Harvard University Press, 2006.

Blyth, Lance R. "The Presidio of Janos: Ethnicity, Society, Masculinity, and Ecology in Far Northern Mexico, 1685–1858." PhD diss., Northern Arizona University, 2005.

Boehm, Christopher. *Blood Revenge: The Enactment and Management of Conflict in Montenegro and Other Tribal Societies*. Philadelphia: University of Pennsylvania Press, 1987.

Bolton, Herbert E. "French Intrusions into New Mexico, 1740–1752." In *Bolton and Spanish Borderlands*, ed. John Francis Bannon, 150–71. Norman: University of Oklahoma Press, 1964.

Bolton, Herbert E., ed. *Spanish Explorations in the Southwest, 1542–1706*. New York: Charles Scribner's Sons, 1916.

Bonner, Robert C., and Andrés Rozental, co-chairs. *Managing the United States–Mexico Border: Cooperative Solutions to Common Problems*. Full Report of the Binational Task Force on the United States–Mexico Border. Los Angeles CA: Pacific Council for International Policy (PCIP)–Consejo Mexicano de Asuntos Internacionales (COMEXI), 2009.

Bowles, Samuel. "Group Competition, Reproductive Leveling, and the Evolution of Human Altruism." *Science* 314 (2006) 1569–72.

Brinckerhoff, Sidney B., and Odie B. Faulk. *Lancers for the King: A Study of the Frontier Military System of Northern New Spain, with a Translation of the Royal Regulations of 1772*. Phoenix: Arizona Historical Foundation, 1965.

Brooks, James F. *Captives and Cousins: Slavery, Kinship, and Community in the Southwest Borderlands*. Chapel Hill: University of North Carolina Press, 2002.

———. "Life Proceeds from the Name: Indigenous Peoples and the Predicament of Hybridity." In *Clearing a Path: Theorizing the Past in Native American Studies*, ed. Nancy Shoemaker, 181–205. New York: Routledge, 2002.

———. "Reshaping Our View of Slavery and the Southwest." *Chronicle of Higher Education*, Colloquy Live, May 16, 2003, http://chronicle.com/ colloquylive/2003/05/slavery (accessed February 12, 2008).

———. "Review Essay: Violence, Exchange, and Renewal in the American Southwest." *Ethnohistory* 49 (2002): 205–18.

———. "Seductions and Betrayals: La frontera gauchesque, Argentine Nationalism, and the Predicaments of Hybridity." In *Small Worlds: Method, Meaning, and Narrative in Microhistory*, ed. Christopher Brooks, R. N. DeCorse, and John Walton, 247–63. Santa Fe NM: School for Advanced Research Press, 2008.

Carroll, Joseph. "Human Nature and Literary Meaning." In *The Literary Animal: Evolution and the Nature of Narrative*, ed. Jonathan Gottschall and D. S. Wilson, 187–216. Chicago: Northwestern University Press, 2005.

Chávez, José Carlos. "Extincion de los Apaches Victorio." *Boletin de la Sociedad Chihuahuense de Estudios Historicos* 1 (1939): 336–40, 346.

Catlin, George. *Episodes from Life Among the Indians and Last Rambles*. Ed. Marvin C. Ross. Norman: University of Oklahoma Press, 1959.

Chacon, Richard J., and Rubén G. Mendoza, eds. *Latin American Indigenous Warfare and Ritual Violence*. Tucson: University of Arizona Press, 2007.

———. *North American Indigenous Warfare and Ritual Violence*. Tucson: University of Arizona Press, 2007.

Chamberlain, Kathleen P. *Victorio: Apache Warrior and Chief*. Norman: University of Oklahoma Press, 2007.

Chartrand, René. *The Mexican Adventure, 1861–67*. London: Osprey Publishing, 1994.

Chirot, Daniel, and Clark McCauley. *Why Not Kill Them All? The Logic and Prevention of Mass Political Murder*. Princeton: Princeton University Press, 2006.

Choi, Jung-Kyoo, and Samuel Bowles. "The Coevolution of Parochial Altruism and War." *Science* 318 (2007): 636–40.

Christiansen, Paige W. "The Presidio and the Borderlands: A Case Study." *Journal of the West* 8 (1969): 29–37.

Clark, LaVerne Harrell. *They Sang for Horses: The Impact of the Horse on Navajo and Apache Folklore*. Rev. ed. Boulder: University Press of Colorado, 2001.

Clarke, A. B. *Travels in Mexico and California*. Boston: Wright and Hasty, 1852.

Cole, D. C. *The Chiricahua Apache, 1846–1876: From War to Reservation.* Albuquerque: University of New Mexico Press, 1988.

Colwell-Chanthaphonh, Chip. "Western Apache Oral Histories and Traditions of the Camp Grant Massacre." *American Indian Quarterly* 27 (2003): 639–66.

Conrad, Paul. "Military Service, Captive Exchange and the Formation of a Hispanic-Apache Community in the Late-Colonial Chihuahua Borderlands." Paper presented at the 2007 ILASSA Conference, Austin, Texas.

Cook, Colleen W. "Mexico's Drug Cartels." *Congressional Research Service*, October 16, 2007.

Cope, R. Douglas. *The Limits of Racial Domination: Plebian Society in Colonial Mexico City, 1660–1720.* Madison: University of Wisconsin Press, 1994.

Cortés, José. *Views from the Apache Frontier: Report on the Provinces of New Spain, 1799.* Ed. Elizabeth A. H. John, trans. John Wheat. Norman: University of Oklahoma Press, 1989.

Creed, Gerald W., ed. *The Seductions of Community.* Santa Fe NM: School of American Research Press, 2006.

Cremony, John C. *Life among the Apaches.* San Francisco: A. Roman and Company, 1868; Lincoln: University of Nebraska Press, 1983.

Crimmins, Martin L. "Colonel Buell's Expedition into Mexico in 1880." *New Mexico Historical Review* 10 (1935): 133–42.

Cunningham, Bob, and Harry P. Hewitt. "A 'lovely land full of roses and thorns': Emil Langberg and Mexico, 1835–1866." *Southwestern Historical Quarterly* 98 (1994–95): 387–425.

Cutter, Donald C., ed. and trans. *The Defenses of Northern New Spain.* Dallas TX: Southern Methodist University Press, 1994.

Daly, Martin, and Margo Wilson. *Homicide.* New York: A. de Gruyter, 1988.

Dawson, Joseph C. III. *Doniphan's Epic March: The 1st Missouri Volunteers in the Mexican War.* Lawrence: University Press of Kansas, 1999.

de la Teja, Jesús F., ed., and John Wheat, trans. "Ramón de Murillo's Plan for the Reform of New Spain's Frontier Defenses." *Southwestern Historical Quarterly* 107 (2004): 501–33.

Debo, Angie. *Geronimo: The Man, His Time, His Place.* Norman: University of Oklahoma Press, 1976.

DeLay, Brian. "19th-Century Lessons for Today's Drug-War Policies." *Chronicle Review*, July 27, 2009.

———. *War of a Thousand Deserts: Indian Raids and the U.S.-Mexican War.* New Haven: Yale University Press, 2008.

Dennen, Johan M. G. van der. "Ambivalent War-Lovers?" *Evolutionary Psychology* 6, no. 1 (2008): 3–12.

Dykstra, Robert R. "Field Notes: Overdosing on Dodge City." *Western Historical Quarterly* 27 (1996): 505–14.

Ebright, Malcolm, and Rick Hendricks. *The Witches of Abiquiu: The Governor, the Priest, the Genízaro Indians, and the Devil.* Albuquerque: University of New Mexico Press, 2006.

Echo-Hawk, Roger C. "Ancient History in the New World: Integrating Oral Traditions and the Archeological in Deep Time." *American Antiquity* 65 (2000): 267–90.

Eisner, Manuel. "The Uses of Violence: An Examination of Some Cross-Cutting Issues." *International Journal of Conflict and Violence* 3, no. 1 (2009): 40–59.

Emory, Deborah Carley. "Running the Line: Men, Maps, Science, and Art of the United States and Mexico Boundary Survey, 1849–1856." *New Mexico Historical Review* 75 (2000): 221–65.

Espinoza de Luján, Josie. *Los Moros y Cristianos: A Spectacular Historic Drama.* Chimayó NM: J. Espinoza de Luján, 1992.

Farmer, Jared. "Borderlands of Brutality." *Reviews in American History* 37 (2009): 644–52.

Faulk, Odie B., trans. and ed. "Projected Military Colonies for the Borderlands, 1848." *Journal of Arizona History* 9 (1968): 39–47.

Fenn, Elizabeth A. *Pox Americana: The Great Smallpox Epidemic of 1775–82.* New York: Hill and Wang, 2001.

Ferguson, Niall. *The War of the World: Twentieth-Century Conflict and the Descent of the West.* New York: Penguin, 2006.

Ferguson, R. Brian, and Neil L. Whitehead, eds. *War in the Tribal Zone: Expanding States and Indigenous Warfare.* Santa Fe NM: School of American Research Press, 1992; 2nd printing, 1999.

Flint, Richard, and Shirley Cushing Flint, eds. and trans. *Documents of the Coronado Expedition, 1539–1542: "They Were Not Familiar with His Majesty, nor Did They Wish to Be His Subjects."* Dallas TX: Southern Methodist University Press, 2005.

———. *The Coronado Expedition: From the Distance of 460 Years.* Albuquerque: University of New Mexico Press, 2003.

Forbes, Jack D. *Apache, Navaho, and Spaniard.* 2nd ed. Norman: University of Oklahoma Press, 1994.

———. "The Appearance of the Mounted Indian in Northern Mexico and the Southwest, to 1680." *Southwestern Journal of Anthropology* 15 (1959): 189–212.

Freeman, Laurie. *State of Siege: Drug-Related Violence and Corruption in Mexico.* Washington DC: Washington Office on Latin America, 2006.

Gálvez, Bernardo de. *Instructions for Governing the Interior Provinces of New Spain, 1786.* Ed. and trans. Donald E. Worcester. Berkeley: Quivira Society, 1951.

Gat, Azar. "The Human Motivational Complex: Evolutionary Theory and the Causes of Hunter-Gatherer Fighting, Part I: Primary Somatic and Reproductive Causes." *Anthropological Quarterly* 73 (2000): 20–34.

———. "The Human Motivational Complex, Part II: Proximate, Subordinate, and Derivative Causes." *Anthropological Quarterly* 73 (2000): 74–88.

———. *War in Human Civilization.* New York: Oxford University Press, 2006.

Gearhard, Peter. *The North Frontier of New Spain.* Rev. ed. Norman: University of Oklahoma Press, 1993.

Geronimo. *Geronimo: His Own Story.* Ed. S. M. Barrett. New York: Meridian, 1996.

Griswold del Castillo, Richard. *The Treaty of Guadalupe Hidalgo: A Legacy of Conflict.* Norman: University of Oklahoma Press, 1990.

Gottschall, Jonathan. "Explaining Wartime Rape." *Journal of Sex Research* 41 (2004): 129–36.

———. *The Rape of Troy: Evolution, Violence, and the World of Homer.* New York: Cambridge University Press, 2008.

Griffen, William B. *Apaches at War and Peace: The Janos Presidio, 1750–1858.* Albuquerque: University of New Mexico Press, 1988; reprint, Norman: University of Oklahoma Press, 1998.

———. "The Chiricahua Apache Population Resident at the Janos Presidio, 1792–1858." *Journal of the Southwest* 33 (1991): 151–99.

———. "The Compás: A Chiricahua Apache Family of the Late 18th and Early 19th Centuries." *American Indian Quarterly* 7, no. 2 (1983): 21–49.

———. *Indian Assimilation in the Franciscan Area of Nueva Vizcaya.* Tucson: University of Arizona Press, 1979.

———. *Utmost Good Faith: Patterns of Apache-Mexican Hostilities in Northern Chihuahua Border Warfare, 1821–1848.* Albuquerque: University of New Mexico Press, 1988.

Gutiérrez, Ramón. *When Jesus Came, the Corn Mothers Went Away: Marriage, Sexuality, and Power in New Mexico, 1500–1846.* Stanford: Stanford University Press, 1991.

Gutiérrez, Ramón, and Elliot Young. "Transnationalizing Borderlands History." *Western Historical Quarterly* 41 (2010): 27–53.

Guy, Donna J., and Thomas E. Sheridan, eds. *Contested Ground: Comparative Frontiers on the Northern and Southern Edges of the Spanish Empire.* Tucson: University of Arizona Press, 1998.

Haas, Jonathan, and Winifred Creamer. "Warfare among the Pueblos: Myth, History, and Ethnography." *Ethnohistory* 44 (1997): 235–61.

Hackett, Charles Wilson. *Historical Documents relating to New Mexico, Nueva Vizcaya, and Approaches Thereto, to 1773.* 3 vols. Washington DC: Carnegie Institution, 1926.

———. *Revolt of the Pueblo Indians and Otermín's Attempted Reconquest, 1680–1682.* 2 vols. Albuquerque: University of New Mexico Press, 1942.

Haefeli, Evan. "A Note on the Use of North American Borderlands." *American Historical Review* 104 (1999): 1222–25.

Hagle, Paul. "Military Life on New Spain's Northern Frontier: The Presidio of Janos, 1787–1800." MA thesis, University of Texas at Austin, 1962.

Hammond, George P., and Agapito Rey, eds. and trans. *Don Juan de Oñate: Colonizer of New Mexico, 1595–1628.* Albuquerque: University of New Mexico Press, 1953.

Hanson, Stephanie. "Mexico's Drug War." Council on Foreign Relations, June 28, 2007.

Hämäläinen, Pekka. *The Comanche Empire.* New Haven: Yale University Press, 2008.

Harris, Benjamin Butler. *The Gila Trail: Texas Argonauts and the California Gold Rush.* Ed. Richard H. Dillon. Norman: University of Oklahoma Press, 1960.

Harris, Max. *Aztecs, Moors, and Christians: Festivals of Reconquest in Mexico and Spain.* Austin: University of Texas Press, 2000.

Hendricks, Rick, and W. H. Timmons. *San Elizario: Spanish Presidio to Texas County Seat.* El Paso: Texas Western Press, 1998.

Herman, Daniel J. "Romance on the Middle Ground." *Journal of the Early Republic* 19 (1999): 279–91.

Hoijer, Harry, and Morris Edward Opler. *Chiricahua and Mescalero Apache Texts.* Chicago: University of Chicago Press, 1938.

Jackson, Robert H. *Race, Caste, and Status: Indians in Colonial Spanish America*. Albuquerque: University of New Mexico Press, 1999.

Jacoby, Karl. *Shadows at Dawn: A Borderlands Massacre and the Violence of History*. New York: Penguin, 2008.

Jastrzembski, Joseph C. "An Enemy's Ethnography: The 'Mexican' in Nineteenth Century Chiricahua Apache Ethnographic Practice." PhD diss., University of Chicago, 1994.

———. "Treacherous Towns in Mexico: Chiricahua Apache Personal Narratives of Horrors." *Western Folklore* 54 (1995): 169–96.

Joseph, Gilbert M., and Daniel Nugent, eds. *Everyday Forms of State Formation: Revolution and the Negotiation of Rule in Modern Mexico*. Durham NC: Duke University Press, 1994.

John, Elizabeth A. H., ed., and John Wheat, trans. "Views from a Desk in Chihuahua: Manuel Merino's Report on Apaches and Neighboring Nations, ca. 1804." *Southwestern Historical Quarterly* 95 (1991): 138–76.

Jordán, Fernando. *Crónica de un País Bárbaro*. Chihuahua: Centro Librero la Prensa, 1975.

Katz, Friedrich. *The Life and Times of Pancho Villa*. Stanford: Stanford University Press, 1998.

Keeley, Lawrence. *War Before Civilization: The Myth of the Peaceful Savage*. New York: Oxford University Press, 1997.

Kessell, John L. *Kiva, Cross, and Crown: The Pecos Indians and New Mexico, 1540–1840*. Washington DC: Government Printing Office, 1979.

———. *Pueblos, Spaniards, and the Kingdom of New Mexico*. Norman: University of Oklahoma Press, 2008.

Kessell, John L., and Rick Hendricks, eds. *By Force of Arms: The Journals of Don Diego de Vargas, 1691–1693*. Albuquerque: University of New Mexico Press, 1992.

Knight, Alan. *The Mexican Revolution*. 2 vols. New York: Cambridge University Press, 1981.

Lafora, Nicolas de. *The Frontiers of New Spain: Nicolas de Lafora's Description, 1766–1768*. Ed. and trans. Lawrence Kinnaird. Berkeley: Quivira Society, 1958.

Lamadrid, Enrique R. *Hermanitos Comanchitos: Indo-Hispano Rituals of Captivity and Redemption*. Albuquerque: University of New Mexico Press, 2003.

Lane, Frederic C. "Economic Consequences of Organized Violence." *Journal of Economic History* 18 (1958): 401–17.

Langfur, Hal. "Moved by Terror: Frontier Violence as Cultural Exchange in Late-Colonial Brazil." *Ethnohistory* 46 (2005): 255–89.

LeBlanc, Steven A. *Prehistoric Warfare in the American Southwest.* Salt Lake City: University of Utah Press, 1999.

LeBlanc, Steven A., with Katherine E. Register. *Constant Battles: The Myth of the Peaceful, Noble Savage.* New York: St. Martin's Press, 2003.

Lekson, Stephen H. *Nana's Raid: Apache Warfare in Southern New Mexico, 1881.* El Paso: Texas Western Press, 1987.

———. "War in the Southwest, War in the World." *American Antiquity* 67 (2002): 607–24.

Lloyd, Jane-Dale. *El proceso de modernización capitalista en el noreste de Chihuahua (1880–1910).* Coyoacán, México: Universidad Iberomericana, 1987.

Lorenz, Joseph G., and David Glenn Smith. "Distribution of Four Founding mtDNA Haplogroups among Native North Americans." *American Journal of Physical Anthropology* 101 (1996): 307–23.

Lucero-White Lea, Aurora. *Literary Folklore of the Hispanic Southwest.* San Antonio TX: Naylor Company, 1953.

Mahli, Ripan S., Holly M. Mortensen, Jason A. Eshleman, Brian M. Kemp, Joseph G. Lorenz, Frederika A. Kaestle, John R. Johnson, Clara Gorodezky, and David Glenn Smith. "Native American mtDNA Prehistory in the American Southwest." *American Journal of Physical Anthropology* 120 (2003): 108–24.

Martin, Cheryl English. *Governance and Society in Colonial Mexico: Chihuahua in the Eighteenth Century.* Stanford: Stanford University Press, 1996.

Maschner, Herbert D. G., and Katherine L. Reedy-Maschner. "Raid, Retreat, Defend (Repeat): The Archaeology and Ethnohistory of Warfare on the North Pacific Rim." *Journal of Anthropological Archaeology* 17 (1998): 19–51.

Mason, Ronald J. "Archaeology and Native North American Oral Traditions." *American Antiquity* 65 (2000): 239–66.

Matson, Daniel S., and Albert H. Schroeder, eds. "Cordero's Description of the Apache—1796." *New Mexico Historical Review* 32 (1957): 335–56.

McCarty, Kieran. "Bernardo de Galvez on the Apache Frontier: The Education of a Future Viceroy." *Journal of the Southwest* 36 (1994): 103–30.

McMurtry, Larry. *Oh What a Slaughter: Massacres in the American West: 1846–1890.* New York: Simon and Schuster, 2005.

Meyer, Michael C. "Health and Medical Practice on the Northern Frontier of New Spain, 1550–1821." *Locus* 2 (1993): 111–30.

Meyers, Deborah Waller. "U.S. Border Enforcement: From Horseback to High-Tech." *MPI Insight*, November 2005.

Moore, Mary Lu, and Delmar L. Beene, eds. and trans. "The Interior Provinces of New Spain." *Arizona and the West* 13 (1971): 265–82.

Moorhead, Max L. *The Apache Frontier: Jacobo Ugarte and Spanish-Indian Relations in Northern New Spain, 1769–1791.* Norman: University of Oklahoma Press, 1968.

———. *The Presidio: Bastion of the Spanish Borderlands.* Norman: University of Oklahoma Press, 1975.

———. "Spanish Deportation of Hostile Apaches: The Policy and the Practice." *Arizona and the West* 17 (1975): 205–20.

Navarro García, Luis. *Don José de Gálvez y la Comandancia General de las provincias internas del norte de la Nueva España.* Seville: Escuela de Estudios Hispanoamericanos, 1964.

Naylor, Thomas H., and Charles W. Polzer, eds. *Pedro de Rivera and the Military Regulations for Northern New Spain, 1724–1729.* Tucson: University of Arizona Press, 1988.

———. *The Presidio and Militia on the Northern Frontier of New Spain: A Documentary History,* Vol. 1: *1570–1700.* Tucson: University of Arizona Press, 1986.

Nirenberg, David. *Communities of Violence: Persecution of Minorities in the Middle Ages.* Princeton: Princeton University Press, 1996.

Nugent, Daniel. "'Are We Not [Civilized] Men?': The Formation and Devolution of Community in Northern Mexico." *Journal of Historical Sociology* 2 (1989): 206–39.

———. *Spent Cartridges of Revolution: An Anthropological History of Namiquipa, Chihuahua.* Chicago: University of Chicago Press, 1993.

Nugent, Daniel, ed. *Rural Revolt in Mexico: U.S. Intervention and the Domain of Subaltern Politics.* Expanded edition. Durham NC: Duke University Press, 1998.

Opler, Morris Edward. *An Apache Life-Way: The Economic, Social, and Religious Institutions of the Chiricahua Indians.* Chicago: University of Chicago Press, 1941; Lincoln: University of Nebraska Press, 1996.

———. "Cause and Effect in Apachean Agriculture, Division of Labor, Residence Patterns, and Girls' Puberty Rites." *American Anthropologist* 74 (1972): 1133–46.

———. "Chiricahua Apache." In *Handbook of North American Indians*, vol. 10: *Southwest*, ed. Alfonso Ortiz, 401–18. Washington DC: Smithsonian Institution Press, 1983.

———. "A Chiricahua Apache's Account of the Geronimo Campaign of 1886." *New Mexico Historical Review* 13 (1938): 360–86.

———. "An Outline of Chiricahua Apache Social Organization." In *Social Anthropology of North American Tribes*, ed. Fred Eggan, 173–239. Chicago: University of Chicago Press, 1937.

———. "Mountain Spirits of the Chiricahua Apache." *Masterkey* 20 (1946): 125–31.

———. *Myths and Tales of the Chiricahua Apache Indians*. New York: American Folk-Lore Society, 1942; reprint, Lincoln: University of Nebraska Press, 1994.

———. *Myths and Tales of the Jicarilla Apache Indians*. American Folk-Lore Society, 1938; reprint, Lincoln: University of Nebraska Press, 1994.

———. "Three Types of Variations and Their Relation to Cultural Change." In *Language, Culture, and Personality: Essays in Memory of Edward Sapir*, ed. Leslie Spier, A. Irving Hallowell, and Stanley S. Newman, 146–57. Menasha WI: Sapir Memorial Publication Fund, 1941.

Opler, Morris Edward, and Harry Hoijer. "The Raid and War-Path Language of the Chiricahua Apache." *American Anthropologist* 42 (1940): 617–34.

Orozco Orozco, Victor. *Las guerras indias en la historia de Chihuahua: Antología*. Juárez: Universidad Autónoma de Ciudad Juárez, Instituto Chihuahense de la Cultura, 1992.

Parker, Bradley J. "Toward an Understanding of Borderland Processes." *American Antiquity* 71 (2006): 77–100.

Patrick, Stewart M. "Are 'Ungoverned Spaces' a Threat?" Council on Foreign Relations Expert Brief. January 11, 2010.

Pattie, James O. *The Personal Narrative of James O. Pattie of Kentucky*. Cincinnati: E. H. Flint, 1833.

Pike, Zebulon Montgomery. *The Expeditions of Zebulon Montgomery Pike*. 2 vols.. Ed. Elliott Coues. 1810; New York: Dover Publications, 1987.

Pinker, Steven. *The Blank Slate: The Modern Denial of Human Nature*. New York: Penguin, 2002.

Pérez de Villagrá, Gaspar. *A History of New Mexico*. Trans. Gilberto Espinosa. Alcala, 1610; Chicago: Rio Grande Press, 1962.

————. *Historia de la Nueva México, 1610.* Ed. and trans. Miguel Encinias, Alfred Rodríguez, and Joseph P. Sánchez. Albuquerque: University of New Mexico Press, 1992.

Perry, Richard J. *Western Apache Heritage: People of the Mountain Corridor.* Austin: University of Texas Press, 1991.

Putnam, Robert D. "*E Pluribus Unum*: Diversity and Community in the Twenty-first Century." *Scandinavian Political Studies* 30 (2007): 137–74.

Radding, Cynthia. *Landscapes of Power and Identity: Comparative Histories in the Sonoran Desert and the Forests of Amazonia from Colony to Republic.* Durham NC: Duke University Press, 2005.

————. *Wandering Peoples: Colonialism, Ethnic Spaces, and Ecological Frontiers in Northwestern Mexico, 1700–1850.* Durham NC: Duke University Press, 1997.

Reedy-Maschner, Katherine L., and Herbert D. G. Maschner. "Marauding Middlemen: Western Expansion and Violent Conflict in the Subartic." *Ethnohistory* 46 (1999): 703–43.

Ridley, Matt. *The Origins of Virtue: Human Instincts and the Evolution of Cooperation.* New York: Penguin, 1996.

Reséndez, Andrés, and Brian M. Kemp. "Genetics and the History of Latin America." *Hispanic American Historical Review* 85 (2005): 283–98.

Rickard, T. A. "The Chino Enterprise—I." *Engineering and Mining Journal-Press* 116 (1923): 753–58.

Roberts, David. *The Pueblo Revolt: The Secret Rebellion that Drove the Spaniards out of the Southwest.* New York: Simon and Schuster, 2004.

Robins, Nicholas A. *Native Insurgencies and the Genocidal Impulse in the Americas.* Bloomington: Indiana University Press, 2005.

Ruxton, George Frederick. *Adventures in Mexico and the Rocky Mountains.* New York: Harper and Brothers Publishers, 1848.

————. *Adventures in the Rocky Mountains, 1846–1847.* Glorieta NM: Rio Grande Press, 1973.

Sanchez, Esther. "Aumenta Nivel de Violencia del Narco." *El Universal,* January 1, 2010.

Santiago, Mark. *The Jar of Severed Hands: Spanish Deportation of Apache Prisoners of War, 1770–1810.* Norman: University of Oklahoma Press, 2011.

Schaafsma, Curtis F. *Apaches de Navajo: Seventeenth-Century Navajos in the Chama Valley of New Mexico.* Salt Lake City: University of Utah Press, 2002.

———. "Ethnohistoric Groups in the Casas Grandes Region: Circa AD 1500–1700." In *Layers of Time: Papers in Honor of Robert H. Weber*, ed. Meliha S. Duran and David T. Kirkpatrick, 85–98. Albuquerque: Archaeological Society of New Mexico, 1997.

———. "Truth Dwells in the Deeps: Southwest Oral Traditions and Archaeological Interpretations." *Journal of the Southwest* 46 (2004): 621–42.

Seabright, Paul. *The Company of Strangers: A Natural History of Economic Life*. Princeton: Princeton University Press, 2004.

Simmons, Marc. *The Last Conquistador: Juan de Oñate and the Settling of the Far Southwest*. Norman: University Oklahoma Press, 1991.

Smith, David Livingstone. *The Most Dangerous Animal: Human Nature and the Origins of War*. New York: St. Martin's Press, 2007.

Smith, Ralph A. *Borderlander: The Life of James Kirker, 1793–1852*. Norman: University of Oklahoma Press, 1999.

———. "The Scalp Hunt in Chihuahua—1849." *New Mexico Historical Review* 40 (1965): 117–40.

Spicer, Edward. *Cycles of Conquest: The Impact of Spain, Mexico, and the United States on the Indians of the Southwest, 1533–1960*. Tucson: University of Arizona Press, 1962.

Spielmann, Katherine A. "Interaction among Nonhierarchical Societies." In *Farmers, Hunters, and Colonists: Interaction between the Southwest and the Southern Plains*. Ed. Katherine A. Spielmann. Tucson: University of Arizona Press, 1991.

Stockel, H. Henrietta. *Shame and Endurance: The Untold Story of the Chiricahua Apache Prisoners of War*. Tucson: University of Arizona Press, 2004.

Strategic Forecasting (Stratfor). "The Geopolitics of Mexico: A Mountain Fortress Besieged." www.stratfor.com, November 17, 2009.

———. "Mexico and the Failed State Revisited." www.stratfor.com, April 6, 2010.

———. "Mexican Drug Cartels: Two Wars and a Look Southward." www.stratfor.com, December 16, 2009.

Strickland, Rex W. "The Birth and Death of a Legend: The Johnson 'Massacre' of 1837." *Arizona and the West* 18 (1976): 257–86.

Swann, Michael M. *Tierra Adentro: Settlement and Society in Colonial Durango*. Boulder: Westview Press, 1982.

Sweeney, Edwin R. *Cochise: Chiricahua Apache Chief*. Norman: University of Oklahoma Press, 1991.

————. *From Cochise to Geronimo: The Chiricahua Apaches, 1874–1886*. Norman: University of Oklahoma Press, 2010.

————. "'I Had Lost All': Geronimo and the Carrasco Massacre of 1851." *Journal of Arizona History* 27 (1986): 35–52.

————. *Mangas Coloradas: Chief of the Chiricahua Apaches*. Norman: University of Oklahoma Press, 1998.

Terrazas, Joaquín. *Memorias*. Ciudad Juarez: El Agricultor Mexicano, 1905.

The War of the Rebellion: A Compilation of the Official Records of the Union and Confederate Armies. Washington: Government Printing Office, 1893.

Thomas, Alfred Barnaby, ed. and trans. *Forgotten Frontiers: A Study of the Spanish Indian Policy of Don Juan Bautista de Anza, Governor of New Mexico, 1777–1787*. Norman: University of Oklahoma Press, 1932.

Thrapp, Dan L. *The Conquest of Apacheria*. Norman: University of Oklahoma Press, 1967.

————. *Juh: An Incredible Indian*. El Paso: Texas Western Press, 1973.

————. *Victorio and the Mimbres Apaches*. Norman: University of Oklahoma Press, 1974.

Towner, Robert H. *Defending the Dinétah: Pueblitos in the Ancestral Navajo Homeland*. Salt Lake City: University of Utah Press, 2002.

Truett, Samuel, and Elliot Young. "Making Transnational History: Nations, Regions, and Borderlands." In *Continental Crossroads: Remapping U.S.-Mexico Borderlands History*, ed. Truett and Young, 1–32. Durham: Duke University Press, 2004.

Turcheneske, John Anthony. *The Chiricahua Apache Prisoners of War: Fort Sill, 1894–1914*. Boulder CO: NetLibrary, 1999.

Tyerman, Christopher. *God's War: A New History of the Crusades*. Cambridge: Belknap Press, 2006.

United States Congress. *Condition of the Indian Tribes: Report of the Joint Special Committee, Appointed under Joint Resolution of March 3, 1867*. 39th Cong, 2d sess., 1867.

United States Department of State. *The Executive Documents of the House of Representatives for the Second Session of the Forty-Ninth Congress: 1886–'87*. Washington DC: U.S. Government Printing Office, 1886–87.

Vandervort, Bruce. *Indian Wars of Canada, Mexico, and the United States: 1812–1900*. New York: Routledge, 2006.

Vanderwood, Paul. *The Power of God against the Guns of Government: Religious Upheaval in Mexico at the Turn of the Nineteenth Century*. Stanford: Stanford University Press, 1997.

Vázquez, Josefina Zoraida. *México al tiempo de su guerra con Estados Unidos (1846–1848)*. México: El Colegio de México, 1997.

Wade, Nicholas. *Before the Dawn: Recovering the Lost History of Our Ancestors*. New York: Penguin, 2006.

Walker, Billy D. "Copper Genesis: The Early Years of Santa Rita del Cobre." *New Mexico Historical Review* 54 (1979): 5–20.

Walker, Dale L. *The Boys of '98: Theodore Roosevelt and the Rough Riders*. New York: Forge Books, 1998.

Wasserman, Mark. *Capitalist, Caciques, and Revolution: The Native Elite and Foreign Enterprise in Chihuahua, Mexico, 1854–1911*. Chapel Hill: University of North Carolina Press, 1984.

Weber, David J. *Bárbaros: Spaniards and Their Savages in the Age of Enlightenment*. New Haven: Yale University Press, 2005.

———. *The Mexican Frontier, 1821–1846: The American Southwest under Mexico*. Albuquerque: University of New Mexico Press, 1982.

———. "The Spanish Borderlands, Historiography Redux." *History Teacher* 39 (2005): 43–56.

———. *The Spanish Frontier in North America*. New Haven: Yale University Press, 1992.

Weber, Max. *The Theory of Social and Economic Organization*. New York: Free Press, 1964.

Werner, Michael S., ed. *Encyclopedia of Mexico: History, Society and Culture*. Chicago: Fitzroy Dearborn, 1997.

White, Richard. *The Middle Ground: Indians, Empires, Republics in the Great Lakes Region, 1650–1815*. New York: Cambridge University Press, 1991.

Wilcox, Cadmus M. *History of the Mexican War*. Washington DC: Church News Publishing Company, 1892.

Wilcox, David, and W. Bruce Masse, eds. *The Protohistoric Period in the North American Southwest, AD 1450–1700*. Anthropological Papers no. 24. Tempe: Arizona State University, , 1981.

Williams, Phil. "Violent Non-State Actors and National and International Security." International Relations and Security Network (ISN), 2008.

Worcester, Donald E. "The Spread of Horses in the Southwest." *New Mexico Historical Review* 19 (1944): 225–32.

Wunder, John R., and Pekka Hämäläinen. "Of Lethal Places and Lethal Essays." *American Historical Review* 104 (1999): 1229–34.

Index